Stranded *in the* Philippines

Professor Bell's Private War against the Japanese

SCOTT A. MILLS

NAVAL INSTITUTE PRESS
Annapolis, Maryland

Naval Institute Press
291 Wood Road
Annapolis, MD 21402

Library of Congress Cataloging-in-Publication Data
Mills, Scott A., 1924-
  Stranded in the Philippines : Professor Bell's private war against the Japanese / Scott Mills.
    p. cm.
  Includes bibliographical references and index.
  ISBN 978-1-59114-497-7
  1. Bell, Henry Roy, b. 1896. 2. Guerrillas—Philippines—Negros Island—Biography. 3. World War, 1939-1945—Underground movements—Philippines—Negros Island. 4. Negros Island (Philippines)—History, Military—20th century. 5. Philippines—History—Japanese occupation, 1942-1945. 6. Missionaries—Philippines—Negros Island—Biography. 7. Americans—Philippines—Negros Island—Biography. 8. Negros Island (Philippines)—Biography. I. Title.
  D802.P52N435 2009
  940.54'8673092—dc22
                                        2009020380

14 13 12 11 10 09   9 8 7 6 5 4 3 2
First printing

All photos are from the Bell family.

Contents

Editor's Note

The author, in writing *Stranded in the Philippines*, relied heavily on the unpublished memoirs of Professor Roy Bell and his wife, Edna. Since much of the dialogue and many of the individuals' thoughts presented in the memoirs can no longer be verified (the Bells are deceased, as is Don, their son and a friend of the author), the reader should assume that those conversations and internal reflections reproduced by the author here came to the Bells secondhand or were re-created by the Bells based on their experiences.

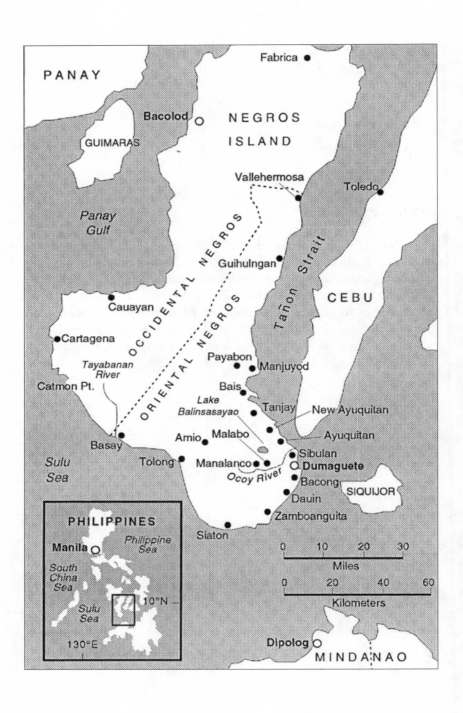

Prologue

Nineteen-year-old Henry Roy Bell shouted, "Halt!" to his mule and they stopped plowing in the middle of the field. It was midmorning in the spring of 1915 in central Kansas. Roy and the mule were not tired that early in the day—both had been working on this farm for most of their lives. A straw hat protected Roy's head from the sun, but drops of perspiration trickled off his forehead and tickled his face. But one drop had gotten into an eye, causing him to pause and pull out his handkerchief. As far as finding protection from the already blazing sun, Roy might as well have stopped there in the middle of the field as anyplace else around. There were no shade trees on the farm except the scrawny ones around the house.

Roy could look in all directions and see level fields plowed or being plowed for spring planting. In the near distance were a few farmsteads—most with a house, barn, windmill, and chicken shed. The flatland stretched to the horizon. Beyond, the same mostly treeless terrain extended for hundreds of miles in all directions—westward to the Rocky Mountains and eastward to the Ozarks of Missouri. To the north the Great Plains stretched through Kansas and across Nebraska, South Dakota, and North Dakota into Canada. To the south, the flatland stretched from Kansas and then across Oklahoma and Texas into Mexico. Roy had never seen any other landscape. Sometimes he wondered what the Rocky Mountains would look like—or New York City.

Roy's forebears on his father's side were Scotch-Irish frontier farmers who had moved westward successively from Ohio, Indiana, Illinois, Kansas, Oklahoma, and back to Kansas. But in 1890, six years before Roy's birth, the frontier had ended—no longer could a north-south line be drawn between settled and unsettled land. The famous historian Frederick Jackson Turner worried about the end of the frontier—it would no longer provide a safety valve for settlement by adventurous or discontented Americans as the population increased in the East and industry expanded. Roy, unlike his ancestors, could not look forward to the challenge and sometimes danger of seeking new farmland farther west. Yet Roy's future would hold risks to him and his family comparable to any harrowing experiences his pioneering ancestors might have had.

But that spring of 1915 was different for Roy. He was looking forward to being a student that September at Emporia College in east-central Kansas. The college had been founded in the town of Emporia by Presbyterians principally to serve the Scotch-Irish and other Presbyterians in the region. Roy had finished high school two years before, but at that time the Bell family had no extra money for college. They were just scraping by on the farm's income, which was down because of the low price of wheat. For the same reason, some neighboring farms badly needed painting, but the Bell family had not gone that far downhill. Yet after World War I began in 1914, the price of wheat soared and so did the fortunes of the Kansas wheat farmers. But Roy's father, Thomas Bell, still could not afford to send both Roy and his twin brother, Robert, to college. But the boys decided who should go by themselves—Roy had liked high school better than Robert and wanted to take on college, while Robert was not eager for more study and preferred to help his father keep the farm going.

On Roy's departure that crisp September day, the twins' four younger sisters cheerfully waved good-bye to him as he and Robert drove off in the family's farm wagon. It would take overnight to reach the nearest railroad station, so it was impractical for the four girls to see him off on the train. Besides, they were needed on the farm to do chores.

Their smiling farewell was sincere in wishing their brother well, but they also looked forward to being free of his oversight in doing their farm chores. Their father, Thomas, gladly left the girls' supervision to their mother. But she relied on Roy to settle quarrels among the girls, such as who would do the milking and other tedious chores. Roy was probably not very diplomatic in doing this, so the girls hoped he would like college well enough to stay for a time.

During his first year, Roy listened intently to the lectures of his professors, who gave him fresh outlooks on history and literature. But he was more intrigued when listening to the Presbyterian missionaries who were back from overseas on their sabbatical year of leave. Roy soaked up the accounts of their lives and challenges at missions all over the world.

When Roy came back to the farm for the summer, his sisters and Robert found him a changed person. Their often taciturn brother now enthusiastically told them about college life and his fellow students from cities and other states. His sisters had changed too. They stopped bickering while willingly working harder to keep the farm going—the whole family had more to do in Roy's absence. Yet now Roy did as much of the farmwork as possible to make up for his absence at school.

Roy enjoyed his second year at Emporia even more. Of only average size—he was 5'9" and weighed 160 pounds—he was strong, quick, and compactly built. He became a regular on the Emporia football team. He also took up tennis and soon competed with the strongest players in school.

But the most wonderful thing happened in his life one evening while he was listening to a Presbyterian missionary who taught at the Silliman Institute in the Philippines. Roy found the subject interesting, but his attention lagged. He discreetly looked around to see if any girls had come to hear the missionary. His gaze was rewarded when he spotted a beautiful young freshman who was paying more attention to the speaker than he was. After the missionary had finished, Roy walked over to the girl and could only think of blurting out, "Would you like to be a missionary and go to the Philippines?" To his surprise she answered quite seriously, "Yes, I think I would like being a teaching missionary." Roy thought, *What luck! To find an attractive girl who wants to be a missionary—something I was thinking a lot about myself.* He soon learned that her name was Edna Mae Elliot and that she came from a prosperous farm near Paola, Kansas, in the northeastern part of the state. By the end of the winter, Edna Mae and Roy were planning to go into missionary work together. But this plan had to be put on hold after April 6, 1917, when America entered World War I.

Roy, eligible for the draft in the summer of 1917, did not wait to be called. He enlisted in the Army Medical Corps and was sent to training camp and then Texas. A sad note at this time was the death of Roy's twin brother, Robert—the worldwide flu epidemic took his life. His death, while Roy survived, was ironic. Soldiers in training camps died by the thousands because the flu was highly contagious. Yet Robert, who on the farm was less likely to catch the flu from others, was stricken.

During the war Roy and Edna kept their dreams alive with frequent letters between Kansas and Texas. When the war ended in 1918, Roy returned to college and Edna. After Roy's graduation with a degree in history in 1920, he taught high school in western Kansas while waiting for Edna to graduate from Emporia.

In the meantime they applied to the Presbyterian Board of Foreign Missions to teach at the Silliman Institute in the Philippines. Even before Edna's graduation on June 3, 1921, the board hired the young couple—he would teach history and she would teach home economics and assist with music at the school's church.

Before they could proceed to the Philippines, however, the board required them to attend a weeklong training course in New York. But first there was something important that had to be done. Edna and Roy were married at Edna's home church in Paola. The bride and groom happily headed eastward on their first long trip together, taking the train to Chicago and connecting with the overnight train to New York. After the training course, the eager young couple proceeded by train and ship to their assignment at the Silliman Institute on Negros Island, one of the larger Philippine islands. The institute's president, David Hibbard, greeted his new teachers. He was already impressed by their credentials, but upon meeting them he thought they would greatly strengthen the school.

Twenty-one years before, Rev. Hibbard had been chosen by the Presbyterian Board of Foreign Missions to establish a school in the Philippines. The board was acting on a request by businessman Horace Silliman, who donated $10,000 to get the school started. Silliman's interest stemmed from the recent U.S. acquisition of the Spanish colony as a result of the Spanish-American War of 1898.

In starting the school, Hibbard had to think about competing with Catholic schools, which had existed over centuries of Spanish rule. Part of his solution was to establish his Protestant school far from Manila, where many of the Catholic schools were located. Hibbard chose Dumaguete, a provincial capital that was three hundred miles south of Manila.

Now, twenty years after starting the Silliman Institute in 1901, President Hibbard proudly showed the youthful Bell couple around the campus next to downtown Dumaguete, a town of 22,000. When Roy and Edna asked about the number of students, President Hibbard told them, "We now have several hundred boys and 55 girls—scattered in elementary and high schools and in our college. By the way, Roy, would you like to coach our athletic teams?"

Roy gladly added coaching to his duties, and in the following years Roy and Edna Mae lived up to Hibbard's expectations. In their ninth year Hibbard was so confident of Roy's ability that he asked him to spend his sabbatical year at the University of Chicago to obtain a master's degree in physics. Then Roy could teach physics at the university level—a requirement for fulfilling Hibbard's dream of making Silliman a university.

Roy was dubious. "I majored in history at Emporia, and I haven't done any academic work since. It was not my field in college, but I will do my best." That was good enough for President Hibbard, so next year Roy, Edna, and their sons, Kenneth and Donald, were off to Chicago for Roy's year of study. The outcome confirmed Hibbard's judgment. The following year Roy returned to Silliman with his master's degree and established the Department of Physics.

Silliman finally became a university in 1938—in large part because of the urging and planning of Hibbard, who was now a trustee. The next year Arthur L. Carson arrived to take over the presidency of the new university. With an enrollment of 1,228 high school and college students, it had become the largest educational institution in the Philippines outside Manila. To catch up with the increased number of students, Carson started construction of a main classroom building and a campus church.

While Silliman prospered, the situation in Europe became frightening. World War II had started on September 1, 1939, with the German invasion of Poland—a campaign that lasted only a month. By the summer of 1940, France and the Netherlands had fallen to German forces. Great Britain was left to fight alone in what seemed a hopeless battle against the German war machine. Almost unbelievably the British air force prevailed over German aircraft seeking to gain control of the air over Great Britain—the forerunner of the expected invasion, which consequently didn't happen.

But in the Far East Japan had benefited from the fall of France. On July 24, 1941, the supine Vichy government yielded the French colony of Indochina to Japan. Over the next four days, the Japanese occupied all of Indochina. In the meantime President Roosevelt halted U.S. scrap iron and oil shipments to Japan on July 26. This embargo seriously hindered the large ongoing Japanese military operations in China.

The Philippines were a special situation in the Far East. The United States had promised the islands independence in 1945, but until then America had pledged to protect them. So the Philippines seemed a likely target for a Japanese attack in retaliation for the U.S. embargo. Fearing such a move, the U.S. War Department recalled General Douglas MacArthur to active duty in

1940 to build up a joint American-Philippine force. But this buildup was not far along by the fall of 1941.

Yet there was no great anxiety in Manila and even less in Dumaguete, located on the agricultural island of Negros—the home of Silliman University. Local people thought that a Japanese landing could not succeed—it would be opposed by the U.S. Navy, the world's largest and most powerful. In any case the people in Dumaguete felt safe on their nonstrategic island of Negros.

Their island was about the size of Connecticut with a population of only 900,000. The mountainous interior made up the bulk of its area and was thinly populated and empty in some areas except for some reported pygmies. The interior hills and mountains were roadless, while the coastal roads had gaps that precluded a continuous traverse around the island.

Half of Roy's colleagues at Silliman were Filipino and also little concerned about the Japanese. But Roy feared an attack might be imminent because the American buildup in the Philippines would eventually threaten the rear of expected Japanese moves against the Dutch East Indies—defenseless after the German conquest of the Netherlands. While such conjectures were running through his mind during the 1941 fall semester, Professor Roy Bell kept busy with a full schedule of teaching and coaching.

Chapter 1

Pearl Harbor
Stuns Dumaguete

At 6:00 AM on December 8, 1941, Professor Henry Roy Bell was hurrying through the streets of Dumaguete, a small city of 22,000 on Negros Island in the Philippines. He was up early as usual on Mondays to teach his 7:00 AM physics class at Silliman University. Most of the classes at Silliman were held early in the morning or late in the afternoon to avoid the unbearable midday heat.

Walking briskly, the fit-looking, forty-five-year-old professor heard more noise than usual from the town dock where the interisland steamer *Panay* normally stopped every Monday morning to pick up mail and passengers bound for Manila—three hundred miles to the north. Professor Bell headed for the dock to see what was going on.

As he came closer, he found a much larger than normal crowd had gathered.

The *Panay* was tied up to the dock, but instead of an orderly procession of boarding passengers, the gangplank was crowded with people, some boarding and a few squeezing back down—seemingly having changed their minds about boarding. Instead of standing on the upper deck to benevolently watch his passengers board, the skipper, Captain Clemente Sumcad, was down on the main deck to help handle the overflow.

The captain's son, Ricardo, was in Roy's physics class, so Roy called out, "What's going on here, Captain?" The harassed skipper was so busy he merely answered, "I'll talk to you before we shove off, Roy." But a bystander answered Roy's question: "The Japs have bombed the American fleet at Pearl Harbor. I guess everyone with somebody dear in Manila wants to go and get them and bring them back here. The Japs would never bother to attack our small island."

Roy realized he shouldn't have bothered Sumcad, but he didn't wait to smooth things over. He had something that had to be done even if he didn't make his class that morning. He headed downtown to see Major Balolong, who had recently been assigned to command the Philippine constabulary soldiers in Oriental Negros Province, comprising the eastern half of Negros Island and a neighboring island, Siquijor. At Roy's knock, Balolong came to the door, still in his pajamas. The major recognized Professor Bell but had never spoken with him in the short time he had been on the job.

Now the sleepy major looked at Roy skeptically. "What is this about, Professor Bell?" Roy answered, "I'm sorry to bother you this early, but you need to know that the Japanese have bombed Pearl Harbor and have probably done a lot of damage. Some of the Japanese merchants in town may be spies." Major Balolong quickly replied, "I'll be with you in a moment. Maybe you can tell me about the merchants."

Soon the pudgy, now wide-awake Filipino major faced Professor Bell in the office adjoining his quarters. Roy spoke first: "About these Japanese merchants, a few months ago a clerk named Takuda bragged to me and others that the Japanese army could capture the Philippines in a few weeks. But I've been more suspicious of Morio, owner of the largest Japanese store in town. He's asked me details about how to reach the best hunting locations in the mountains, and he wanted to know if there were still Negritos [Asian pygmies] there. Morio already seemed to know a lot about the geography and sugar refineries on the island when he came here and bought the store a couple years ago."

Major Balolong assured Roy, "I have sealed orders in my safe to carry out in such an emergency. I'm not to open them until directed. I have no doubt I will soon receive word and then will deal with the merchants and other Japanese." Roy left somewhat confident that the new officer would act quickly and effectively.

Roy glanced at his watch and, unbelievably, found he could still get to his physics class on time. Everyone was there and all were in a high state of excitement. A determined professor, Roy tried to teach them for a while, but for the first time in his life he did not compel a class to complete its instruction period. After dismissing his students, he thought about the regular Monday morning chapel at 10:30 AM—he might have to say something as a senior faculty member. But not being fond of public speaking, Roy was pleased that President Arthur L. Carson would do most of the talking for the university.

Having some time on his hands, Roy walked slowly and full of thought over to his family's home on the campus. It was one of a number of faculty houses provided by the university—whitewashed and sturdy with steep, peaked roofs that were thatched with nipa palm fronds. The houses stood on stilts a full story off the ground for coolness and were surrounded by lush gardens and lime, orange, and avocado trees.

Inside Roy sank down on a comfortable chair to enjoy the airy coolness under the high ceiling woven from split bamboo stalks. But not for long; restless as usual, Roy got up and began to fiddle with his ham radio, hoping to learn more about Pearl Harbor or other Japanese moves. Then he could pass on any new developments at chapel. As for saying anything else, he would just support the comments of his friend, President Carson, as he had often done in the past.

That Monday morning all the students were at chapel—normally some didn't make it, although the Presbyterian school urged full attendance. Besides all the students, many people from town crowded into the Silliman University chapel, and many more stood outside hoping to hear anything important that was said. All waited expectantly and noisily to hear from President Carson as well as Guillermo Villanueva, governor of Negros Oriental Province—his office being located in Dumaguete. The crowd mostly chattered about how soon the Japanese forces would attack the Philippines and then their own island. The boarding students talked worriedly about returning to their home islands before the Japanese attacked Negros.

Roy could hear the buzzing crowd as he left his house. At the chapel he slipped in a side door that brought him near the podium. President Carson immediately spotted him and urgently motioned Roy to join him. Once Roy was seated, Carson bent toward him and made himself heard over the noisy crowd. "Roy, I want to keep our university going as long we can—at least until the end of the semester. Back me up on that point as strongly as possible." Roy assured him, "Arthur, I'll do the best I can, but I'm certain you'll make the case strongly. The Japs won't bother to come here that soon even if they're capable of doing so."

Already on the stage were Governor Villanueva and Major Robert Vesey, commander of U.S.-Philippine forces on Negros Island.[1] Carson had no trouble quieting the throng in front of him. Everyone was eager to hear from the leaders about the chances of a Japanese invasion. Major Vesey spoke first. He looked the part of a leader and an officer of his rank. He stood ramrod straight in his immaculate uniform. To build up his joint American-Philippine force, Vesey trained thousands of young Filipino recruits. Now, instead of training them, Vesey would have to lead his still unready young soldiers into battle. If he was concerned about that prospect, Vesey didn't show it.

As to the crowd's worry about the future, Vesey predicted firmly, "Dumaguete and Negros Island are in no immediate danger—they would be of little strategic value to the Japanese army." Vesey said nothing about the six-hundred-man Silliman Reserve Officers' Training Corps (ROTC). The cadets had been asking each other, "When will we be called into active duty?" Nevertheless, when Major Vesey concluded by declaring his confidence in eventual victory, he left the crowd in a more relaxed mood.

The next speaker was Governor Villanueva. He had a pleasant face and in office had done little to attract the attention of the university or the townspeople of Dumaguete. It was well known that he had investments in Japanese companies. Yet it was too soon to think of his being disloyal. In addressing the anxious audience, Villanueva did not speculate on the safety of Negros Island, but promised, "As governor of Oriental Negros province, I will cooperate in every way possible with the military and university authorities in the uncertain times ahead." The audience listened quietly to the governor, and then perked up when the university coach, Professor Roy Bell, began to speak.

Roy was better known as the coach in town, but on campus his physics classes were respected. However, the coach merely echoed Major Vesey's views that there was little danger to Negros Island. Bell spoke in short sentences, punctuated by occasional laughs that were his habit when making light of a subject. He insisted to the students, "Negros Island is neither rich, nor populous, nor strategic. If you live on this island, Dumaguete is a safe place, and it is easy for you to go home if you have to. If you live on another island, it is safer to stay here than risk a boat trip now."

President Carson spoke last "in a very unalarmed and diplomatic way," according to Edna Mae, Professor Bell's wife. Carson urged the students, "Stay for at least the six weeks that remain in the current semester. In that short time the Japanese will not bother to come to this unimportant island even if they capture Manila before American forces come to the rescue. Silliman University will stay open! Let's go back to class." The students listened attentively. As they left the chapel, they talked quietly and were less apprehensive than before—though not persuaded about finishing the last six weeks of the semester.

As the speakers came off the stage, Roy Bell brought up the question of the Japanese merchants with Major Vesey. He reported, "I visited Major Balolong earlier this morning to ask about the Japanese and German residents here in Dumaguete." Before Roy could continue, Vesey interjected, "There are thirty Japanese aliens and six Germans here in Dumaguete.

Major Balolong should be picking them up right now. We'll put the Japs in the provincial jail and keep the Germans under guard at the Bais Central Sugar plant north of here."

But Roy Bell was worried. "Most of the Japanese merchants have been in Dumaguete for years and are accepted by the community because of fair dealing and courtesy. However, I suspect the newcomers. I would hate to have the others who have been here for some time treated unfairly—most are probably innocent." Vesey assured Roy, "Well, we'll find out quickly if any of them have been subversive. Balolong's men will check their homes and store records. If they haven't done anything, they have nothing to fear. I'll have Balolong let you know what we find out." Reassured about the Japanese merchants, Roy headed home for lunch with his family. As always, Edna gave the blessing, but this time she also fervently prayed for the family's safety.

Any success the chapel speakers might have had in calming the students that morning was soon undone. The Manila broadcast reported that at about 1:00 PM—less than a day after the Pearl Harbor attack—Japanese bombers and Zero fighters had unleashed a devastating attack on American airpower in the Philippines. Many of the American fighter aircraft stationed around Manila were caught on the ground, as well as sixteen new B-17 Flying Fortress bombers at Clark Field.

The B-17s had been ordered aloft in early daylight to keep them safe while the high command in Manila determined what to do with them. They finally decided to bomb Japanese facilities on Formosa. But by this time the bombers were short of fuel and so landed at Clark to refuel for the three-hundred-mile flight to Formosa. They were still on the ground when the Japanese aircraft struck. Sixteen of the B-17s at Clark Field were destroyed. The eighteen other B-17s in the Philippines had recently been withdrawn to Del Monte Airfield on Mindanao—well out of the range of Japanese bombers based on Formosa.[2]

But that same afternoon, Japanese naval aircraft showed that none of the Philippines was safe from attack. Carrier planes bombed Davao, a large coastal city on Mindanao—the southernmost island. When Modesta Hughes and other Silliman students from Mindanao learned of this attack on their home island, they rushed down to the city dock, hoping to find some way home. But they found no ship bound for Mindanao and no likely future passage since the *Panay*'s normal weekly service south would probably end. The *Panay* never called at Dumaguete again; it was sunk by enemy bombers and Captain Sumcad lost on January 2.

Modesta, a twenty-year-old freshman, dejectedly trudged back to the campus. She was just finishing her first year at Silliman—the first time she had been away from home for any long period. Her father, a veteran of the Spanish-American War of 1898, had stayed in the Philippines after the war and bought a farm near Davao. Modesta was homesick at school. Yet she had stuck it out. Now, instead of walking back to her dormitory, Modesta went to President Carson's office and pleaded for help—her natural shyness had been overcome by not knowing how or when she could get home. The harassed president immediately invited Modesta to stay with his family until she could get home, so she gathered up her belongings at the dormitory and crossed the campus to the Carsons' residence, where Edith Carson warmly welcomed her. A few days later the Bell family, like the Carsons, took in another stranded female student, Arnaldy Ramos; Nelly, as she was called, was also from Davao City.

That evening Roy and Edna Bell heard from their sons about how their fellow students felt about the Japanese attacks on the Philippines. Nineteen-year-old Ken reported, "Everyone I talked to from another island wanted to go home right now! And most from our island were almost as eager to leave. But I think we should stay here and fight." But seventeen-year-old Don pointed out, "The Japs aren't even here yet! Maybe it will be a long time—they haven't even landed and taken any territory yet."

Roy didn't let on how worried he was. He feared the Japanese had won a big advantage in the Philippines with their initial attacks, just as they had inflicted heavy losses of American ships at Pearl Harbor—something he had gleaned from his ham radio. Roy didn't express his gloomy thoughts to his family, nor did he mention Major Balolong's task of rounding up the Japanese and German inhabitants of Dumaguete. He thought it best not to bring up that subject until it was determined which of them were enemy agents and which were not.

After the boys were asleep, Edna had subjects she wanted to bring up for just the two of them to discuss. Because of her job as dean of women at Silliman, Edna asked Roy, "What shall we do about our girls who live in the dormitory? They'll be eager to go home, but they'll face more danger than the boys. The thirty girls from Thailand are a special worry—they'll have to go by passenger ship." Roy replied, "Answers will be found tomorrow." But even as he was about to drift off to sleep in his chair, Edna persisted: "What does our family do if the Japanese land on Negros? It is probably impossible for us to go back to America. We should be thinking about what we should do if the Japs come here."

Roy controlled his drowsiness and assured her, "We'll find answers as we go along. We'll plan as much as possible as we know more. For now, we should retire and get some sleep." Once in bed, though, Roy couldn't follow his own advice. He kept mulling over the Japanese merchants. Finally he promised himself to check with Major Balolong first thing in the morning. Then sleep finally came.

Chapter 2

Buckling Down
to War

P rofessor Bell awoke early the day after the war had begun. But unlike the day before, he didn't have to awaken Major Balolong early. Today Roy waited until after breakfast to visit the major, who cheerfully announced, "We have more than 30 Japanese in the provincial jail and six Germans under guard at the Bais Central Sugar Refinery complex north of town. We searched Morio's large store and other Japanese stores and store-owners' homes. Many of them were officers in the Japanese army, and their stores had been subsidized by the Japanese government." The professor nodded in approval and commented, "I always wondered how the groceries and other items could be so cheap—part of their scheme to be well thought of and trusted, I guess."

At lunch with the family that day, Edna reported, "At the office, we had calls from parents far and near for their daughters to return home immediately. But other parents from areas of Luzon and Mindanao that had already been attacked pleaded for our faculty to take care of their children—believing they would be safer here." Roy had seen some students board overcrowded buses while others were picked up by parents or relatives, who had driven miles to reach Dumaguete. Their boys, Ken and Don, likewise noticed friends waiting impatiently to leave town. On the other hand, the six hundred members of the Silliman ROTC were proud to be staying on campus, as ordered by Major Vesey.

With most of the students gone after the war began on Monday, Professor Bell had no classes to teach and no teams to coach. Roy was uncertain as to what he could do to help the war effort. So on Friday he hustled down to the city dock to watch a group of American officers come ashore. They said they had come from General William F. Sharp's headquarters on the island of Cebu and wanted to see the town's mayor.

Roy pointed them to Mayor Perdices' office, which was a short walk from the dock. One of Roy's colleagues, Professor Ben Viloria, and some interested townsmen followed Roy, also hoping to learn what American military leaders had in mind for their island. Ben asked Roy, "Does this visit of high-ranking officers mean they think we will be attacked?" Roy answered his old friend, "In that case, I hope I can find a way to resist the enemy."

In less than a half hour, Mayor Perdices came out of his office with the officers and stood before the expectant group. Perdices was a trim, confident young man, never at a loss for words. He explained, "These officers from General Sharp have informed me that substantial army forces are being sent here to protect Negros Island. In an hour we will have a town meeting in the university chapel. Please spread the word to all Dumaguete citizens to attend because important business will be carried out."

An hour later, Perdices opened the meeting by explaining, "Dumaguete and the province will have many soldiers stationed in and around our provincial capital here. They will need to be supported with provisions, supplies, and transport. An orderly process would be needed for the purchase of supplies and services at fair prices. Vehicles might have to be requisitioned." The mayor paused and continued, "Therefore, we are going to choose a civil affairs officer to mediate disputes and keep good relations between the Army and civilians."

Then the mayor asked for nominations. First to stand up was Dr. Ponce de Leon, director of the Presbyterian Mission Hospital in Dumaguete. He confidently declared, "Dr. Arthur Carson, president of Silliman University, would make an excellent civil affairs officer. He has done a wonderful job in leading the university and gives good support to the Presbyterian hospital, which serves the whole province. Furthermore, he has excellent relations with our townspeople." No one wanted to challenge the popular and respected doctor.

The crowd was silent while President Carson paused to gather his thoughts. He had not expected to be nominated. While pleased with the sincere appreciation of his work, Carson instantly thought to himself, *I have only been here two years. Before coming here as president, I have spent my whole life teaching. I want to help in any way I can. But how useful would I be in such a job? My main effort here has been to add new university buildings.*

Finally Carson stood up—resolute and relaxed now that he had made up his mind. He declared, "I appreciate your confidence in considering me for your civil affairs officer, but my two years here are not long enough for me to serve effectively in this job. Silliman University will do everything possible to support the war effort—a 600-student ROTC unit has remained on the campus, and the faculty and staff will do anything they can. The university can even provide the perfect civil affairs officer, Professor Roy Bell—a coach and professor here for 20 years."

Whoops of approval came from the town meeting at the mention of Roy Bell. The loudest shout came from Mr. Angel Jornales, father of Victor, who played on Coach Bell's football team. Angel had been grateful for Coach Bell's steadying influence on the boy. Now the meeting joined in a unanimous voice approval for the coach. Everyone was familiar with Professor Bell's coaching, if not his physics courses.

Roy was not against taking the job, but he was never happy about making a speech. Yet now words came to him. "I do not feel very qualified for this job. My military experience consists of being in the Army Medical Corps in Texas daring World War I. In Dumaguete, I've just been a citizen—never having worked for the government. But I will do my best to stand up for the interests of the civilians and our local government on issues that come up with the Army. And I will do my best to help everyone get ready to defend our province and Negros Island."

As the town meeting broke up, Governor Villanueva came up to Roy and told him how pleased he was to have Roy's help as civil affairs officer and said, "With your new job, you should have an office in town. You must take the empty office next to mine." This was in line with the governor's promise on the first day of the war to help in the crisis.

But now Villanueva surprised Professor Bell by adding, "Instead of me, I want you to take over chair of the weekly meetings of the heads of the emergency committees that the Philippine government has had me establish." The committee heads were from Silliman University and had responsibility for Public Health and Sanitation; Beach Patrol; and Food, Transportation, and Fuel, which Roy himself headed.

Roy respectfully answered, "I am willing to try this, Governor, but insist you attend the weekly meetings and give us advice and direction."

Villanueva did attend the meetings, though Roy noticed the governor was reluctant to assert himself. He attributed this to Villanueva's Japanese investments. Roy did not question Villanueva's loyalty and urged him to take a more active role. And for a time the governor did speak up more.

On his first day in office, Roy received a call from Major Vesey, who explained, "We're going to need help with transportation as well as food and clothing for the troops—no more supplies can reach us from Manila.

I've invited Felix Montenegro to meet with us at your office. He has offered to turn over some trucks to the Army from his sugar plantation." That afternoon, the relaxed, patriotic Montenegro signed over all of his plantation trucks to a delighted Major Vesey.

During the following days, Roy requested food, clothing, and vehicles from a diverse group of citizens—Filipinos, a few of strong Spanish descent, a few Americans, and a few Chinese merchants. Most of them gave gladly, but Felix Montenegro and the others were later disillusioned when the young enlisted Army quartermaster in Dumaguete failed to compensate them— they rightly believed the Army had plenty of money. Felix came to Roy after being told that he would have to wait some time to be paid for his trucks. Roy listened sympathetically to the disturbed planter and said he would look into the matter.

The next day Roy took a boat to the nearby large island of Cebu to seek help from Colonel Cooke, who was in charge of Army finances in the islands south of Luzon. Cooke listened attentively, but could or would not help after Roy insisted that such patriotic citizens should be paid. Yet Cooke did not wish to antagonize this determined civil affairs officer. Hoping to divert Roy's attention, Colonel Cooke motioned to one of his young officers waiting outside to come in. Cooke explained to Roy, "Captain Redmond here has a problem that maybe you can help him with since you were a physics professor in civilian life." Turning to Redmond, Cooke requested, "Tell Mr. Bell the details, Captain."

Redmond then explained to Roy, "Sir, a fisherman on the north shore of Cebu thought he had a prize when he snagged and tied up a large ball encased in metal that had floated ashore. Unfortunately some of his friends have done the same thing. These mines had broken loose and drifted down from the minefield the enemy had laid in the Surigao Strait. We know that other mines have drifted farther south to Siquijor. But we don't know how to safely detonate them."

Thoroughly interested in Captain Redmond's problem, Roy suggested to Redmond, "I believe I can detonate the mines. Could you come back to Dumaguete with me and we'll tackle the mines that have drifted down to Siquijor? Then you'll know how to handle the others." Captain Redmond eagerly assented, and Colonel Cooke was relieved to have Roy out of his hair. When Roy and the captain reached Siquijor, they found the locals had left alone six mines that had drifted to a deserted beach. There Roy showed Captain Redmond how to detonate them. They were large and had German-made components. Then the captain went back to Cebu and detonated the mines there himself.

On January 3, 1942, three weeks into his job as civil affairs officer, Roy Bell joined President Carson to witness the induction of the six-hundred-student Silliman ROTC unit into the American-Philippine armed forces. After the war began, the cadets had been ordered to stay on campus. Since then, Captain Salvador Abcede and Lieutenant Ceferino Galvez had been rigorously training them. Now Roy Bell and President Carson looked on proudly but soberly as the student-cadets fell into a perfect formation and were sworn into service by General Guy O. Fort.[1] President Carson and Professor Bell bade them farewell, since the next morning the young soldiers were to move as a complete battalion to the northern part of the province to face the expected enemy invasion.

Civil Affairs Officer Bell and President Arthur Carson faced a dangerous future themselves. They had no feasible way to leave the Philippines with their families. The war news was bad—Japanese troops marched into Manila on December 22, 1941, after General MacArthur had declared it an open city. He was withdrawing his forces to Bataan Peninsula for a last stand—without having stored enough rice there for a prolonged siege. U.S. naval forces withdrew to the Dutch East Indies, leaving MacArthur with neither air nor naval support.

Yet, like most Americans and Filipinos, Bell and Carson did not realize the bleakness of their situation—they still thought American forces would come across the Pacific on a rescue mission in six months or so and doubted that the Japanese would bother about their agricultural island of Negros.

However, Roy had plenty to do without worrying about the uncertain future. At his weekly meeting with the emergency committees' heads, the chairman of the Food Committee, Professor James Chapman, reported, "I have persuaded people to plant thousands of banana plants and even introduced two new plants—that is for the future—but now the local stores have run out of corn and rice. Jap warships have stopped our regular imports from Mindanao." Roy nodded respectfully to Dr. Chapman, a world-renowned entomologist, and said, "I'll try to think of something." Dr. Chapman replied, "It would be wonderful if you could, but I don't see what we can do."

In fact Roy had noticed the local grain shortage and was about to work out a solution—it involved the grain supply on the neighboring island of Mindanao. But he hadn't told anybody about it, wisely believing there had to be traitors in Dumaguete after its people had been bombarded for weeks by enemy broadcasts that promised a bright future for the Philippines. So Roy kept to himself what he had observed of the movements of the enemy destroyer that had been sinking the boats bringing grain from Mindanao. He noticed that the enemy warship was patrolling on a regular schedule—one day it would pass eastward and the next day westward to cut off north-south shipping on the fifteen-mile-wide sea separating Negros from Mindanao. The times of passing were quite predictable.

Roy scheduled his project for the day after Dr. Chapman's report. Late that afternoon, after telling his family about his plans, Roy climbed aboard a motor launch and waited patiently until the enemy destroyer passed westward into the setting sun. Now Roy pushed away from shore and chugged steadily southward toward Mindanao. It was a moonlit night, but the enemy was no threat—Japanese aircraft usually did not fly after dark, and the destroyer should not be back until morning.

Before dawn Mindanao came into sight. Coming closer, Roy could see enough detail of the shoreline to find the landing spot described by Roy's friend on Mindanao, Father O'Toole. Roy had arranged with him for delivery of grain to the deserted cove. Now O'Toole was there with the sacks of grain. They worked quickly, but it was dawn before they finished. Daylight return was out of the question because of enemy aircraft, so O'Toole took Roy to a nearby parishioner's house, where Roy enjoyed a welcome sleep after his all-night crossing.

The next night Roy again was chugging until dawn—this time in the opposite direction with a load of grain—and again avoided the destroyer which kept to its patrolling schedule. Roy made several such trips before the Japanese landed on the north coast of Mindanao.

Chapter 3

Wives Retreat
to Malabo

Roy was soon busy on his new job as civil affairs officer while Edna was left to deal with the safety of their children. Yet an additional concern for Edna, as dean of women, was the welfare of the university girls from the other Philippine islands and other countries. The weekly boat service to Manila and south to Mindanao—Dumaguete's only scheduled link with the outside world—was not likely to continue. Those girls could be stranded.

Edna had worried out loud to Roy about these problems as they were going to bed the first evening of the war, but no solutions were possible that early. The next morning, after a fitful sleep, Edna walked across the campus to President Carson's house. At the door Edna's friend, Edith Carson, the president's wife, invited her in for a cup of coffee. After they were seated, Edna blurted out, "What are we going to do if the Japs land here today or tomorrow?" A calmer Edith replied, "I don't believe they're coming that soon. Yet we should have some plan to get the stranded girls and our children out of town quickly when and if they come."

Edith's comment settled Edna down. Edna picked up on the idea of getting out of town, saying, "There is an empty elementary school five or six miles away where the road ends at the foot of the mountains. Our own children and the stranded University girls could hike out there on short notice." But Edith, not as familiar with the countryside as Edna, asked, "Won't the Japs be able to catch up with us by driving along the road?" Edna explained, "The hiking trail cannot be seen from the road and, if we get them going soon enough, the Japs won't even know about the flight." Edith nodded and Edna went on. "Let's have a practice hike right after lunch. I'll get the Thai girls and you round up the Philippine girls who are still here."

The girls assembled early in the afternoon in front of the president's house for the westward trek to the schoolhouse at the village of Palimpinon. Before the hike started, a now composed Edna explained to the girls, "We're just doing this for practice. The Japs may never reach Dumaguete. But if they do, we want to get out of the way of the fighting as quickly as possible." The hike was successful—most of the girls treated it as a lark.

The next day another practice hike wasn't so much fun because the students were discouraged by news of strong Japanese attacks on Mindanao and Luzon—the largest Philippine island, where Manila is located. So the uneasy girls hurried and made the round-trip in less than three hours.

Now Edna became more concerned. That evening she told Roy, "I believe we should move our children and the stranded girls to the schoolhouse at Palimpinon right away." Roy quickly answered, "Yes! Moving would be safer. But the school's wood floors won't be comfortable. I guess you can buy food from the local farmers, but it will be a job to prepare meals for the crowd. President Carson and I can stay on the campus and make an escape by car." Edna agreed; "I know there will be hardships but we have to keep our children and our students as safe as we can."

The next day the Bell and Carson children and college girls took their clothes and personal belongings to the schoolhouse, where each chose a floor space for sleeping. To feed the crowd, Bob Carson and Ken Bell built a cooking shack outside the school, and some of the college girls helped Edna and Edith cook rice and chicken and serve fresh bananas and avocados. It was easy to buy food, but sleeping on the hard floor was a comedown from the dormitory beds and beds in the faculty houses. Edna recalled, "Those first nights were difficult and we woke up more tired than we were when we went to bed, but we were to find in the days ahead there were times when we looked back on a dry, smooth, hard wood floor for sleeping as a luxury."

One day Edna decided to come down to town from the schoolhouse to buy some clothes. She had just finished shopping at the large Chinese store on Main Street when the air-raid bell rang from the old Moro tower downtown.[1] Merchants frantically closed their shops, but ten enemy aircraft had already come in sight—there was no early warning system.

Edna rushed to the lumberyard, clutching her purchases, and pushed herself and packages into a large, crowded culvert. She and the others froze in terror as the sound of the aircraft became louder and louder. Then Edna, being the last in the culvert, could see the planes circling lazily over the town. Fearing they would land rather than bomb, Edna, still clutching her bags, squeezed out of the culvert and began the hike to the schoolhouse retreat.

But just out of town Edna was picked up by Silliman professor Ramon Tapales and his wife, who had been frightened by the aircraft into driving their car toward the hills.

Back at the schoolhouse, Edna joined Edith in worried discussion. Both were aware of General MacArthur's retreat to Luzon's Bataan Peninsula and were now still more concerned by the flight of enemy aircraft over Dumaguete. They briefly felt safe at the Palimpinon schoolhouse, but now Edna declared, "It is only a matter of time until the Japs take Luzon. I'm no longer counting on American-Filipino forces fighting much on our island. After taking Dumaguete, the Japs will soon spread out to the ends of all roads out of town, and they will certainly come here. We have to move our families into the mountains—the sooner the better."

Edith agreed but pointed out, "Although a move will be easier because the Filipino girls have found homes with faculty families—like your Arnaldy and our Modesta—we still have the Thai girls on our hands. Shall we try to take them with us?"

Edith replied, "That really worries me. It's hard to conceive of a large enough shelter and the task of feeding the 30 of them in the mountains." Then both women knelt and prayed, believing that somehow a solution would be provided.

Miraculously the next day the Thai girls' student leader shyly reported to Edna and Edith, "We have found a place in the hills where the villagers want to have us as long as conditions are unsettled. But we are grateful to you for taking care of us up to now." Surprised, Edna and Edith asked the girl a few questions, but became convinced the Thai girls would be reasonably safe.

After the girls departed, Edith remarked, "They might be safer anyway by being away from us Americans.[2] Now with the Philippine girls locally placed and Thai girls taken care of, we can attend to our families' safety."

In President Carson's office, their husbands were also discussing what should be done in view of the worsening situation. Roy pointed out, "Most faculty members already have vacation cottages in the mountains, which should be remote enough to escape the Japs' notice. I had a rough hut way up by a mountain lake some years ago, but we haven't kept it up and it is not livable for even one family. I know you have been too busy with the campus construction program in your two years here to think about a vacation cottage. Since we both should have a place to go if necessary, why don't we join forces? Besides, our wives have already worked together in establishing the temporary retreat at Palimpinon."

Carson delightedly replied, "That would be wonderful and helpful because of your familiarity around here. Have you thought about a desirable location?"

Roy was stumped. "Even though I've been here for most of 20 years I can't readily think of a good place—the other faculty members have already taken many good spots in this region. Anyway, it would be safer to find a new place not very close to them to attract less attention."

During this discussion Ben Viloria dropped by the office. He was a good friend of both and a tenured professor in the history department. Since Viloria had lived all his life in Dumaguete, Carson asked his professor if he could suggest a suitable location in the hills. Ben Viloria pondered carefully, realizing that his advice very well could be followed and might be dangerous after the Japs actually came.

Viloria began by hedging. "I know a village that has no Americans, but is considerably closer to Dumaguete than my cabin or the retreat cabin of any of the faculty. But it has the advantage of requiring a very difficult hike to get there. It is the farming village of Malabo, located on a farming plateau only five or six miles from Palimpinon—yet almost straight uphill. The villagers should be friendly. Why don't you send your wives and children up there and look it over." Roy and Arthur Carson liked the Malabo described by Ben Viloria. So they decided to send their wives and children first because the villagers might more readily accept them rather than the complete families. The husbands would not need to come at that time anyway.

So on January 7, 1942, Edna, Edith, and their children left the schoolhouse at Palimpinon and followed a trail upstream along the Ocoy River, which came out of the mountains near the school. After a short distance they reached a ford across the swift-flowing river and waded ankle-deep to the other side. From there they followed a horse trail that ran beside a branch of the Ocoy and led them upward to the village of Pulangbato, where the horse trail ended. Here, at an elevation of nine hundred feet, they felt a welcome coolness while they rested. From there a steep path took them past huge red boulders, around which the stream swirled downward. As they continued the trail had to zigzag sharply for them to ascend beside the plunging waters.

Two hours after leaving the schoolhouse, the families found themselves at the edge of an open plateau that clung like a shelf to the mountainside at an altitude of 1,710 feet. Edna and Edith were captivated by what they saw—an open area of coconut trees amid small, tilled fields, covering about six hundred acres, and close by the thatched dwellings of the farmers' village.

Scrub jungle growth reached down to the edge of the fields while mountains towered beyond. Nearby a large spring of water gushed out of the ground.

A confident-looking, middle-aged woman came out of one the village's thatched homes and stood smiling before them. Edna tried to start a conversation in Tagalog, the common village language in the Philippines, but apparently she wasn't proficient enough because the woman didn't say a word, but just kept smiling. Edna then tried Spanish and finally English, but all she received was a bigger smile. Soon the woman's children came out and clung to her. Finally her husband appeared. He smiled and asked in understandable English, "Where are all of you going?"

Edna answered, "This is where we planned to come to. Right here. We live down in Dumaguete but expect Japanese soldiers to land there soon. They are enemies of Filipinos and Americans so we would like to live here until they're gone. Our husbands may come later, but they don't want to farm—in fact we would like to buy food at your village while we're here."

The man listened carefully and, smiling broadly, said, "You are welcome to stay close by this spring near us. My name is Pedro, and my wife's name is Maria. I will tell my neighbors. They will like to have you here too. When are you coming?"

Edna and Edith were flabbergasted by this welcome. When Edna told Pedro they would like to move tomorrow, Pedro pointed to an old weaving shed that could provide temporary shelter for them. When Edith told Pedro of their need of help to bring cooking gear from Palimpinon, he sent his wife to a nearby neighbor. Maria soon came back with two young men who agreed to carry the cooking equipment from the schoolhouse for a few pesos. The move was accomplished the next day. Edna and Edith felt safer than they had since the war began.

This sense of security helped them to adjust to the one-room weaving shed, which was about the size of a small bedroom and had to accommodate the six sleepers at night. Besides being crowded, the sleepers soon experienced damp bedding during a four-day rainstorm because of leaks in the roof. The floor became a sea of mud, but Edna and Edith kept cheerful even when they had a frustrating time cooking because the damp wood made only a smoldering fire.

While Edna was doing her first washing in the spring nearby, she lost the diamond from her wedding ring. Her sons had never seen her in tears before. They hurried over to her. But the boys could see nothing on the sandy bottom of the crystal clear spring. Yet when Don delved into the sand, he grasped it right away. His joyous mother thanked both boys and then God in silent prayer.

The wives hired some laborers to build a permanent house close to the spring. The workers understood the wives' eagerness to get into a larger house and hurried. They used split bamboo for the walls and floor and abaca shingles for the roof.[3] The house was to be long and relatively narrow and would have three rooms plus a kitchen at the end.

While they were living in the weaving shed, the teenage boys, Ken and Don Bell and Bob Carson, complained about their mothers' cooking. The mothers astutely sent the boys on an overnight hike with Filipino guides. The boys enjoyed the hike, but upon their return they felt differently about their mothers' cooking. Bob Carson wrote, "The guides wouldn't fix food for us so we were left on our own. The result was not so good. From then on we felt blissful about our mothers' meals."[4]

Bob was also eager to get back with his mother because Modesta, the college girl staying with the Carsons, would soon rejoin them. Modesta and Arnaldy, the Bells' college girl, had temporarily stayed on the campus until the larger place in Malabo was completed. Bob Carson, age sixteen, was eager to have Modesta, who was twenty, back in the family again. He thought she was the most beautiful girl he had ever seen. Modesta, who had been homesick at Silliman all year, had sought out the Carsons the day after the war began. She despaired of getting home because of Japanese attacks near her home on Mindanao.

The new house at Malabo was still not finished when two Filipinos in ragged clothing suddenly appeared and excitedly announced to the wives, "The Japanese landed south of Dumaguete, causing a mass flight into the mountains." After they unsteadily stumbled off, Edna remarked to Edith, "Well, those fellows must have drunk too much *tuba* at our little market here.[5] Roy and your husband would certainly already have sent a messenger or come themselves if the Japs had actually landed." Despite her skepticism, Edna sent a messenger to Roy to make sure there had been no landing. Roy answered, "The Japs have not come ashore here. This is a rumor that might have started because of a recent landing on Mindanao."

After four weeks the workers completed the house, which gave the two families some space, but their dry food, belongings, and furniture were down the difficult trail at the Palimpinon schoolhouse. To transport the families' goods, their neighbor Pedro called on Ambrosio, chief of the mountain carriers, or *cargadores*. He assigned a dozen of them to carry the two families' possessions to Malabo.

Late the next morning, the wives' neighbors gaped at the procession of heavily laden *cargadores* who emerged on the Malabo plateaus, amazed that they were looking at the possessions of only two families. The *cargadores* used large woven baskets that had hemp straps that were wrapped across their shoulders and foreheads to bear the weight. They filled the joint house with rice, corn, cassava flour, salt, canned goods, bedding, and clothes.[6] The inside of the house became a mess. When Ken Bell brought his pet turkeys inside, his mother exploded for once in her life, yelling, "You put those turkeys back in the weaving shed. I don't want them in the new house ever again."

The next day was Sunday and the new dry floor was practically covered with all the stuff the *cargadores* brought up. For the first time in their memories the wives forgot about any kind of religious service. Finally, after straightening things out, Edith commented, "We're still cramped for space, but at least we have a roof over our heads that can keep us dry."

At night the large household arranged itself to accommodate everyone—the Bell adults had double-decker beds at one corner; the college girls, Arnaldy and Modesta, were lodged in another corner; the Carsons' ten-year-old daughter, Jean, slept on a sofa bed on the first floor; and Donald and Kenneth Bell and Robert Carson slept on the second floor.

The village neighbors continued to be curious, stopping by the new house on their way back and forth from the community spring. They lingered to watch the American women cook and wash dishes. For their part Edna and Edith noticed how the neighbors used the spring—to wash clothes, sponge themselves, and fill bamboo tubes with water to carry home. Often Pedro's wife, Maria, and others brought the Americans a few eggs, onions, or tomatoes. In turn the Americans helped Maria and others whose cooking fires had died out during the night with a stick of fire in the morning—the American wives carefully banked the glowing logs from evening cooking to hold embers overnight. The villagers had no matches, while Edna and Edith hoarded theirs, having no prospect of getting more. For lighting lanterns, the American women used scrap paper to bring flame from the log fire.

One day, after noticing an infected cut on a neighbor's wrist, Edna treated it with sulfanilamide. Afterward word of the rapid care spread beyond the Malabo plateau into the mountains. Soon people were coming from all directions for treatment of sores, ulcers, boils, and bolo cuts.[7]

Another day a twenty-year-old named Julio came to their "clinic" with his right arm in a sling and bleeding profusely from the large vein on the back of his right hand. The wives had him lie down and put on a tourniquet, but the bleeding continued long enough to scare the amateur doctors. However, it gradually slowed and stopped by the time Roy Bell and Arthur Carson returned in the late afternoon from their usual workday in Dumaguete.

Edna greeted Roy abruptly: "We've had a time today with a boy with a bad cut. Our tourniquet took forever to stop the bleeding. We put him in the weaving shed for the night. If he starts bleeding again, we'll need your help."

After the families finished their joint dinner, a worried Edith Carson pointed out, "What would we do if we got a patient with a serious problem such as Julio's who could be saved, but we didn't know enough to give him the right treatment?" Arthur agreed: "That is a problem that could come up." He turned to Roy and said, "We should have an experienced doctor here since there will be a greater need here with various faculty families moving into the mountains. You've known Dr. Ponce de Leon, Director of the Mission Hospital, much longer than I. Why don't you talk to him tomorrow about our clinic and need for professional help?"

The next day Roy spoke to Dr. Ponce at the Mission Hospital in Dumaguete. Within days Ponce sent Dr. Vicente de Juan and two nurses to Malabo, where they became a branch of the hospital in town. Their arrival brought great relief to Edna and Edith.

Chapter 4

The Fall of Cebu

W hile Edna Bell and Edith Carson and their children coped with their new life on the Malabo plateau, American and Filipino soldiers were battling the Japanese on Bataan Peninsula. They lacked air and naval support, and their rations had been cut in half since their retreat. The need to make a stand on Bataan had not been expected, so little rice—the staple food in the Philippines—had been stored on the peninsula.

By March 11, 1942, the U.S. government realized American defeat and surrender on Bataan were quite likely. Yet General MacArthur, a symbol of American defiance, must not be part of that surrender. So the U.S. Army ordered General MacArthur to seek safety in Australia.

After turning over his command to General Jonathan Wainwright, MacArthur waited until after dark to board PT-41. The PTs were rough-riding patrol boats designed to close with enemy warships at fifty miles per hour, fire torpedoes, and use their speed to escape. But PT-41 could only manage twenty-six miles per hour because of bent struts and propeller. The skipper, Lieutenant John Bulkeley, was to deliver MacArthur to Cagayan, on the northern coast of Mindanao—the southernmost Philippine island.

The bouncing, jarring ride quickly made everyone sick or queasy. MacArthur himself suffered most—he lost everything in his stomach and kept retching as he lay gray-faced on the deck. After thirty hours of misery, the general's nausea eased as PT-41 passed into the calmer waters of Mindanao Sea. A revived MacArthur aroused his aide and outlined how he would retake the Philippines.

Lieutenant Bulkeley delivered the general to Cagayan, which had not yet been occupied by the enemy. MacArthur had to wait there four days before a B-17 Flying Fortress picked him up and flew him to Darwin, on Australia's north coast. There an enemy air raid was in progress, so he landed forty miles inland, from where another plane flew him beyond range of enemy aircraft and into Australia's vast interior.

In the Philippines John Bulkeley took his PT-41 and PT-34—which operated under his command—to Cebu City for repairs. Bulkeley hoped his bent propeller and struts could be repaired to restore PT-41 to its designed performance. PT-34 just needed maintenance.

The Filipino workers at the drydock assured him and Lieutenant Bob Kelly, the skipper of PT-34, "We'll fix up your boats. They'll be as good as new." Bulkeley and Kelly nodded politely, but as they walked into town for a drink, Kelly worried out loud, "The only equipment I saw in that shop was heavy wire, large pliers, and a ten-pound hammer." Bulkeley replied in a resigned tone, "Well, we'll know how good they can do tomorrow when we pick up the boats. Meanwhile let's relax and have a good drink."

Next day Bob Kelly took his PT-34 out for a test run and found its operation greatly improved. He was still thanking the Filipinos for their work when his boss, John Bulkeley, interrupted. "We have to get going now. A Japanese heavy cruiser and destroyer are moving south on the west side of Cebu. The Japs won't be able to see us if we head south on this side of the island, so we can surprise them in the middle of the night at the southern tip of the island—if we can get there in time."

In a short time Bulkeley's tiny two-boat squadron was churning southward on the eastern side of the long, narrow island of Cebu. Bulkeley had hoped the enemy warships were continuing their course and speed, and his timing turned out to be perfect. As the PTs rounded the southern tip of Cebu in the early hours of April 9, their lookouts could make out the dark hulls of the enemy warships heading toward them. Bulkeley steered his PT-41 at full throttle toward the enemy cruiser while Kelly's PT-34 slowed its motors and hung back, unnoticed. After a Japanese searchlight found PT-41, enemy guns opened fire, causing the boat to zigzag. This action took place just twelve miles east of Dumaguete on neighboring Negros Island.

That night Roy Bell had stayed in his campus home in Dumaguete. By the time the gunfire had awakened him, many people were already hurrying down to the waterfront to see what was going on. Roy dressed quickly and joined the crowd at the town dock in time to see the zigzagging PT-41 finally swerve free from the searchlight, causing an outburst of cheers from the crowd. Somebody told Roy, "That PT was in closer and fired a torpedo that missed. It looked like it took a lot of gunfire, but it was still moving fast when the searchlight lost it."

The cheers were cut short when the enemy searchlight found the other PT boat. It had started to charge toward the cruiser while the Japanese were trying to sink Bulkeley's PT-41. When the searchlight finally located Kelly's PT-34, it was so close to the cruiser that its two torpedoes couldn't miss. Seconds later Roy and the watching crowd erupted with shouts when they saw big, black chunks of debris flying through the searchlight's beam, apparently torn off the cruiser. Then the searchlight dimmed, and its last glowing showed the cruiser dead in the water.

With the searchlight out, Kelly's retreat in the dark was no longer challenged, although he had to pass only two hundred yards astern the stricken cruiser. Both PTs returned to Cebu City safely. But the next day enemy planes damaged Kelly's PT-34 beyond repair and killed some of the crew. Kelly survived, however, and commanded a PT squadron in the Solomon Islands campaign (1942–1945).[1]

The apparent destruction of the enemy cruiser did not result in any sense of security in Dumaguete despite the cheers of the watchers at the dock. The appearance of these big warships might mean the Japanese were about to land. Would Dumaguete then be punished for the heavy damage suffered by the cruiser? A good many of the onlookers hastened home, threw their belongings in cars, and headed for the hills. The number of cars on the roads out of town caused such traffic jams that some people spent the rest of the night in their vehicles.

The next day the town seemed calm enough, and late in the afternoon Roy was talking to Professor Chapman about the grain ship from Mindanao that was expected soon. But that conversation halted when ten enemy ships came into view near the site of the previous night's battle off the tip of Cebu.

Seeing the ships and fearing a landing or a bombardment, most people with cars drove out of town—like they did the night before after the attack of the PT boats on the enemy warships. Many of them had returned, but the ten Japanese warships convinced the returnees to flee again while others who had stayed in town the night before now joined the exodus.

Before Roy and Dr. Carson headed for their car to join the mass flight, Roy said, "Wait for me here at your office. I'm going to walk down to the dock and take another look at the enemy convoy." Roy found it still idling along but not yet heading directly for Dumaguete. While he was standing there trying to figure out what the enemy ships were going to do, Roy heard a familiar feminine voice: "Roy, Roy! It's me!"

He turned around and saw to his amazement his wife coming toward him. If he wondered about the bad timing of her coming to town from the safety of Malabo, he didn't show it. Companionably, they watched the convoy hover in the distance. It was not leaving but not coming closer. Single Japanese warships had done the same thing before—a silent message that the Filipinos were helpless against Japanese imperial forces.

Meantime the continued presence of the ships had thrown the townspeople who didn't have cars into a panic—it made the confusion of the night before look mild. Now Roy felt it was his duty as civil affairs officer to stay in town until things settled down. He asked Edna, "Why don't you go and wait with President Carson in his office while I use my official car to drive around town and hopefully keep things relatively calm?" Edna answered, "No, Roy! I'm staying with you. Maybe my presence will help people feel more secure. But first we can go tell President Carson not to wait for us."

So the two of them drove around various parts of town during most of the night, stopping to talk with people who seemed upset. Both, having years of teaching experience, were successful in calming the townspeople. At one stop, Major Roque, a Filipino officer of the Army battalion stationed in Dumaguete, noticed Edna and asked, "What do you mean being in town on a night like this?" Edna declared, "My place is with my husband when I believe I can help him!" Not until 4:00 AM did the convoy turn definitely northward away from Dumaguete.

Now there was a general relaxation in town, so Roy drove to their old home on the Silliman campus, hoping they would have a good nap before daylight. Yet they were too keyed up to fall asleep right away. They were still awake an hour later when a knock on the door caused them to jump out of bed, expecting more excitement.

Roy opened the door cautiously to find President Carson standing there: He explained, "I stayed in town to do my scheduled patrol with the Emergency Patrolling Committee and have finished. But now I've found another worry. Please come and see what you can make of this noise."

Roy and Edna obediently followed President Carson, though they were still in nightclothes. He led them under an avocado tree in back of a faculty home and whispered, "Be quiet and listen closely. Do you hear that droning sound, like many airplanes at a distance?" Then all three looked around and began to think they were hearing a large air fleet. But then Roy walked to the back of the garden, where he found the noise was much louder. He suddenly stopped and exclaimed, "Our fleet of aircraft is a massive swarm of Asian bees here among the flowers of an acacia tree in fall bloom.[2] There is just enough pre-dawn light for me to pick them out or I might have gotten a bad stinging."

Back at their campus home, Roy and Edna didn't even try to sleep again even though the bee episode finally relaxed them. Roy stayed in town to work with his emergency committees and Edna went back to Malabo to look after their boys.

The next day Melchior Siao, a Chinese student at Silliman who had returned home to Cebu City when the war began, showed up at Roy's office. Melchior reported excitedly, "The Japs have taken Cebu City. I got out of town just as they were landing. Before that seven of their planes started fires downtown so bright that the sun looked like the moon. Then ships joined in by firing into the city. My parents told me to come down here and stay with my relatives, the Sycip family."

Roy replied, "Thanks for the information, Melchior. Those ships must have been the ones that recently hovered for hours off Dumaguete to scare us before going after Cebu City. I'm glad you're stopping with the Sycips— you're in good hands." After Melchior left, Roy wondered, *I don't understand this destructive attack on Cebu City, the second largest Philippine city. Maybe the enemy thinks it would be easier to control Filipinos by showing willingness and capability to destroy on a large scale.*

Roy also thought the Japs would soon overrun Cebu Island and force him to join his family at Malabo, because Negros Island was so close to Cebu. The two islands were separated by the 15-to-24-mile-wide Tanon Strait, which extended between the islands for 125 miles. Cebu City was on the northern end of Cebu and Dumaguete was on Negros, at the southern end of the strait.

But on the sixteenth day after Cebu City was taken, the enemy had not moved on Negros and Roy was still in Dumaguete. On that day he happened to be at the bus station when the truck-bus rattled in from Bais, twenty miles to the north. Four young American soldiers in ragged uniforms stepped out and looked like they didn't know what to do next. Roy greeted them and asked, "Do you soldiers know anything about the Japs on Cebu? I understand they wrecked Cebu City a couple weeks ago."

One of the soldiers introduced himself as Edward Weiss and answered, "We've just escaped from Cebu with the help of Captain Cushing, who seems to be staying in the hills to harass the Japs."[3] Immediately curious, Roy wanted to know, "Exactly how did that happen and how did you get here?"

Weiss, the articulate leader of the group, willingly explained that the other three were signalmen on the steamer *Don Esteban,* which supplied Corregidor. When it sank, they fled south and reached Cebu City just ahead of the Japanese assault on April 10. As they moved on through the jungles of Cebu, Weiss joined Jim Cushing, a mining engineer, on a brief errand to seek information. By chance the two came upon, ambushed, and apparently killed a detachment of six Japanese soldiers. Then Weiss rejoined his shipmates, and they continued their flight to the shore of Tanon Strait, where they boarded two leaky boats to cross the strait to Negros. But the strong current prevented them from crossing there. Instead they paddled and bailed all night while the current carried them sixty miles southward—luckily away from the enemy. By daybreak they had paddled to where they were twenty miles across the strait to Negros—in time to cross before the daytime enemy patrols. After a three-day rest at the plantation of Charles W. Bryant, they rode the truck that morning to Dumaguete. They were eager to keep going on their way to Australia. They wanted help in reaching the next island, Mindanao.

Worried that the soldiers would never reach Australia alive, Roy pointed out, "Australia is 1700 miles from here, and the enemy is already moving in front of you—also heading for Australia." But the soldiers insisted: "We're going on. We escaped from our sinking ship, and with the help of Captain Cushing took care of a few pursuing Japs on Cebu. We can take care of ourselves."

Roy proposed, "Since you're determined to keep going, you're welcome to ride with me on a launch I'm taking across to Mindanao tomorrow night. I'm going over there to pick up grain—we're short of bread here in Dumaguete. Tonight you can stay in our empty dormitory—we've had to close down the university."

But as they were waiting for the sun to set the next day before making the thirty-five-mile crossing, Roy received word that the Japanese had landed near the spot where he had been picking up the grain in recent weeks. Before the dejected soldiers retired to the empty dormitory beds for the second night, Roy promised, "Tomorrow, we'll try something else to get you on your way."

The next morning Roy was waiting with the soldiers for the bus to Tolong, forty miles to the west on the southern coast of Negros, where the road ended. Roy told them, "When you reach Tolong, see the mayor and ask him to find a sailboat for you to cross over to Mindanao. He's an old friend of mine."

But final farewells were delayed because the bus ran out of fuel—it used alcohol, a by-product of the sugar refinery at Bais. While the driver went scrounging for fuel, Roy suddenly found himself saying, "I know you are all eager to be on your way so I didn't say anything about this before. But

I could make good use of one of you signalmen if he would stay. I plan to operate a radio station in the mountains here to send military intelligence to American commands. I already have a transmitter, receiver, and a 500-watt, 220-volt generator. Unfortunately, I can't handle Morse code so I need a skilled operator badly. But if one of you stayed, there would always the danger of capture and brutal treatment. You would have the rough food and accommodations my family has."

Taken by surprise, the three signalmen discussed the pros and cons of Roy's sudden offer. There were different but uncertain risks in staying or going. Then the tediousness and responsibility of standing long radio operator watches could be compared with the discomforts of trekking the seventeen hundred miles to Australia. Nobody had decided yet to stay when the bus driver called out, "We're ready to go now. I found some fuel." The three signalmen stopped talking. Then after a pause, one of them, Edward Chmielewski, turned to Roy and said, "I'd like to stay. Maybe I can help with the radio station." So a surprised and elated Roy was joined by his new signalman in waving farewell to the other soldiers as the noisy bus headed for Tolong.

Roy furnished the traveling soldiers with trousers and shirts to replace their uniforms—he thought it would be safer to appear as American civilians rather than American soldiers, who would attract more attention on Mindanao, where the Japanese had already landed. But nevertheless, Ed Weiss faced a hostile Filipino at Tolong and had to draw his .45 revolver to scare him off. But that was the only hostility shown by Filipinos as they continued through the Philippines.[4]

After Edward Chmielewski's companions were out of sight, Roy welcomed his new radio operator by saying, "I'm sure you'll be a big help for my intelligence project, and together we may help the war against the Japs. As I've said, my family is living up in the hills, and we're not expecting the enemy to bother us for awhile. Arthur Carson and I of Silliman University and our families are living together at a cabin we built on a high plateau. They'd all like to meet you. You are welcome to stay with us, but you are not obligated. So why don't you come up for dinner tonight and see what you think." After a couple weeks of fleeing from the enemy, Edward was amazed by his good luck. He immediately replied, "I would like to come up and meet everybody. I believe I can help with the radio project."

It was easy for Edward to decide to join the friendly household even before a tasty meal of chicken and sweet potatoes. The relaxed soldier told the group, "My first name is Edward like my buddy, Edward Weiss, who has gone on toward Australia. So to avoid confusion, my friends called me 'Ski'—the last three letters of my Polish last name, Chmielewski. I like 'Ski' so it would be fine if you used it." Then Ken, the oldest Bell son, advised the lanky 6' 2" signalman, "Ski, you should stop wearing those good shoes of yours and go barefooted like us. You might need your shoes for emergency mountain climbing if we have to move suddenly."

A few days later, Roy saw four more bedraggled and somewhat bewildered young men across the street in downtown Dumaguete. Like the signalmen, they looked to Roy as though they were on the run from the enemy, although they did not wear uniforms.

Always looking for information about the enemy, Roy crossed the street, hoping to strike up a conversation. They stopped and smiled, but only one could speak English, and that only barely. He was a tall blond and said his name was Tore. He haltingly explained to Roy, "We are Norwegian sailors. A fisherman brought us here. We aren't sure where we are. He tell us. We not understand him. He pull us out of the water. Our merchant ship, MS *Bavnass*, sank. It first day of the war. We have hard time since. Now we're going to Australia."

Realizing the language barrier, Roy explained as simply as he could, "It is too dangerous for you to go south. The Japs are fighting ahead of you already on the way to Australia. Your lives mean nothing to them. As you go through the Philippines, only educated Filipinos speak English. But you don't know the common Filipino spoken language at all. You will be safer by staying here and taking to the mountains. Even then, you would have the language problem with the mountain people. They would have to feed you and warn you of Jap raids."

Tore replied, "We stay here a day or so. We think about staying safe—what you say." Roy wished them luck and walked away, heavy at heart. He realized that the sailors had no good choice. But after a few steps Roy turned and walked back to them. As clearly as possible, Roy said to Tore and his friends, "All of you meet me here at noon tomorrow. I may have an idea to help you."

That night Roy told Edna and the Carsons about the Norwegians' plight. They also worried about them, and agreed to Roy's suggestion of inviting the four up to Malabo for dinner. The next night the Norwegians enjoyed a bountiful meal of fried bananas, sweet potatoes, and chicken. The husbands had left the decision of having them join the already large household to Edna and Edith. After dinner the wives immediately agreed to ask them, so Edna addressed Tore: "We would like the four of you to stay with us here in the hills until the Japs are driven out. It is too dangerous for you to keep on toward Australia."

Tore understood and smilingly answered, "You very kind to help us. It dangerous for us to keep going. I take my friends outside. I explain in Norwegian. They know little English." Full of good food, it didn't take much explaining in Norwegian for the sailors to decide to stay.

Tore Knudsen was the student of the group—he spoke some English, and was tall and blond. Ole Torgrimsen, the oldest, craved tobacco so much that when he couldn't buy cigarettes, he rolled his own from local leaves—his smoking later unexpectedly helped his new household while he was on guard duty. Arne Hansen, the youngest Norwegian sailor, was quick and energetic and told tall tales about his romantic affairs. Ragnvald Myhre was the household's "singing cowboy"—he could never find a situation so dark that he could not come up with a cheerful song.

They brought the number in the Bell-Carson household to fifteen—four in the Bell family, the four Carsons, the two stranded college girls, the radio operator Ski, and now the four Norwegian sailors.

Chapter 5

The Japanese Land
at Dumaguete

May and June 1942

By the end of April, the Japanese had not yet landed on Negros. Roy Bell and Arthur Carson still came to their university offices daily, but they returned to Malabo for the night. In the morning they hiked down to the road at Palimpinon and then drove a car to Dumaguete; afternoons it was a drive and then a hike back up to Malabo.

About this time two non-Silliman Americans visited Roy Bell's university office, trying to decide whether they should surrender to the Japanese. One of them was Charles W. Bryant, the plantation owner who had recently sheltered Ski, Roy's radioman, and his friends after their flight from Cebu. Both Americans had already evacuated their families into the hills along with five single American women. Soon Mr. Parhem, the local superintendent of schools, joined the two men in Roy's office with the same issue to decide.

All three men had come to doubt the wisdom of their retreat to the hills now that it had been accomplished. They reasoned they might be in the hills for months, even years, during which they would have to depend on warnings from Filipinos to escape capture by Japanese forays. Moreover, they felt it would go harder for them if they seemed to be keeping away from the Japanese military administration. In the hills they would need to live much like the subsistence farmers who would provide them with their food. The three Americans had pretty much talked themselves into surrendering to the Japanese rather than being captured later.

During the discussion President Carson dropped in. He listened for only a short time before he declared, "Those who want to may surrender, but Professor Bell and I have no such thoughts—no matter what the enemy promises. I speak from experience. As a missionary professor in China during Japan's ongoing war there, the Japs took me off a train and put me in a cell with two Chinese—they had been tortured and would soon die. Fortunately a Japanese officer released me since I had a passport, and we were not at war with Japan then. But now with Japan at war with the U.S., I want to avoid any chance of me and my family becoming Japanese prisoners!"

Nevertheless, Arthur Carson and Roy could not change the minds of the three Americans. When the visitors left, Carson and Roy exchanged looks of frustration and sadness, worried about what might happen to the Americans.

On May 6, 1942, General Wainwright surrendered his Filipino-American forces on Corregidor and Bataan to General Masaharu Homma. As mentioned earlier, General MacArthur had already been ordered to retreat to Australia by the American government. General Wainwright was left in charge and now had to surrender—his troops lacked food and had no air support.

Once Wainwright was a prisoner, Homma ordered him to surrender the Filipino and American troops on the other Philippine islands. But as a prisoner himself, Wainwright knew he no longer had such authority. Yet he complied because Homma declared he would execute the eight to ten thousand Allied troops surrendered on Bataan and Corregidor the day before if the Allied troops throughout the Philippines were not surrendered also.

To speed up the surrender on Roy Bell's island of Negros, General Homma sent four Filipino officers captured on Bataan. They had thus escaped the perils of the Bataan Death March, but danger awaited them on Negros. It came about after the deputy American commander on Negros, Colonel MacLennan, rebuffed the four officers and confined them. He assigned Corporal Justo M. Lusoc to guard the emissaries.

Lusoc slept fitfully the first night—every time he awoke, he became more convinced that the Filipino officers should be considered traitors because they came as willing emissaries of the Japanese. Shortly after dawn, Lusoc walked into his prisoners' bedroom with a Browning automatic rifle and shot them.

But a few days later the surrender effort went forward anyway when an American officer was sent to Negros by General Sharp, the senior American officer after the capture of General Wainwright. That emissary carried an order to surrender Negros. It was accepted by Colonel Roger Hilsman, the physically ill Negros commander. On May 22, 1942, Hilsman gathered his five commanders and many of their troops at Fabrica in northern Negros.

The ailing Hilsman was able to persuade only three of his five commanders to surrender. Of the total force of forty-five hundred soldiers, only a thousand surrendered. The surrendered troops turned in their weapons and scattered in various directions.

Among the thirty-five hundred soldiers who did not surrender were the six hundred members of the Silliman University ROTC. They remained as a battalion under Major Abcede, their peacetime commander at Silliman. Another commander who ignored the order to surrender was Major Mata, who kept his organization mainly intact. Many of the soldiers in the units in which their officers had surrendered took up their Enfield rifles and walked into the jungle. These thousands of armed men could wait and see how they wanted to use their weapons during the coming Japanese occupation.

If they formed bands to resist the enemy, the geography of Negros favored them. More than three-fourths of the island was mountainous and was roadless and sparsely populated. It would take a large enemy force to patrol this area frequently enough to prevent the ex-soldiers from forming guerrilla bands and operating with the still-intact Filipino units.

Because of the surrender, Roy could have looked back ruefully at his efforts as civil affairs officer to prepare for the defense of Negros—he had persuaded citizens to give up cars, trucks, and food to the U.S. Army on the island. These contributions would pass into the hands of the enemy. Yet now Roy doubted if the Filipino soldiers would have had enough weaponry to be effective. He commented to Arthur Carson, "Half the Filipino troops have only small arms and the rest are armed with obsolete 1903 Enfield rifles, which the U.S. Army no longer uses. Besides, General Homma might indeed have executed the Filipino and American troops, he had already captured on Corregidor and Bataan—as he threatened."

The Japanese drive toward Australia had been stalled for five months by mostly American soldiers on Bataan. Now the bulk of the enemy troops in the Philippines were hurried south to join the main drive on Australia. On Negros a small Japanese detachment oversaw the surrender of Filipino soldiers, and the actual occupation of the island was a low Japanese priority. But the Bell-Carson household did not wait tensely and idly for the occupation forces to arrive.

After the officer from General Sharp arrived to call for surrender of Allied forces, Arthur Carson said to Roy, "We are only 15 miles from the dock at Dumaguete and just an hour's hike from the end of the road at Palimpinon. We've been making the trip daily ourselves. What would stop an enemy patrol from walking up the trail and finding us?" Roy answered, "I remember taking my family higher into the mountains for a vacation a few years before you came to Silliman. We camped and then I built a small cabin by a volcanic lake—to escape the summer heat. Maybe we should go up there and look around."

The next morning the two fathers, the three sons, and the four Norwegian sailors set out to find a safer retreat. Since the enemy had not yet landed, it was decided that the wives, little Jean Carson, and the two college students would be safe if left at Malabo with Ski, the radioman. Anyway, Ski's feet were not yet tough enough to go barefooted—Ken Bell had advised him to save his only pair of shoes for an emergency.

The exploring party started at 6:00 AM to take advantage of the morning coolness. Roy led the party up from the Malabo plateau on a slippery trail that took them steeply upward on hillsides open except for shoulder-high cogon grass that bent over their path. Its sharp edges sometimes drew blood on their bare hands and wrists. In time, when they passed into a cool, upland forest, leeches latched onto them from overhanging bushes. The party had to stop while Roy Bell carefully removed a leech that had grabbed Ken under one eye.

Yet Arthur Carson observed with wonder the giant trees of the tropical forest, its top layer known only to the birds and monkeys. Below these giants were palms that were stunted by perpetual shade, where the party hiked in semitwilight even though the day was clear. Next the party walked among huge vines and climbing bamboo and rattan. Occasionally they passed small clearings, which were fast being grown over by vegetation that grew all year round.

After leaving the forest, they continued upward along the top of a knife-like ridge, where a slip on either side could send a hiker tumbling. Then the trail became so steep that they had to grasp roots and bushes to climb farther. In one place a maze of roots was their only footing over a deep hole. When they heard the roar of waters somewhere underneath them, they cautiously hastened their steps.

Two and one-half hours after leaving Malabo and wringing wet with perspiration, they halted at the rim of an ancient crater. They had reached an altitude of thirty-six hundred feet and looked down on a small lake that lay eleven hundred feet below—the core of an old volcano. They could just make out the rough summer cabin that Roy had built on the shore of the lake several years before. But this remote dwelling was not big enough for their large household, and Roy pointed out, "This place is sure to be known by our curious Japanese storekeeper Morio and probably the other Japanese in Dumaguete, who were interned by Major Balolong the first day of the war. They will all soon be freed and will be eager to tell the Japanese commander all they know."

Arthur Carson suggested, "Why don't we take a look on the other side of the lake?" Yet Roy could not find the path he had used to reach the lake before, and descent on the sheer stone side of the old volcano was impossible. Finally young Bob Carson noticed a slight break in the heavy brush some distance back from the volcano's rim. When he pushed through, he could make out the faint trace of a path that angled downward. It wasn't the one Roy had used before, but all agreed there was nothing to do but see where it led. It took them steeply downward from thirty-six hundred to eighteen hundred feet above sea level and around to the other side of the lake.

Finally on the lake's shore, they looked a mile across the water to the old Bell cabin. For the new cabin, they chose a site shielded from the shore by trees and bushes to make it invisible from the water. Yet the house would be close enough for convenient drinking, washing, and swimming. The site also had the advantage of being impossible to approach along the lake's shore—it was too steep and rocky.

The party started back in a hurry to hike in daylight as long as possible but didn't reach Malabo until after dark. The wives had stayed up—not going to bed as usual as night fell. They were not worried, but eager to hear what the party had to say. In the faint moonlight Roy reported briefly, "We found a good spot on a volcanic lake—across the lake, Edna, from where our old cabin is—this new site should be safe from the Japs but so difficult to get to that we doubt that we'll be able take much of our stuff with us, even using *cargadores*."

Edna Bell and Edith Carson were not concerned about the problem of transporting household goods. But Edith turned to Edna and said, "Let's go and take a look at this location. We're liable to be there a long time." When Edna agreed with Edith, the wives could not see the frustration on their husbands' faces—the moon had gone behind a cloud. And the men said nothing about the danger they perceived in delaying the move. Instead, Roy made the best of the situation by suggesting, "You two should go tomorrow and take Ambrosio with you to see how much stuff his *cargadores* can take up there if we decide. Arthur will take you up there because I will be busy with Professor Chapman—we're receiving a final shipment of grain from Mindanao before the Japs come."

The next day, while Roy was in town with Dr. Chapman, Arthur Carson led the wives and Ambrosio up the trail to the rim of the volcano and then to the building site by the lake. The strenuous hike convinced them of the safety of the location. While the party rested before turning back, Edna asked Ambrosio, "How can you possibly get our belongings up here?" He assured them, "My *cargadores* won't have any trouble doing this job!" Arthur Carson—who was in the habit of buying milk from a farmer at Malabo— had one last question for Ambrosio: "Would it be possible to get a cow up to the lake?" After a moment's thought, Ambrosio answered, "We could do it, but the cow might not be alive when we got it here."

With the wives now satisfied with the lake site, the men and teenage sons were eager to start construction. As there was still no sign of the actual enemy landing, it was decided that the wives and girls could remain safely behind in the comfortable Malabo cabin. The next day all the males loaded up with tents, food supplies, and tools before beginning the long hike. They were soon exhausted by their burdens, and their progress was slower than in their earlier hike to the lake. Shortly before dark, they finally reached the construction site and set their tents up. The next morning they were still weary after sleeping on blankets on the ground.

Nevertheless, at dawn the Norwegians and the boys started clearing brush from the house site. Suddenly everyone stood stock-still when a half-dozen roughly clad Filipinos came out of the jungle on the faint trail the Americans used to reach the clearing. It flashed through Roy's mind that their location had already been discovered.

There was no reason for concern, however. As their leader explained to Roy and Arthur Carson, "Ambrosio sent us to help you build the house. We'll make shingles from strips of abaca bark and make floor boards from the large trees around here. Abrosio's *cargadores* will bring the bark we need and the rattan for making nails."

Roy and Arthur could only express their gratitude for what the mountain sawyers and Ambrosio were doing for them—they believed their eagerness to help went beyond what the Americans were paying them. They also realized the Filipinos would build a better house, and do it much faster, than they could alone.

On May 26, 1942, the same day construction started near the lake, a confident-looking, smiling Captain H. J. Tsuda of the Japanese army stepped onto the Dumaguete dock. He was pleased that a quiet group of Filipinos had gathered to see him and forty soldiers land. Tsuda figured the watchers were mainly curious, but at least they were peaceful. He had only a small force to occupy Negros Oriental Province, which had an area almost half the size of Connecticut. By that time, most people who had cottages in the hills moved out of Dumaguete. But Frederico Tatel, a Silliman student, had stayed and was now in the crowd watching the Japanese as they came on the dock. Yet once Frederico had seen them, he wanted to get as far away from them as possible. Not wishing to attract attention by hastening away, Frederico mingled with the dispersing crowd before heading for the edge of town. Then he used the shortest path to the foot of the mountains. There, at Palimpinon, he was breathing hard but did not pause before heading up the trail to the Malabo plateau, where he knew the Bell-Carson household had settled.

Frederico was red-faced and wobbly by the time he found Edna and Edith washing clothes at the spring near their Malabo cottage. He reported between gasps for breath, "The Japs have landed—at least 100 of them led by an officer in full uniform. I don't know what they'll do but there are enough of them to fan out over the countryside and even get up here." To which Edna added, "We are well-known and not far away. Right away the Japs could bribe someone to lead them to us."

The wives were going to flee immediately, but Arnaldy, the Bell's college student, pointed out, "We might not be able to get back to pick up our pans, pots, dishes, clothes, and furniture and take them up the mountain." This practical comment caused the wives to stop and consider. Their minds ran together—both exclaimed at the same time, "We need Ambrosio to get started right away now that the Japanese have landed."

Luckily Ambrosio was nearby, but he did not have *cargadores* immediately available. Yet by noon he gathered a dozen men whom the wives and college girls quickly loaded with household goods. Then, skipping lunch, the women followed the *cargadores* on the trail beyond Malabo, feeling much safer. The *cargadores* kept up a brisk pace, but the energized women and girls stayed right with them.

At dusk the exhausted women and girls and the still-fresh *cargadores* reached the construction site by the volcanic lake. The Norwegians and the boys were still working while Roy and Arthur were trying to start a fire to heat some food—a job so difficult they had resorted to using precious matches.

When Roy and Arthur saw the women, the girls, and then the group of *cargadores* come out of the jungle, they feared that something had really frightened them. Roy asked quietly, "What has happened? We've just started on the house. It won't be ready for weeks." Edna explained, "[Frederico] Tatel hurried up to Malabo this morning to report that the Japs had landed at Dumaguete. There were about 100 of them. As he said, they were enough to patrol the countryside in different directions. I was afraid some townsmen would lead them to Malabo. So we're here with the household goods."

Roy thought, *Frederico Tatel panicked Edna and Edith. He may not have actually seen that many soldiers.* But Roy only said, "There's a dry spot for you, Edith, and the girls under a part of the roof we have finished. The Norwegians and boys will keep sleeping in the tents."

Edna understood from Roy's tone his doubt of the need for their early and sudden appearance. But she thought, *We did the safe and right thing in coming up here. Besides, the men obviously will need help cooking and keeping a fire going.* Then she quietly pointed out to Roy, "With us here you won't have to try to cook so more of you can work on construction and get the house finished sooner." Neither said more. The whole household was listening—the fifteen of them would be living together for no one knew how long. Roy and Edna knew that they should try to create a friendly spirit in the household in order to give everyone the best chance of survival.

The builders cut down all the large trees around the building site to make floorboards; they were the closest source of wood. But eliminating these large trees was more important because of the common occurrence in the tropics of large, leafy trees blowing over after excessive rain diminished their roots' ability to hold in the soggy ground during strong winds. The two American families remembered vividly the stormy night back at Malabo when they were aroused from sleep by a crash that seemed frighteningly close. They rushed outside in time to see an massive uprooted tree roll ponderously toward their house. Fortunately a large clump of banana trees stopped the tree short of their flimsy dwelling.

Now, at the lake house, the cleared space was also perfect for a vegetable garden, so the Norwegians and the American boys cleared the brush. A few weeks after sweet potato vines were planted in the rich soil, they provided plenty of greens for the large household.

Meanwhile Edna and Edith took care of the weekly washing. They put on bathing suits and stood waist-deep in the lake under a sunny sky to rinse the clothes they had scrubbed while sitting on flat stones in shallower water. Edna gave credit to the beautiful blue water and sunshine for keeping them healthy.

They all felt fairly safe there, but Roy still worried about the Japanese civilians who had been interned on the first day of the war. Some of them had lived in Dumaguete for years as agents of the Japanese government. Now they would eagerly brief Captain Tsuda on what they knew about places and people. They could guide soldiers to the old Bell cottage on the lakeshore, but they probably didn't know as yet about the new house on the other side of the lake or the trail there. To guard against a water approach, Roy had the small boats at the old cottage brought across the water to the new one.

The mountain builders completed the large new house to take care of the fifteen-member household in just a few weeks. But Edna's sunny experience of washing the clothes in the lake's blue water ended a few days after the families had all moved inside the new house—the rainy season began. At the altitude of twenty-five hundred feet, everyone felt damp and chilly much of the time, even though the temperature was seldom lower than 65° Fahrenheit. In the dampness shoes disintegrated with normal wear, so everyone went barefoot all the time. On the rare bright day, the clothesline was always full. Then Ski devised a stove so clothes could dry inside, and everyone stayed warmer.

Late one afternoon a bored Roy went outdoors, even though it was wet and misting. He was strolling around the perimeter of the clearing when he heard a slight rustle in the jungle growth that covered the entrance to the household's trail to the outside world. Roy stepped out of sight, concerned as always by the prospect of unexpected visitors. But he relaxed when he recognized Rev. Alvin Scaff, a new Silliman faculty member. Alvin, bedraggled by his hike through the wet jungle, suddenly looked relieved to see Roy.

Inside the cabin, Alvin explained his visit. "A few days ago I was visiting a patient at the Mission Hospital, which has evacuated inland to Pamplona to avoid being in Japanese control. As I was leaving after seeing a patient, the hospital's treasurer, Alice Fullerton, wanted to have a word with me. She told me she had kept in reserve $40,000 from the Presbyterian Board of Foreign Missions. She hadn't told anyone else, but she wanted me to help her prevent the Japs from getting the money. Alice said to me, 'To do this, I need your help tonight.' So I arranged to stay overnight. At midnight I met Alice just outside the hospital at the edge of the jungle. We found a spot in heavy brush and buried the money there. Then I rolled a downed tree over the disturbed ground."

A suddenly enthused Roy interrupted: "So it's still there!" Alvin replied, "It should be. But I keep worrying about the money. The Japs might torture its location out of Alice after the hospital moves back to town under Japanese control." Roy exclaimed, "That will not happen. This is a Godsend, Alvin! Like Alice Fullerton and you, I don't trust the Japs to use that large chunk of money on the hospital. As far as upkeep of the hospital goes, the Japs should pay for it since they want to move it back to town. We'll use the money to pay the Silliman faculty—they have fled to the hills. The Board in New York won't mind since it supports Silliman University also. We'll start early tomorrow and go dig it up."

Alvin was dumbfounded that Roy should move so quickly. Yet he had worried about the enemy getting the funds, so he contentedly joined Roy on the long trail to Pamplona. As they departed the next morning, Roy was in high spirits, pleased to be on a worthwhile project that involved travel and escape from the crowded cabin that was besieged by dampness.

Alvin and Roy found the still-hidden money, which allowed Roy to disburse pay to the evacuated faculty members for a considerably longer time than President Carson had expected.

Chapter 6

Return to Malabo

T he worry about numerous Japanese occupation troops combing the interior hills of Negros had driven the Bell and Carson families into their urgent recent flight to their house on the mountain lake. But it turned out there were forty enemy troops stationed at Dumaguete, rather than about a hundred, the number Frederico Tatel had reported coming ashore. When they learned the Japanese were sticking to the coastal plain, Roy told Arthur Carson, "I'm planning to take my family and Ski, my Signal Corps radio operator, back to Malabo—there we will be 15 miles from the coast and should be safe." Roy explained that he was going to set up the radio station at Malabo as he had earlier planned; Ski was still available to operate the station. As before, Roy hoped to provide intelligence on Japanese military operations to General MacArthur, who had been ordered to Australia to await reinforcements for his promised return to the Philippines. Roy added, "I believe it will be feasible to set up a station in Malabo. It will be like the ham radio station I have operated in Dumaguete."

But Arthur Carson differed. "Roy, I believe Malabo may become a center of resistance and thus subject to destruction. I saw what the Japanese did to the villages in China in retaliation for harboring guerrilla activities." Carson added, "I do not believe it to be an obligation for American missionaries to take part in resistance. It is for the Filipinos to do."

Roy Bell listened politely to his friend's comments—he was not surprised by them. To avoid capture, both families had evacuated to Malabo and then to the lake. Arthur Carson's aim was still to stay safe at the lake with his family. On the other hand, Roy's first priority, if he could keep his family safe, was to aid the American cause with his radio station. Roy's family liked the idea of leaving the rain at the lake for the sunshine at Malabo as much as he did, so he easily persuaded them to move.

In June 1942 the Bell family, Arnaldy, and two of the Norwegians loaded themselves up with clothes and kitchen gear for the trek down to Malabo. Roy and Edna saw no need to have *cargadores* carry back the bulk of household goods that they had carried up to the lake about a month before. If they were to do so, another sudden retreat from Malabo might well cost them all their goods there, even if they escaped capture. After a relaxed but strenuous hike with their belongings on their backs, the members of Roy's household piled their loads in the same house they had shared with the Carsons a month before. There was a lot more space now.

In early July, a few days after the Bell family's return, Professor Ben Viloria and his wife, Victoria, hiked a few miles down to Malabo to see how Roy and Edna were getting along. Ben had been on active duty as a lieutenant in the Philippine Army at the time of surrender but had returned to Dumaguete to find his home destroyed. Now the Vilorias were settled in the hills a few miles from Malabo. Ben supported Roy's idea of a radio station at Malabo even though it could draw enemy attention and force Ben and his wife to move farther into the mountains.

While Ben and Victoria were walking back home, Ben remarked to his wife, "Roy looks really tall in his khaki shorts and Army shoes with a small hat on his gray head. He doesn't look like a professor any more in his faded coat and a haversack over his shoulder." Victoria answered, "Well with that old shotgun in his hand, he looks more like he's ready to fight the Japs than start up the radio station he talks about." (At 5'9" Roy was average height for an American then, but he was considerably taller than most Filipinos.)

A few days after the Vilorias' visit, Edna was out washing clothes at the spring when she noticed five young men come into sight over the edge of the plateau from the trail that led down to Palimpinon and the road to Dumaguete. As they headed for the Bells' house, Edna rushed inside and reported with alarm, "Five men are coming this way. What shall we do?" Roy cut short his talk with Ski, picked up his shotgun, and strode to the door, where he stood waiting for the men—gun in hand and Edna and Ski at his side.

Soon the visitors were close enough for Roy and Edna to recognize one of the young men. He was Victor Jornales, a star football player Roy had coached the previous season. As though reporting to Coach Bell on one of his somewhat rare academic achievements, Victor proudly announced, "Look at these weapons we've stolen from the Japs!" As Victor spoke, he and his friends proudly displayed a dozen assorted guns and emptied their pockets of even more pistols. Victor explained about the weapons: "My friends and

I crawled into a garage at Japanese headquarters in Dumaguete and found the guns—we were told about them from fellows who work as servants to the Japanese officers. What shall we do now, coach?" Shocked and uncertain of his role, Roy could only counsel, "Keep the weapons hidden for the time being and don't tell anyone about them." The young men were not happy with this advice. Little more was said before they headed down the trail.

Edna and Ski had heard and seen everything. She said in a weak voice, "Someone will certainly report to the Japs that we have been talking here with a group of armed young men. Then they will come after us." Roy disagreed, pointing out, "The villagers up here are our friends. In any case they wouldn't want the Japs to come up here." Somewhat calmed, Edna went into the house, leaving Roy and Ski outside.

The next day Arthur Carson came down to Malabo to check on the disbursement of the Mission Hospital funds that Roy and Rev. Scaff had recently dug up. When Carson learned of Victor's theft of guns from the Japanese, he commented, "I remember Victor's last grades at Silliman. He got a C in Bible and A in Military Science/ROTC."

Arthur spent the night at Malabo. In the morning he answered a knock on the door and faced a particularly scruffy-looking pair of Filipino ex-soldiers. Roy was soon there and said, "I'll talk with them, Arthur." Then one of the soldiers said, "I'm glad we found you, Mr. Bell. We were told you were Civil Affairs Officer for the province and you didn't surrender. We didn't surrender either and want to keep up the fight against the Japs. Have you gathered some soldiers to resist the enemy and could we join up with them?"

Roy paused for a moment but couldn't think of any advice to give them, although he understood their desire to resist the Japs. Finally he just said, "I can't take any such leadership job because I have to be available to protect my family. But if a group organizes around here I will let you know." At this, the ex-soldiers looked disappointed, and the one who had spoken before said, "Well, we'll try to find some other soldiers ourselves to join with. We'll let you know if we get a unit together." After they had left, Arthur Carson declared, "I'm afraid such leaderless men, many with guns, will turn to outright banditry."

That night Arthur slept fitfully. He was worried about the Bell family, who were exposed to danger from possibly lawless ex-soldiers as well as the Japanese by staying at Malabo. Then he remembered the two Norwegian sailors who had stayed at the lake to protect the Carsons while the other two had come with the Bells to Malabo.

Before leaving next morning, Arthur insisted to Roy Bell, "You need the two Norwegians who stayed behind with us more than we do. Besides the Viloria family will send us the word if the Japs reach Malabo so we can retreat farther into the hills." Roy thankfully accepted Arthur's offer, saying, "We might need all the Norwegians, but we'll make sure that you are warned if the Japs come up this far. One of the Norwegians will bring the word to you if necessary." As Roy watched Arthur striding across the plateau toward his family's lake retreat, Roy felt thankful to have such a friend.

In the days that followed, many soldiers sought advice from Roy—if less dramatically than Victor Jornales and his friends. Roy realized that in many minds, his having been civil affairs officer now meant that he was considered the senior American-Filipino military authority outside the coastal strip occupied by the Japanese. So ex-soldiers kept dropping by, and Roy still could not answer their question about how should they fight the Japanese. Roy could not help because no resistance leaders had arisen thus far. He was trying to decide what he should do himself now that the Japanese had landed. Roy remembered that President Carson had said that it wasn't the job of American missionaries to fight the Japanese, and that the Filipinos had to do it themselves.

Yet Roy believed that the United States had a responsibility to protect the Philippines until independence.[1] So Roy thought, *Maybe as a missionary I don't have responsibility to resist the Japs, but as an American citizen, maybe I do. If so, is there any practicable way to oppose the Japs without endangering my family? I'll just have to wait and see what develops while keeping free of the enemy.*

However, Roy had an easy decision to make about keeping his family safe. Edna brought up the issue of safety at Malabo when she and Roy happened to be alone in the house. She remarked, "Since Victor Jornales startled us with the gun he had taken from the Japs, I've asked ex-soldiers stopping by to see you. But there is no warning of any such visits. What if a few Japs in Philippine clothes walk up here?"

As Roy listened to Edna, the Norwegians crossed his mind. He now had all four of them available since President Carson sent the two of them who originally had stayed at the lake house to protect the Carson family. So Roy answered, "You're right, Edna! We need to have a warning system. The Norwegians can stand watch half-way down the trail to Palimpinon— everyone coming from the coast has to use that trail. Two of the sailors can stand watch at a time and then be relieved by the other two—making a constant watch. If the Norwegians can't handle the intruders, they'll hurry up here in time for us to get away." The relief on Edna's face made Roy happier than the idea itself. Could the Norwegians bring warning to them soon enough?

Whatever Roy's concerns, the watch had hardly been established when it was tested. Ole Torgrimsen, the oldest sailor, and Arne Hansen, the youngest, were down the trail one afternoon. While waiting to be relieved by the other two Norwegians. Ole, a heavy smoker, expelled the last cloud of smoke from his strong local cigarette. When the smoke settled over a dense clump of bushes, a loud noise like a sneeze startled the sailors. They aimed their rifles at the thicket and shouted, "Come out now or we'll shoot." Two Filipinos came out, even though they didn't understand Norwegian. After a glance at the huge sailors, they must have sensed a lack of ruthlessness, for they bolted. Their instincts were right. The sailors did not shoot them. Back at Malabo, Roy and Edna praised Ole and Arne for frightening the spies and not killing them.

A few days later Victor Jornales paid Roy another visit. The nineteen-year-old had completely ignored Roy's advice to be cautious. He reported, "I've recruited a few more friends and raided Dumaguete twice. I don't think the Dumaguete police try very hard to stop us." While Roy liked the idea of annoying the enemy, he nevertheless warned Victor, "I'm afraid the enemy will execute you if you're captured."

Victor just changed the subject. "I was stopped by two of your Norwegians on my way up here, but I had no trouble explaining myself. I wasn't surprised because the story in Dumaguete is that you have an organization of huge blond soldiers who are guarding the approaches to Malabo." Roy explained, "Yes, we have a constant guard of two Norwegian sailors on the trail up here from Palimpinon. Recently they flushed two Filipinos out of the bushes who were trying to sneak up here. Ole and Arne didn't shoot them when they bolted. Probably just as well. From what you say, the scared spies have spread the word that we are well-guarded here. I hope the Japs are taken in too."

A few days later Victor was back at Malabo. He was worried that what he had to say would upset Edna, so he stuck his head in the door and said, "Mr. Bell, come outside where it's cooler. I have a little more news from Dumaguete." Outside, Victor said, "On August 22, one of my new men was pointed out to the Japs in the Dumaguete public market by Teodorico Lajato, who has become a collaborator. The Japs threw my man into the city jail to await execution. The next night three of us slipped into town. It was dark but not late when we asked a guard at the jail if we could talk with our friend a last time before his execution. But at the jail door, we fired a few shots over the heads of the guards—they ran for their lives. Then we fired point-blank into the padlocks and then pried the doors open. We released all the prisoners except an elderly American and his son—they refused to leave. They must have been picked up some place else, and not knowing where to go here, they figured they would soon be captured again and get worse treatment by trying to escape."

Victor's shots during the jailbreak had attracted a lot of attention in town because it was still early in the evening. Attention grew into general excitement when the jailers were seen fleeing toward Governor Villanueva's home. Although Villanueva had stayed in office at Captain Tsuda's request, the scared jailers sought the governor to report the jailbreak, hoping for more leniency than they would receive from Tsuda. But Villanueva wouldn't even come to the door, not wanting to show any forbearance for the jailers.

The next day Villanueva did speak to Captain Tsuda on behalf of the guards, but Tsuda insisted he would execute them. Yet on the day they were to be hanged, Tsuda reinstated them as guards and then warned, "You will be executed immediately if any other prisoner escapes."

Tsuda's leniency was part of his effort to get along with the Filipinos. Besides keeping Governor Villanueva in office, Captain Tsuda had persuaded Mayor Perdices and his staff to reassume their positions as well. Tsuda wanted all the Filipinos who had fled to come back and restore normal life in Dumaguete. Hanging the two jailers could hamper such efforts.

One morning a few days later, however, Tsuda had something else to worry about. Curious people had gathered at different places in downtown Dumaguete to study new posters that had been put up in place of announcements of Japanese victories. The Japanese posters now lay on the ground; they had probably been ripped down overnight. The new posters boldly instructed: ALL FORMER SOLDIERS ARE TO REPORT TO CIVIL AFFAIRS OFFICER ROY BELL AT MALABO ON AUGUST 28.

Victor Jornales was taken aback. He asked his friend Juan Dominado, "Who put up those signs about ex-soldiers reporting to Coach Bell? He and his family may have to move farther into the mountains to escape a Jap foray." Juan, also one of Roy's football players, explained apologetically: "A group of us were talking about how furious we were about Jap soldiers forcing every passerby to bow to them. Then someone pointed out that Coach Bell was still Civil Affairs Officer. Since he hadn't surrendered, he should do something about the Japs. Unfortunately there were some high school boys in the group. Some of them must have taken this idea to an immediate extreme. They probably tore down the Jap posters in the middle of the night and put up the new ones that put Coach Bell on the spot. Could you go up to Malabo to warn the Bell family right away?"

A worried Victor slipped around the Japanese guard at the edge of town and hurried up to Malabo to report the situation to Roy Bell—for once he did not come to report about his own exploits. His information alarmed the Bell family and caused them to carefully plan what they should do on August 28—the day the posters had ordered former Filipino soldiers to report to Roy. They thought Japanese soldiers might show up that day to capture them and their sons as well as any ex-soldiers coming to join the resistance. But Roy was not interested in fighting the intruders. So the evening before the possible crisis, Roy sent Ole and Arne, two of the Norwegian sailors, back to the Carsons at the lake house. The other two, Tore and Ragnvald, insisted on staying to help the family.

Roy had a hard time sleeping that night, even though he and Edna had already decided what to do. To start with, everyone was to get up before dawn and eat early. Normally the two Norwegians who had been on watch down the trail since before dawn joined the family for breakfast. Today only Ragnvald came up. His partner, Tore, stayed halfway down the path to Palimpinon to provide a constant watch. Tore was tall, blond, slim, and the fastest runner of the sailors.

Because of his speed, Tore had volunteered the night before to be the single guard to start the day. Rather than the Norwegians' usual job of turning back intruders, Tore's only purpose that day was to see Japanese soldiers soon enough for him to warn the family at Malabo in time for them to retreat. That morning Tore figured that the farther down the trail he discovered the intruding enemy soldiers, the more warning time he could give the Bell family. Tore knew he could move much faster than the Japanese soldiers could on a trail new to them.

So Tore began to ease down the trail, enjoying a banana after Ragnvald headed up for breakfast at Malabo. At first Tore thought he might just descend a few hundred yards to a good vantage point, but the logic of finding the soldiers as far down the trail as possible kept him descending farther and farther. Finally he knew he had to stop when he looked down on the Palimpinon schoolhouse at the edge of the coastal plain.

Now Tore relaxed behind a thicket, but he had only a few minutes to wait before forty or so soldiers and at least one Japanese officer gathered in front of the school. Tore immediately headed back up the trail to Malabo.

The Bell family and Ragnvald had just finished breakfast when Tore burst into the house. Between gasps for breath, he reported, "I've just run up from Palimpinon as fast as I could after I saw forty Jap soldiers gathered around the schoolhouse. I think I got away without their seeing me." Roy replied, "You've given us plenty of time to get away by going way down to Palimpinon. Now take along something to eat as you and Ragnvald head for the lake house. We'll be along soon." Both refused to leave without the family.

Then, as Roy and Edna had planned, each member of the family picked up the items that had been assigned to him or her and carried them to a storage hut in the jungle. Then the family and the Norwegians hastened up the trail that led eventually to the hidden path to the lake retreat. After climbing as fast as they could for an hour, they finally stopped at a spot where they had an open view down the mountain. They half expected to see billows of smoke rising from the destruction of Malabo, but they did not. After several more stops without seeing smoke below, Roy, his younger son, Donald, and Tore turned back to investigate. Edna, Kenneth, and Ragnvald continued onward to a still better vantage point to determine if the village had been destroyed. By the end of the day, all of them had returned to the still intact and peaceful village of Malabo.

While the Bell family was scurrying for safety up at Malabo, Captain Tsuda was thinking himself into a quandary as his troops rested at Palimpinon. He had set out early from Dumaguete with the idea of coming to grips with Roy Bell before he could recruit more resistance soldiers—the posters had announced that this was the day for recruitment. Tsuda already believed Bell had a sturdy group of Norwegians. Now Tsuda worried that the Norwegians could easily ambush his party of soldiers on their way up the trail to Malabo as they passed the dense thickets and climbed steeply beside plunging waterfalls. His fears were embellished by the report of the collaborators whom the Norwegians had frightened.

Tsuda was also nagged by what the Japanese authorities in Manila expected him to do the next day. They had ordered him to deliver three American prisoners to a ship for transport to Manila—the same three Americans who had surrendered despite the efforts of Roy and Arthur Carson to dissuade them. That task bothered Tsuda because of the recent jailbreak in Dumaguete, carried out by Victor Jornales.

After some consideration, Tsuda decided it would be wiser to handle Roy Bell another time. So he marched his company of soldiers back to Dumaguete. There they would be ready to handle the deportation of the three Americans. In fact, Captain Tsuda was so concerned about rescue attempts that he posted soldiers at the edge of Dumaguete during the night, hoping to forestall such efforts. Furthermore, Tsuda moved the prisoners from their comfortable housing on the Silliman campus to a concrete building in the middle of town and surrounded it with sandbags.

Yet these precautions were not necessary because neither Victor Jornales nor Roy Bell had the means or the desire to rescue the prisoners. These Americans had made clear their intention to surrender before the Japanese had landed.

Thus Captain Tsuda's caution was evident on the day Roy was supposed to be recruiting. Afterward Captain Tsuda continued his conciliatory policy of bringing Filipinos back to town. Two weeks later Tsuda countered the posters announcing that Roy was recruiting at Malabo on August 28 with his own appeal to Filipino ex-soldiers.

This time the ex-soldiers were urged to come back to town. If they came, Captain Tsuda promised to be lenient.

I, Commander-in-Chief of the Japanese Imperial Forces in Dumaguete . . . advise all Filipino ex-soldiers that I am sure to forgive you for your past in case you surrender to us now, with your arms.

If you love your family and are willing to cooperate with us to build a new Philippines, just accept my advice . . . We will forget everything in your past and allow you to live with your family without any worry. This is your best chance. Come to me and surrender right now for the sake of everybody.

—H. J. Tsuda

Chapter 7

Roy Bell Joins
the Resistance

In the days that followed Captain Tsuda's intense effort on August 29 to see that the three American prisoners boarded a ship to Manila, still more Filipino ex-soldiers sought out Roy Bell at Malabo, drawn by the posters announcing that Roy was recruiting. Most of them did not have weapons, believing that Roy had the six hundred rifles that had belonged to the Silliman University ROTC. But the ROTC members had taken the rifles when they were mustered into the combined American-Philippine force and sent north under command of their ROTC officer, Major Abcede.

Roy's only weapons at Malabo were several shotguns and six rifles of various calibers. In fact, Roy mused, *Why should I be thinking about resistance? I don't even have any guns to speak of. On the other hand, I've already attracted enough unfavorable attention to put my life at risk. Victor tells me that people in Dumaguete believe I masterminded the jailbreak he carried out. Then the overnight appearance of the unwelcome posters that identified me as a guerrilla recruiter must have convinced the Japs of my hostility. So maybe I should help fight the invaders since I'm marked as their enemy and thus already in danger.*

Roy was in that conflicted frame of mind when several more of his football players came to see him. They were led by Juan Dominado, who, after surrendering as a lieutenant in the Philippine Army, had come to Dumaguete with his bride, Maria, to be with her aging parents. But he had become bored and admired the exploits of Victor Jornales against the Japanese.

Yet fast-talking Juan was already active as a resistance spy. He had persuaded Captain Tsuda, the garrison commander, to let him help bring Filipinos back to normal life in Dumaguete from the hills where they had fled when the Japanese came. To carry out this assignment, Juan was allowed to move freely into the mountains and back into town. Yet hoodwinking Captain Tsuda into providing information to Roy was not enough for Juan.

So in front of Roy's house at Malabo, Juan confronted his old coach and declared, "Coach, you have been Civil Affairs Officer for the province and did not surrender. You are the lawful authority in the province except for Dumaguete and the strip of coastal plain where the Japs move freely. We would like you to support us in the formation of a resistance group to harass the Japs and eventually drive them out. We hate to have to bow every time we meet a Jap soldier on the street."

Roy answered, "I understand how you feel, and American forces with Philippine help will surely drive them out in time. But I don't know how I would be of any help to the unit you want to put together. I've never been a combat soldier. In World War I, I only served in the Medical Corps. If you want to consider being supported just by supplies of food and clothing, I might be able to help, but I'll have to let you know about that in a few days. I have to check on a supply source." Juan quickly replied, "Your help with food and supplies and just knowing you would be backing us are all we need to get started. We hope to hear from you very soon."

As Roy watched the patriotic young men head down the trail, his heart yearned to give them all the support he possibly could. He believed that Manuel Sycip, head of the Chinese merchants in Dumaguete, would support a resistance band—the Chinese merchants had already paid about $2 million in fines to the Japanese. But Roy's mind told him that he should first think carefully of the consequences of helping Juan. For a couple restless days, Roy mulled over the situation.

On one hand, Juan's guerrilla band could galvanize Captain Tsuda into more aggressive operations. Roy's support of Juan's group would eventually become known to Captain Tsuda, which could endanger both Roy's family and possibly the Carsons, as well as Roy's projected radio station.

On the other hand, Tsuda might become even more cautious if another guerrilla group joined Jornales' unit in threatening the Japanese. Tsuda had already been discouraged from advancing toward Malabo by the report of an inflated number of Norwegians guarding the trail up there. And then, in Dumaguete, Tsuda had taken elaborate defensive steps to forestall a supposed attempt by Victor Jornales or others to rescue the three American prisoners. Thus Roy could conclude that an additional armed Filipino group would make Tsuda more cautious and less aggressive.

But Roy's final and deciding thoughts were *These young men are looking to me because I have gained their respect as their coach in many athletic contests. I am convinced of their sincerity. As a citizen of the United States—at war with Japan—I cannot disappoint these young men who are eager to drive our common enemy from their land.*

His mind made up, Roy sent word of his decision to Juan Dominado. Then he wrote Manuel Sycip, the Chinese merchant: "Some young Filipinos are ready to strike the invaders and need food supplies." The next day a courier brought Sycip's reply: "We have already delivered a truck-load of food for the boys to pick up at the house of our mutual friend in Palimpinon."

Roy was anxious to have the food picked up that night, but Juan—in his role as spy—was busy seeming to serve Captain Tsuda. However, by good luck, Victor Jornales had some men available that afternoon and was eager to help. In the middle of the night, Victor and his men picked out the right house among the half dozen in Palimpinon and carried away some of the food that Manuel Sycip had deposited there.

But Jornales' work in Palimpinon that night was seen by an informer. The next day the collaborator excitedly told Captain Tsuda about the night pickup from the Palimpinon house, which still burst with food. Tsuda promised the informer a reward, but first he had go back to Palimpinon with a raiding party. When the informer pointed out the house where he thought the food had been deposited, the soldiers peppered it with machine-gun fire. But when they looked inside, they found no food supplies—only a ten-year-old girl lying dead on the floor, the victim of their fire.

Dissatisfied, the soldiers left the village and advanced downstream along the level valley of the Ocoy River, feeling safe from ambush on the valley's open ground. Then the relaxed soldiers caught sight of two older Filipinos bathing in the river. When the old men began to run, the soldiers used them as targets.

Later in the day, when the Japanese sergeant reported what had happened to Tsuda, the captain was furious and demoted the sergeant to common soldier on the spot. Tsuda thought, *These killings counter all my efforts to restore normal life here. My men can't be trusted without an officer being present. They've given me the dregs of the soldiers for this sidelight occupation duty. The good soldiers are in the drive toward Australia. I wish I were there.*

The next day relatives of the slain young girl appeared at Malabo to ask Roy for rifles to kill Japanese. But Roy had already given his few extra weapons to Victor Jornales' band. Roy was appalled by the tragedies of the girl and the two old men and his part in them. Then he became more downcast when he felt he had failed in comforting the girl's sorrowing mother.

After the distraught family group left, Edna tried to lessen Roy's feeling of guilt by pointing out, "You couldn't possibly foresee any such consequences when you and Mr. Sycip arranged for the food pickup." Then, knowing her husband's natural restlessness, Edna suggested, "Why don't you hike up to Bob Silliman's hideout and see how they're getting along? You aren't having many recruits coming by just now, and if some do, I'll have them come by tomorrow. And we'll be safe with the Norwegians here."

Edna's idea was just the thing to improve Roy's outlook. He hadn't checked on the Silliman household—consisting of Bob Silliman, the university's senior history professor; his wife, Metta; and her sister, Abby Jacobs—for some time.[1] After a long steep hike, Roy came upon Bob, who was planting sweet potatoes in the clearing by his house. Bob looked up at the now more placid Roy and exclaimed, "I heard Captain Tsuda brought some troops as far as Palimpinon looking for you and then gave up coming into the mountains. Did the Norwegians scare off Tsuda? Has my recent history student, Victor Jornales, harassed the Japs lately? He was always interested in the famous battles of history."

Roy answered, "Oh, Victor doesn't tell me everything he's doing, but he reported recently that a cowardly group of enemy soldiers had gunned down a couple elderly Filipinos when they tried to run away—it was on open ground where the Japs felt safe from ambush. Way up here, though, you are safe. The Japs would never risk this difficult climb—while being subject to ambush all the way."

One morning soon after visiting the Silliman family, Roy was walking across the Malabo plateau when he noticed a horseman riding along in a roughly parallel direction. Roy changed direction slightly to intercept the rider. As they neared each other, Roy recognized Simeon, a policeman in the nearby village of Luzuriaga. Simeon carried a 12-gauge shotgun. After they greeted each other, Roy asked, "What are you going to do with that gun, Simeon?" Simeon explained, "I'm supposed to turn it in to my police chief. He says the Japanese want to collect the guns held by policemen around here."

Roy believed that Simeon would cooperate against the Japs but was not sure how Simeon's chief stood, so he said, "Simeon, would you leave the gun at home and report to your chief without it?" That afternoon, Simeon sought out Roy at home and reported, "I told the chief that you said not to bring my gun. He whispered, 'That's all right.'"

The next day Simeon came back to Roy and said, "The Chief wants you to meet with him and Mayor [Guillermo] Villamil of our village." Roy was suspicious because of the mayor's eagerness for a meeting, so he insisted on a night meeting in the hills outside the village. Roy arrived ahead of time with his son Kenneth and Ski, his radio operator, and hid them in nearby bushes, armed with rifles.

However, it turned out that the two village leaders simply wanted moral support for using their village offices to obstruct the Japanese and looked to future cooperation with Roy. Currently they planned to turn in only an old pistol and an obsolete rifle—not Simeon's 12-gauge shotgun.

While Roy was being drawn into the resistance, Ski had been transmitting daily without having contacted American military stations in Australia or on the U.S. Pacific Coast. Roy's ham radio equipment had been brought up to Malabo earlier in the year when the Bell-Carson household had settled there. Then mountain people had built a small radio shack in the hills close by. Roy believed his equipment was at fault rather than Ski. Therefore Roy learned with interest that the Japanese had captured his former student Louis Vail—now a U.S. Army Signal Corps officer—and were holding him prisoner in Dumaguete.

Roy thought, *Louis has just the skills I need to get my radio station working. I should check with Juan Dominado about how to bring Louis into the hills. Juan still lives in town with his young wife, supposedly helping Captain Tsuda—Juan has not pursued his idea of forming his own guerrilla band. Through no fault of Juan, my effort to supply the unit Juan was to organize became a tragedy. Yet Juan might now make an important contribution if Lt. Vail's escape were accomplished.*

Juan quickly responded to Roy's summons to Malabo, being free to pass in and out of town as Captain Tsuda's agent. At Malabo Juan quickly understood Roy's need for Louis and then explained Louis' situation: "After Louis was wounded, the Japs captured him and he was treated by the Mission Hospital here. He has now recovered and is free to come and go in town and stay at home with his new wife Rosa. But he still must report daily to Japanese headquarters here. By treating him well, Captain Tsuda probably hopes to persuade him and other Filipinos to return to town."

After a pause, Juan went on. "A complication about getting Louis to help you, Mr. Bell, is that he has just married Rosa and may not want to make a break so soon that would risk their lives." Roy quietly replied, "If you think it would be all right to ask him, I will be satisfied with his answer—whatever it is. He was a student of mine, as you may know, and is a friend. I can provide a cottage for Louis and his new wife. He will understand my need for him. You could suggest to him offhandedly that as a prisoner his good life is not necessarily going to last long."

The next evening when Juan brought Roy's offer to Louis Vail, circumstances had changed for the young couple. That morning, while at the Mission Hospital for his daily checkup, Louis had talked with an old friend from his student days at Silliman, Teodorico Lejato. Teodorico was being treated for a deep cut on his right forearm, but he didn't tell Louis how it had happened.

Louis confided to his old friend, "It really gripes me to have to bow whenever I meet a Japanese soldier on the street here. What a difference from when America was in control here! In fact, as you know, I became an American Signal Corps officer. Now the Japs want me to be a civilian here." Lejato made no comment, but Angelo, another patient, overheard the conversation and followed Louis out of the ward as fast as he could in his wheelchair.

But Louis was moving away. Yet Angelo hesitated to call out and attract Lejato's attention. Then Louis stopped to talk to a nurse, and Angelo caught up. Now Louis sensed Angelo had something to say, so he waited for him to catch his breath. At last Angelo spoke carefully. "Your friend Lejato's wound was inflicted by Victor Jornales' guerrillas, who were trying to capture Lejato, who works with the Japs by identifying guerrillas. He drives a Jap car and is accompanied by a Jap guard. This time the guard saved Lejato but was killed himself. I'm afraid Lejato will inform the Japs of your opinions."

Louis and Rosa Vail worried about the friendly Angelo's warning for the rest of the day. When Juan brought Roy's offer of refuge and work at Malabo early in the evening, Louis exclaimed, "I think we had better go tonight. I talked too much to my former friend Lejato—not knowing he had become a traitor. I may have stayed safe this afternoon because of our old friendship. But I'm not counting on being safe in town any longer."

At midnight Louis and Rosa were still waiting inside, spooked by the bright moon. Then heavy clouds brought darkness and they stepped outside. The streets seemed deserted, but they felt still safer when a sudden storm drove sheets of rain against them. As they headed for their rendezvous with Juan Dominado, they saw no one else out in the heavy rain. But finally they could make out Juan, who was waiting patiently despite being soaked.

The three of them left town by a trail that bypassed the Japanese soldier who guarded the main road leading inland toward the mountains. In a couple of hours they knocked on the door of the cottage in the hills where Juan Dominado's parents had recently settled to avoid the invaders. The parents were overjoyed to see them, fearing the worst since the three were late because of the Vails' delay in starting. But there was little talk—the less the parents knew, the less they could tell the Japanese if interrogated. Besides, Juan and the Vails were exhausted and immediately fell into a deep sleep after changing into dry clothes.

The next day the Vails awoke to bright sunlight, but Juan was not there. His worried-sick parents explained, "Juan's friend Carlos came from town after you went to sleep. He reported that the Japs had already missed you and suspected Juan of helping you get away. Juan immediately headed for Dumaguete in hopes of saving his wife."

The Vails—dejected that their escape might be tragic for Juan—made their way on mountain trails to Malabo, where Louis was to work on Roy's radio station. What should have been a happy reunion between Professor Bell and his former student immediately became sad when Louis Vail told Roy of the perilous situation that faced Juan back in Dumaguete. Yet Roy remarked, "I wouldn't give up on Juan yet. Knowing him, I believe he may work himself out of even this difficulty."

The previous night a despairing Juan took the trail toward town. The rain had ceased. Yet the sodden, slippery trail and darkness matched Juan's mood. He imagined over and over how the Japanese must have seized Maria and ransacked his house. Surely they would have found something that linked him to the resistance.

Nearing town in this despondent mood, Juan was startled by a half-dozen shadowy figures coming up the trail in the still-dark early morning. But Juan soon recognized Victor Jornales and some of his followers. Victor sensed worry on Juan's face and wanted to find out what was wrong. Yet first he hoped to cheer up his friend by telling him about his group's raid that night.

Victor said, "Juan, I wish you had been with us tonight. We decided it would be fun to raid Police Chief Severino Pastor's house to show that the Japs can't protect their own puppet Filipino officials. As you know, Tsuda had persuaded the Chief to return to his prewar job. Anyway, we scared the life out of the so-called Chief. Before leaving, I thought it would be nice to have a trophy for our night's work so I took the Chief's revolver."

As Victor proudly handed over Chief Pastor's pistol for Juan's inspection, something clicked in Juan's mind. He said, "Victor, I need that revolver badly. I have to have something to show Captain Tsuda that I'm still helping him. I've just managed the Vails' escape from town but have learned Tsuda may suspect me." Victor cut in: "Say no more. Keep the revolver and best of luck. If they take you, we'll try another jailbreak!" So Juan hustled down the trail, trying to figure out how to make best use of the revolver.

In town, Juan's first stop was his house. He found it in shambles. Certain that Maria had been taken, Juan headed for the house of provincial governor Guillermo Villanueva, who, as a Japanese puppet, still tried to stay friendly with his fellow Filipinos. A servant awakened Villanueva, but the governor refused to see Juan, suspecting his visitor's resistance ties and not wanting to know anything that the Japanese would blame him for concealing.

Playing his last card, Juan strode to the nearby Japanese headquarters and demanded to see Captain Tsuda. The captain was conferring with his officers as Juan entered the room. Without a word, Juan laid the revolver on the table in front of Tsuda. Before the stunned captain could collect his thoughts, Juan declared, "I wasn't able to stop a raid on Chief Pastor's home last night, but afterwards I retrieved the Chief's revolver that the young rascals had taken. I hope to persuade one of them to settle back in town in a few days."

When Juan realized the Japanese officers were being taken in, he raised his voice and demanded, "Why has my house been torn apart?" Tsuda did not answer—his men had thrown things around in Juan's house but found no evidence of guerrilla ties. So now, believing Juan, Tsuda praised him: "Juan, you did good work last night. Take this reward for the revolver—bigger than usual—and see if you can get some of the gang back to town. We'll see that they're well-treated. We just want them to settle down to normal lives." Since Tsuda did not mention Juan's wife, Maria, Juan did not ask about her. He began to hope she had not been picked up. So Juan thanked Tsuda for the reward and left.

Upon stepping outside, Juan became aware of his good friend Carlos, who was loitering across the street. Yet Carlos pretended not to notice him. Juan, understanding Carlos had something to say, started walking along his side of the street at a leisurely pace. Carlos walked along at a good pace in the same direction on the other side for several blocks and then waited for Juan. Carlos' first words relieved Juan's mind. "Maria is safe. She was saved by Mayor Mariano Perdices, who by great luck, had just returned from Manila—where with characteristic aplomb he attended a conference of Philippine puppet mayors. Perdices was back in time to learn of Tsuda's plan to tear up your house and got Maria out in time. She is now waiting for you at your Uncle Ramos' home."

A little later Juan and Maria rejoiced at being together again and stayed indoors for the rest of the day. Late that night they made their way along the deserted streets toward the edge of Dumaguete, restraining their urge to salvage something from their ransacked home. So, with nothing but the clothes on their backs, they hastened along the off-road trail to the edge of the mountains at Palimpinon. Then, heading up the steep trail toward Malabo, Juan and Maria relaxed and slowed their pace under the full moon hanging in the clear sky, its face easily recognizable. The loss of their possessions did nothing to lessen their delight in being safe together.

The next morning a relieved Roy welcomed the couple. His hopeful hunch about their safety had come true, but it had taken great good luck in addition to Juan's resourcefulness. Mayor Perdices, Victor Jornales, and Carlos had all made the successful flight of Juan and his bride possible. As a result, Roy no longer suspected Perdices of being a collaborator—his doubts had been based on Perdices' quick return to serve as mayor under the Japanese after initially resigning.

Juan's escape gained for the guerrillas a full-time officer instead of a casual spy who reported on Tsuda to the resistance while supposedly helping the Japanese captain to persuade Filipinos to return to town. Now Juan became a guerrilla lieutenant—the same rank he had held with the joint American-Philippine forces.

Captain Tsuda's gentle treatment of Vail had just facilitated his escape, and his offer to reopen Silliman University in Dumaguete had been flatly refused by President Carson. Yet Tsuda succeeded in bringing the Presbyterian Mission Hospital back to town after it relocated in Pamplona. He did not know that Roy Bell had also urged the director, Dr. Ponce de Leon, to move back to Dumaguete. Roy declared to Dr. Ponce, "You have the only hospital in the province, and back in Dumaguete is the best place for the most people to use it." Thus pushed separately by Roy Bell and Captain Tsuda, Ponce de Leon gave in and moved the hospital back to town. But Ponce would suffer personally later by being under Japanese control.

Captain Tsuda was pleased with having brought the Mission Hospital back to town. So now to keep town life normal, Tsuda sought to bring back a well-respected surveyor, Lucio Ridad, who had moved to his farm near New Ayuquitan when the Japanese came. But Tsuda lost much control over his effort when Major Honshu, an inspecting officer from Manila, arrived and joined him. Tsuda's first step was to request that Villanueva, his puppet provincial governor, arrange a meeting with Ridad, an old friend of the governor's. Ridad accepted the invitation without hesitation. But at the village office where Ridad was to meet his old friend, he unexpectedly also faced two Japanese officers.

The officer of lower rank addressed him first. "Mr. Ridad, I am Captain Tsuda and command Japanese forces in this province. We wish Philippine life to resume normal activities. Since you are a respected surveyor, we would like you to move back to Dumaguete, the capital." Ridad replied, "I moved out of town to my farm because I'm getting too old to work. I prefer it to town." But Tsuda pointed out, "But in Dumaguete you would be right by the Mission Hospital, which has already come back. We need your surveying knowledge to consult even if you don't work much." But Ridad insisted, "I feel much better out here in the country."

Ridad's last remark caused the other, higher-ranking officer to growl, "Who fired on a Japanese truck near your farm? We have been told it was your wife's nephew. Where is he?" Despite threats, Ridad refused to furnish any information about his relative. He remained silent even after the officers called in a large soldier, who slapped and kicked the small-sized Ridad. The frail surveyor almost lost consciousness after being flung to the floor. This brutality appalled Villanueva, and it frustrated Captain Tsuda to see his conciliatory policy shattered. Yet he was powerless to countermand Major Honshu, who would probably report that Tsuda was too soft on Filipinos in describing his inspection trip.

The Japanese officers left Villanueva kneeling over his prostrate friend, who was too far gone to hear the puppet governor whisper, "I'm sorry, I didn't realize they would be that rough." Then Villanueva sadly informed Ridad's relatives of Lucio's condition. They took him back to his farm. After several weeks, Ridad was not yet himself.

Ridad's beating enraged his sons, Frederico and Honorario. They were eager to form a guerrilla band to get back at the Japanese. But first they moved their parents and younger brothers and sisters much farther into the mountains. Now, knowing of Roy Bell's support of the resistance band of Victor Jornales, the Ridad brothers visited Roy to seek his counsel and assistance.

Frederico, who had recently been a mild-mannered, intelligent engineering student at Silliman, asked Roy, "You have probably learned what the Japs did to our father?" Roy nodded in sympathy and Frederico continued. "We have moved our family deep into the mountains so we are ready to go after the Japs with the armed group we are forming. We'll help Victor Jornales drive the Japs out of here."

Roy replied, "Victor and I welcome you to the resistance and will cooperate in any way we can. Right now, we're short of weapons. But Victor may be able to take some for us sometime soon. Meantime, it would be better to wait until you have a fully armed band before making any moves. When that time comes, the best way to damage the Japanese is to conduct night raids, waylay convoys, or embarrass puppet officials. An open fight with their armed troops is the worst situation for you." The brothers nodded politely and left, disliking the idea of delaying attacks on the enemy.

Chapter 8

The Japanese Challenge the Guerrillas to Open Battle

S till another guerrilla band formed in the Dumaguete area after Sergeant David Cirilo learned of the mistreatment of the elder Ridad and noticed with admiration Victor Jornales' exploits. David was a regular Army sergeant who had not surrendered and had kept his rifle. At first he had settled with his family in the hills, helping on his father-in-law's farm, but he soon became restless. A veteran soldier at the age of thirty, Cirilo knew a number of ex-soldiers, so was able to gather forty-two recruits in a couple of days for his guerrilla band.

Captain Tsuda now faced several guerrilla bands who waylaid his troops when they moved in the countryside outside Dumaguete. After firing at close range from hidden locations, the attackers would disappear. As to Filipinos who took official jobs, the guerrillas only stopped and verbally harassed them and called them puppets. These Filipinos were a big part of Captain Tsuda's effort to promote normal life under Japanese rule. Early in the occupation Tsuda had had a signal success in persuading Mariano Perdices to return to his job as mayor of Dumaguete after staying in the hills for only a few days. But later Roy Bell had learned Perdices' real allegiance when the supposedly puppet mayor saved from capture the bride of spy Juan Dominado. In mid-September the ever-active Victor Jornales and twelve of his men slipped into the village of Sibulan, three miles north of Dumaguete. They overwhelmed the local police and seized their four shotguns and four pistols, causing the Japanese to disarm the local police in the rest of the small towns around Dumaguete. In Dumaguete, however, the Japanese did not disarm the police because they were too numerous for the guerrillas to handle. Meantime the Ridad band had ambushed three truckloads of soldiers near Ayuquitan, inflicting casualties and then fading away before the Japs could regroup.

All this was too much for Captain Tsuda, who had abandoned his failed conciliatory policy of persuading Filipinos back to town, as shown by his brutal treatment of Lucio Ridad. Tsuda publicly complained that the guerrillas wouldn't come out and fight. The young Filipinos had contented themselves with ambushes and random attacks while never standing up for a fight with the trained Japanese soldiers. But now three guerrilla leaders—puffed up by their successful operations—decided to accept Tsuda's challenge.

But first the guerrilla leaders came up to Malabo to consult with Roy, who had encouraged their ambush-type warfare. After being told of their intent, Roy pointed out, "Right now you are causing Captain Tsuda a lot of trouble with your hit-and-run tactics. That is why he's trying to have a face-to-face combat so he can kill enough of your men to put you out of business. Don't fall for his trick."

Victor Jornales, the youngest, answered for the three: "Instead of them putting us out of business, we'll get a lot of them together and wipe them out and drive them out of Dumaguete for good. Our plan is to send rumors into Dumaguete that a bridge over the Ocoy River is about to be blown up. We'll station our soldiers on a ridge close by. If they will assault and try to dislodge us, we should be able to do away with a lot of them." Roy knew he couldn't change their minds, so he answered, "If you can get them to assault up the steep sides of that ridge, you can inflict heavy casualties if you hold your ground."

Two days before the planned battle, Jornales had an unusual opportunity to seize an important collaborator, whom we shall name Ricardo. He was a large, blustering man who had helped Captain Tsuda find and force Filipinos back to town. Jornales had tricked Ricardo into coming to a conference in the village of Luzuriaga. As we have noted, that village kept on good terms with the Japanese by turning over a couple obsolete weapons when ordered to disarm its police. That evening Ricardo showed up but was accompanied by two Japanese soldiers. Nevertheless, Jornales' men nabbed Ricardo. In the confusion the two Japanese soldiers escaped into heavy brush without being hit by the bullets fired after them. Their escape made it a crisis. They would report what happened to Captain Tsuda. Under his new confrontation policy, the village of Luzuriaga was doomed. To save the villagers, the guerrillas went from house to house to urge everyone to flee into the hills.

The next day Jornales slowed the avenging Japanese patrol, but it was able to continue on to Luzuriaga, where it burned down the village's twenty-two empty dwellings. Jornales' men wanted to pursue the patrol. But Jornales reminded his puzzled followers, "We have to hurry now to be in place with

David Cirilo's and the Ridads' bands near the Ocoy River bridge to face—we hope—most of the enemy garrison in Dumaguete."

Earlier that same morning of October 11, Ridad and Cirilo stationed their bands on a ridge three hundred feet north of the Ocoy River Bridge, near the village of Lo-oc, four miles north of Dumaguete. The ridge rose sixty feet above the road and was about one-third of a mile long and two hundred yards wide. Its north slope was almost a cliff, but the other slopes were more gradual and covered with coral rocks, coconut trees, and underbrush. Jornales' agents had planted rumors that the guerrillas were about to destroy the bridge. But Victor Jornales himself had not yet arrived an hour after the leaders had agreed to meet and deploy their forces.

Frederico Ridad was not aware of Jornales' attack on the enemy patrol that morning, which had slowed his arrival, so he sent Victor a message with a joking threat: "If you do not participate in this fight, we shall declare your group a wild group to be hunted down as bandits.' Jornales was grinning about this message when he arrived with his band at 10:00 AM. Hungry after ambushing the enemy patrol, Jornales' men had barely started an early lunch of green bananas when a runner climbed the ridge. He was so short of breath he could barely manage to say, "There are 40 of them and they are right behind me."

The first thing the guerrillas saw was an enemy truck cautiously approaching the cliff from the north. Ridad's brother, Honorario, quickly disabled it, but Japanese soldiers scurried out of the truck. They took cover from the guerrilla fire and began to lob mortar shells onto the Filipino positions.

At the same time, Captain Tsuda launched the main body of Japanese troops up the more gradual slopes of the ridge at a distance from the guerrilla positions. The Japanese troops advanced but could only half-surround the guerrillas because of the steep cliff. And the Filipinos still held the higher ground. Yet Captain Tsuda sensed his troops would soon bring an end to the pesky guerrillas. He recklessly exposed himself as he urged his troops to make the final push. But a guerrilla rifleman on higher ground was seeking a good target among the jumble of huge rocks and bushes where the enemy had taken cover. When Captain Tsuda briefly became visible, the rifleman was ready and fired. The bullet penetrated Tsuda's lower abdomen, and he collapsed. Tsuda's deputy took charge of the assault.

The new Japanese commander was also confident his experienced and better-armed regular troops would kill or capture the trapped Filipinos. But the guerrillas adapted to a new situation for them. Instead of fading into the jungle after an ambush, the Filipinos took cover behind rocks and brush

and turned back repeated assaults. They made good use of their fifty obsolete rifles and shotguns. But their most effective weapon was Frederico's
Browning automatic rifle (BAR)—he drew lots of fire because of its deadly
performance. Yet he kept firing even after a thigh wound caused serious
bleeding. Hour followed hour, but the veteran Japanese soldiers could not
finish off the untrained Filipino irregulars.

Not long before dark a heavy rain set in. In the semidarkness the surviving
guerrillas slipped away, except for the Ridad brothers. They settled behind a
large rock, not being able to move because of Frederico's leg wound.

Tsuda's deputy officer—now in charge—had no stomach for pressing
forward in the rainy half-darkness even after the guerrilla fire ceased for the
time being. So the Ridad brothers were safe behind their rock until the next
morning, when two of their soldiers came to help move Frederico.

In the meantime, amid the darkness and continuing rain, the Japanese
loaded their dead and wounded comrades on trucks and headed back to
Dumaguete. Dr. Ponce de Leon—director of the Mission Hospital, who
had been urged to return his hospital to Dumaguete from the hills by both
Captain Tsuda and Roy Bell—now wished he had not come back. Captain
Tsuda's deputy officer ordered Ponce to bring all the hospital nurses, medicines, and instruments to the Japanese headquarters.

Dr. Ponce could do little for Captain Tsuda, who was taken to Cebu
the next day but did not survive. Ponce did the best he could for six other
severely wounded Japanese at the headquarters building, but one of them
died the next day. In another building the doctor was about to climb the
stairs to treat a wounded sergeant but was stopped and told the patient
would be brought down for treatment. Ponce figured the Japanese did not
want him to go up and see their dying and dead soldiers.

Only after several days did the extent of the Japanese casualties become
evident to Roy Bell. He was greatly surprised by the guerrillas' success.
He had thought it possible only if the guerrillas stood firm in the face of
Japanese assaults—and unexpectedly they had, holding together on higher
ground for hours before slipping away in the growing darkness. The
Japanese admitted to only five dead. Yet Japanese cremations took all of
the grandstand seats of the Silliman University athletic stadium plus timbers
from the local lumberyard.

Bell concluded that the guerrillas had killed about twenty-five or thirty
enemy soldiers, or up to three-fourths of the Dumaguete garrison. He spec-
ulated, *If we had known how great were their losses, we could have easily
taken Dumaguete. But maybe that wouldn't have been such a good idea—we*

could not have resisted a serious effort from Cebu to retake the town. Then the enemy would have burned the town and killed many of its people.

As to guerrilla losses, there were eleven killed and eight wounded. The healthy guerrillas took their wounded comrades into the hills to David Cirilo's camp at Tinpayan, about four miles west of Sibulan. Upon learning of the battle that he had not encouraged, Roy Bell sent Dr. Jose Garcia to treat the wounded.

Dr. Garcia was available and willing at Malabo. After settling his family at Basay on the far southwestern coast of Negros, Garcia welcomed Roy's earlier invitation to come to Malabo to serve the Silliman faculty who had gone to the hills. Then, like Roy, Garcia became an eager supporter of the resistance.

Now at Tinpayan, Garcia stayed all night treating the injured men. The next morning he had the wounded moved again, this time to Malabo, where the doctor had his medical supplies and equipment. Of the eight wounded to be treated, Frederico Ridad's thigh wound came closest to being a fatality.

Frederico's injury had prevented his brother, Honorario, from moving him from their place of hiding at the battle site until next morning. When Frederico continued to bleed during the day, Dr. Garcia knew he had to remove the offending shrapnel. Lacking an X-ray machine to locate the tiny piece of metal, Dr. Garcia undertook to find and extract it without using anesthesia. During the last bit of daylight, the doctor succeeded and sewed up the wound. But three days later Garcia had to reopen the severe wound. Yet Frederico recovered after blood transfusions from his brother and others of his band.

Chapter 9

Control of
Guerrilla Bands

October 1942

After Roy Bell encouraged the formation of three guerrilla bands by two former Silliman students and Sergeant Cirilo, their success in harassing the Japanese was gratifying to the young leaders and to Roy. But Victor Jornales' activities became bolder and bolder while he ignored Roy's cautionary words. Finally Roy mustered all his persuasive power in an effort to prevent Victor from raiding the Mission Hospital to pick up an enemy informer, Teodorico Lejato, who was recuperating there. Lejato had been wounded by Jornales' men but had escaped.

Roy sternly admonished Victor, "If you force your way into the hospital to capture Lejato, the Japs will have a perfect excuse to burn it down. It is the only hospital in the whole province. Besides its chief, Dr. Ponce, secretly sends us medical supplies for guerrilla use." For once Victor Jornales followed Roy's advice, believing the hospital might be destroyed if he went after Lejato.

Roy was worried that he would not be able in the future to prevent crazier projects by Jornales—or by all of the guerrilla leaders, for that matter—such as the ill-considered operation at Lo-oc, where the guerrillas had allowed themselves to be encircled. Roy spent several days hiking in the hills to find and talk to each of the three leaders.

At the Ridad camp, Frederico was still very weak from his leg wound at Lo-oc, so his seventeen-year-old brother, Honorario, did most of the talking. All three leaders greeted Roy with great friendliness, and all agreed to deal more diplomatically with each other regarding desertions from one band to another. Then Roy explained to each leader the value that uniting their three forces under a Philippine Army officer could bring to operations. But none of them wanted to consider it—they were pleased with their own successes.

So Roy returned to Malabo, discouraged by the three leaders' attitude. He didn't know what to do next about the guerrilla bands he had helped create. Wanting advice, Roy invited a group of friends to meet with him at Malabo: President Carson, his boss at Silliman; Professor Ben Viloria, a colleague at the university; and George Fleischer, a sugar plantation owner.

After Roy explained the situation, Fleischer pointed out, "These guerrilla bands may come to consider themselves to be the law since the civil administration ceased in the hills when the Japanese took over Dumaguete, our capital. We need an overall leader of these bands, who will prevent the guerrilla soldiers from taking advantage of the current lack of civilian administration up here, such as looting or settling grudges. Of course he must be an effective military leader. Why don't you take charge of them, Roy? You served in the U.S. Army in World War I." Roy quickly answered, "But George, I was in the Medical Corps and had little military training and no military experience:"

President Carson and Professor Viloria likewise tried to persuade Roy to take military command of the guerrilla bands, citing his twenty years living in the area and his current, though limited, influence, on the guerrilla bands. But Roy rejected the idea, declaring, "Thank you for your confidence, but I don't feel I could do as good a job as a Philippine Army officer of sufficient rank, whom the guerrilla leaders and soldiers would consider to be their legitimate leader. However, I'll do my best to supervise and coordinate them until I can find the right officer for the job." Roy's three friends could only agree to this course.

However, before Roy's visitors had started back home, Frederico Tatel, Roy's student courier, came by to report that Lieutenant Colonel Gabriel Gador, who had commanded all forces on Negros Island before the surrender, had returned from Mindanao Island and was located in the mountains near the center of Negros Island. Realizing that Gador seemed to fill their requirements, Roy and his group agreed to offer command of the guerrillas to him.

Tatel volunteered to take the group's offer of command to Gador despite the danger of travel outside the area controlled by Roy's guerrilla bands. Beyond that area it was not known what group was in control in the absence of peacetime administration from Dumaguete.

In saying farewell to Frederico, Roy advised, "You should meet with Lt. Sibala on the way. His guerrilla camp is in the mangrove thicket just south of Tanjay. He may know the whereabouts of Col. Gador." Roy had earlier consulted with Lieutenant Galicano Sibala about the formation of a guerrilla group near Tanjay; it now had several ambushes to its credit.

Late the next afternoon, after a twenty-mile hike, Frederico found Lieutenant Sibala relaxing deep in the mangroves after ambushing a Japanese column of trucks the night before. When Frederico told him of his mission to Gador, Sibala warned, "You'll be passing through the area around Tanjay where some of Gador's men operate. I don't know whether they'll let you proceed. But if you want to go on, stay with us tonight and give it a try tomorrow."

The next morning Frederico kept on for a mile or so to the edge of Tanjay before he was challenged by a burly guerrilla. When Frederico explained what he wanted, the man said, "If you have a letter, I will get it to our leader, Col. Gador. Otherwise, let Mr. Bell come himself. Anyway I don't think Col. Gador would be interested in working with Mr. Bell. Our leader told us there is no need of attacking the Japanese now. He said we will just hide because the Japanese invasion forces will be sent to Australia and will be wiped out there. We'll just wait."

Frederico handed over Roy's message and hastened back to Malabo. There Frederico's information fit in with a report that Gador had rebuffed an offer from Major Abcede that he serve under the colonel in a combined Negros Island command—Abcede controlled Negros Occidental Province, comprising the island's western and northern sections. Gador had informed Abcede that he would not take island command or engage in active operations unless he were ordered to do so by General MacArthur or the U.S. War Department.

Roy soon learned of another Philippine Army officer, Major Placido Ausejo, who might be willing to take over Roy's guerrillas. After the surrender Ausejo had retreated with his family from Mindanao to the remote seaside village of Basay on the southern coast of Negros, twenty miles beyond the end of the road. It was a safe place for his family; Dr. Garcia had also settled his wife and children there. But Roy thought it possible Ausejo himself wanted to play it safe, just as Gador reportedly did. Roy needed to find out, so he called upon a prewar Dumaguete neighbor now in the hills, Genaro Saavedra, to carry Roy's message across the island to Ausejo. But Saavedra had not returned with an answer when Roy received a request from Gador—apparently in response to Roy's earlier inquiry about commanding his guerrilla bands—to visit him at Payabon in northern Negros.

It was a week's trip on foot each way during the autumn rainy season. And Roy was not ready to offer Gador the job if the report of his passive attitude toward the Japanese was true.

Major Ausejo, a Silliman graduate, would probably be a better choice if he were willing. Nevertheless, Roy thought it would be desirable to establish good relations with Gador, whose men seemed to be located near Tanjay—close to where Lieutenant Sibala operated. So Roy set off on the long trip to see Gador without having learned Ausejo's intentions.

Meantime Saavedra had reached Major Ausejo near Basay. Roy's proposal had come at just the right time. The major was eager to join the resistance now that he had settled his wife and five children at the family's rice farm near Basay. They were indeed safe—decades later Ausejo's adult son told the author that as a child at the farm, he had never seen a Japanese.

In October 1942 Major Ausejo was fifty years old. He had been a career officer since 1917. He was executive officer of the Philippine Bureau of Constabulary (BC) forces on Mindanao at the war's start. Now Ausejo urged Saavedra to hurry back to inform Roy that he would soon be on his way to Malabo. Ausejo bade his family good-bye on October 7, 1942, and headed westward along the southern coast toward Tolong. He started out with five soldiers and Lieutenant Timoteo Oracion, another Silliman graduate, who also had returned to Negros from active duty on Mindanao. At Tolong Ausejo enlisted the mayor, the police, and other leaders in his projected command, contemplating a larger organization than Roy's bands.

Two days later Ausejo reached Siaton, where the resistance leader also joined the new organization. Continuing westward, the major's party stopped at Dauin and Bacong, just south of Dumaguete, and enlisted still more guerrilla leaders.

On October 12 Ausejo brought under his command the large guerrilla unit that ex-professor Ben Viloria had recently formed. After meeting with Roy about guerrilla control, Viloria realized the guerrillas suffered from a shortage of guns and ammunition. So he had formed a band that had the initial purpose of acquiring weapons beyond its own needs. Major Ausejo eagerly questioned Viloria about the recent clash near Lo-oc between the Japanese and the three guerrilla bands that Ausejo was about to take over. The major was surprised that the enemy commander, Captain Tsuda, had fallen along with so many enemy soldiers. Ausejo remarked, "These boys I will have are real fighters, but I will do my best to avoid pitched battles while we harass and frustrate the next enemy garrison."

Then Viloria bragged a little to Ausejo about an earlier encounter with three Japanese agents sent by Captain Tsuda to persuade Viloria return to town. Viloria recounted, "They told me I had only to surrender and I would be welcomed back to Dumaguete and given a respectable job. I told them I liked my present job and suggested that they should stay in Dumaguete."

Major Ausejo reached Malabo on October 14. But Roy Bell was already on his way to see Gador. However, Arthur Carson was on hand to greet the new guerrilla commander, just as Roy had planned in case Ausejo took the job and came soon. So now President Carson faced a barefooted and dusty Major Ausejo.

At first Carson didn't realize who it was. But the man's bearing and confident manner soon convinced Carson it was the officer he and Roy were seeking. Ausejo understood right away that he was being greeted on behalf of Roy Bell. He declared, "I'm here to help Mr. Bell with his young fighters. I've added some other good men to our resistance organization on my way here."

Meanwhile Roy was still heading northward. Because of the slow going in the hills and the rainy season, Roy had only covered two-thirds of the way to Payabon when the messenger from Ausejo overtook him with word that the major was on his way to Malabo and would take charge of Roy's three guerrilla bands. Roy immediately turned back after instructing the messenger, "Continue on to Payabon and tell Col. Gador that I have to get back to Malabo because of pressing guerrilla business. I'll come up to see him as soon as I'm able to get away."

Relieved by the welcome news from Malabo, Roy hardly noticed the rough trail and the discomfort of the rain as he hastened southward. He thought, *I'll go back by my friend Captain Leon Flores' place. His Army days go back to 1917—the time of my World War I service. Maybe he would like to join Major Ausejo's force.* So Roy stopped and explained the situation to his friend Flores. He ended by saying, "Major Ausejo could make good use of you as his executive officer. If you're interested, Ausejo and I will come to see you soon." Flores perked up at the idea, saying, "I thought I was too old to join the resistance, but I would like to talk with the two of you."

On the afternoon of October 18, Roy reached Malabo. He was eager to meet Ausejo. But the major had gone into the hills to find a suitable place for an emergency headquarters. However, Ausejo returned while Roy was still listening to his wife, Edna, and their sons give him their news.

After thanking Ausejo for his promptness in coming, Roy told the major of his own recruiting effort, saying, "Yesterday I stopped by to see an old friend, Captain Leon Flores. I hadn't been able to get him interested in guerrilla activity before—he said he was too old for such fighting. But when I told him you would form a regular military organization in the hills, he seemed a lot more enthusiastic. I told him we would come and see him as soon as you got here. I was thinking he could be the deputy officer in your organization." Ausejo answered, "Yes! Let's go tomorrow. I'll need a good officer to help me, especially with the additional guerrilla units who joined me on the way from Basay."

At Captain Flores' home the next day, Major Ausejo briefly explained his plans. Almost at once Flores declared, "I will form my own guerrilla group from men I know in the hills west of New Ayuquitan and join your organization." Roy Bell and Major Ausejo nodded in agreement to this idea even though they had been planning to ask Captain Flores only to serve as Major Ausejo's deputy. Then Ausejo added to Flores' proposal: "Would you take charge of Mr. Bell's three bands besides the new band you are forming as their battalion commander?" Flores liked the idea of leading the young guerrillas who had decimated Captain Tsuda's command at Lo-oc. Thus Lieutenant Jornales, Lieutenant Ridad, and Sergeant Cirilo would lead companies E, F, and G of the 2nd Battalion.

The next day Roy Bell took Major Ausejo to meet Sergeant David Cirilo. David had modestly not tried to promote himself although he had formed a band of forty-two men who had fought at Lo-oc. But as part of the new 75th Regiment, Major Ausejo promoted a delighted Cirilo to lieutenant.

Ausejo now insisted on returning to his new command post at Malabo, believing he should be available to the various leaders and units he had taken into his command. So he and Roy did not hike farther north to visit Lieutenant Galicano Sibala, whose unit was located just south of Tanjay. But before they headed back to Malabo, the Cirilo assured them, "There is no doubt in my mind that Lt. Sibala will join up with us."

Roy Bell and Major Ausejo returned to Malabo on October 21, 1942. Roy was proud of what Ausejo had accomplished. Ausejo brought under his command Roy's three bands—which would operate directly under Captain Flores—as well as the several units along the southern coast of Negros that Ausejo had picked up on his way to Malabo. With the expected addition of Sibala's unit, Ausejo had formed a carved chain of resistance some seventy miles in length. It extended thirty-five miles from Tolong to Siaton, twenty miles from Siaton to Malabo, and eighteen miles north from Malabo to Tanjay.

The next day back at Malabo, Ausejo sent Rito Dominado, Juan's brother, to the small island of Siquijor to check on those guerrillas. Upon his return, Rito reported that guerrilla soldiers under Major Benito Cunanan had driven off an enemy landing in August. Cunanan added his unit to Ausejo's command. By early December 1942, Major Ausejo had organized his bands to operate as components of the 75th Regiment, consisting of one full battalion, headed by Captain Flores, and scattered elements of three other battalions. As his staff officers, Ausejo selected Captain Ben Viloria as executive officer; Lieutenant Juan Dominado as intelligence officer; Lieutenant Rito Dominado as operations officer; Lieutenant Timoteo Oracion as supply officer; Lieutenant Jose Garcia as surgeon; and Lieutenant Louis Vail as chief signal officer.

Would Ausejo's leadership and paper transformation of the guerrilla soldiers into a regiment make the soldiers more effective? For the time being the answer was yes. Most days in late October and November guerrilla soldiers of Captain Flores' new 2nd Battalion mounted attacks on weakened Japanese forces in their narrow coastal area of control that extended twenty miles from Dumaguete to Bais.

The longer term also looked promising because of Ausejo's efforts to provide for an orderly supply of civilian food to the guerrilla soldiers so as to avoid the kind of guerrilla theft and terrorism of civilians that had occurred at Tanjay. Viloria and other officers of Ausejo's staff made individual agreements with farmers to provide the guerrilla soldiers with food. Each farmer would give a modest amount according to his production. But no guerrilla would demand food or anything else directly from him. After a farmer agreed to his quota, Ausejo sent bolo men to pick up his farm's output.

Bolo men acted locally for resistance forces and helped people in need on many Philippine islands in places where no civil authority existed because of the Japanese occupation of administrative centers. The bolo men were named for the long Philippine knife used to cut the stems of bananas and sugarcane. A bolo man usually worked individually. He carried messages or stood a lonely watch to warn of enemy incursions into the hills. He was usually clad in a shirt made from the rough fibers of the abaca tree. In addition, the bolo men aided in the location and identification of collaborators. These patriotic Filipinos often paid for their brave efforts by having their homes burned or relatives captured and held as hostages.

Roy encountered the work of bolo men while looking after the Winn family. Rev. Gardner Winn and his wife, Viola, were faculty members who, with their three children, had settled in the hills sixty miles north of Dumaguete. Because of the distance, Roy had not visited them yet to pay them—he was paying all faculty members as long as funds lasted. Roy was not in a hurry to make the long trip to see the Winns until he learned through the guerrilla-bolo network that the Japs had blackmailed Gardner Winn into turning himself over to them. Viola Winn and her three children were still in the hills under the care of bolo men.

The next day Roy Bell hastened northward to see how he could help. Four days later Viola Winn met him at the door of her retreat and invited him in. While they sat and ate bananas, Viola explained what had happened. "When we first came up here to get away from the Japs, Pedro, a local Filipino, let us stay in his place until we could get something built for ourselves. During this time, an enemy raid almost reached Pedro's house—forcing both families into flight. Then a collaborator learned how Pedro had helped us—leading to his capture by the Japs. Soon the collaborator brought us word that the Japs would execute Pedro unless my husband Gardner gave himself up to them. We had a terrible time trying to figure out what to do, but in the end Gardner believed he should save Pedro. So my husband is in enemy hands."

After Roy sympathized with her as best he could, he explained his trip there. "I needed to visit you soon anyway because President Carson is paying faculty members as long as Silliman has funds. The Board of Missions in New York by great good luck transferred funds to Silliman University at Cebu City just before the Japs arrived. The money will be the last that we get from the U.S. President Carson wants you to have a double share of this money."

Mrs. Winn just smiled and then astonished Roy by saying, "We won't need any of the finds. The members of our Christian congregation talked with me yesterday about helping us. They're expecting to look after us indefinitely—a couple of them are bolo men who constantly keep track of the Japs so they and the guerrilla soldiers can move us if necessary. Others in the congregation plan to plant a garden and find a water buffalo for us to milk and work." Roy still insisted that she should take the money, but she again declined.

Roy left in an uneasy mood; he was worried about the safety of Viola and the children. He hadn't gone far when he came upon a clearing in the forest where a farmer was plowing sweet potato vines with a water buffalo. Seeing the farmer, Roy crossed the field and with a smile asked, "Do you know Mrs. Winn?" The farmer dropped the carabao's reins and seemed ready to take a break. He eagerly replied, "Yes, she's a member of our church. We're very grateful that Rev. Winn gave up his freedom because the Japs promised to spare Pedro's life. Pedro is an uncle of one of our members and saved the Winns from the Japs and they suspect him of it. We hope he can get away and come up here. Our members will look after Mrs. Winn as long as the Japs are close enough to make raids up here. It may be a long time."

Roy nodded but said nothing about his fear that Pedro would never be released or even that his life would be spared. Yet Roy felt better about Mrs. Winn and her children's chances to survive. He waved good-bye to the farmer and headed toward Malabo.

Mrs. Winn's Philippine neighbors kept their promises. Besides planting a garden and providing a carabao, bolo men repaired the house and moved them away from enemy raids. Guerrilla soldiers later escorted Mrs. Winn and her children on an eleven-day trek to meet a submarine that took them to Australia. Her husband also survived the war as a Japanese prisoner.

Chapter 10

Forming a Free Government

November 1942 to January 1943

U pon returning to Malabo after visiting Viola Winn, Roy found a contented but thoughtful Major Ausejo. The guerrilla commander commented, "Mr. Bell, we have Japanese power confined to the coastal area. But that means there is no civilian authority whatsoever in the hills except the mayors of a few villages." Roy interrupted: "Yes, the prewar center of administration was Dumaguete, but it is now occupied by the enemy."

Ausejo asked, "Shouldn't we try to set up a substitute government for the hills here in the southern part of Negros Oriental Province? Such a government near my military headquarters would make both organizations more legitimate in the minds of the villagers and farmers here in the hills." Roy had thought of the same thing but typically was reluctant to push himself forward. In this case he would probably have to assume authority in the civil administration that was established. Nevertheless he now said to Ausejo, "I will try to think of how exactly to do it."

But Roy didn't have to think much about getting this project started. One bright morning soon after this conversation, a young man stood before Roy out of breath and looking upset. He had just hiked up from Dumaguete after sneaking around the Japanese guard on the main road out of town. He told Roy, "I am Jose Hernandez and was secretary to Governor Villanueva until this morning. Yesterday I told the supposed Governor, 'I don't much like working for the Japanese. We do whatever they tell us to do and [they] give us a nice office as a reward for accepting their orders without complaint.' That complaint yesterday really made the boss angry. He got red in the face and said, 'Any more remarks like that and I'll report you to the Japs.' That was yesterday so I came up here today without going to work. I'd like to stay."

Roy immediately replied, "Jose, you're welcome to stay up here. By the way, how would you like to be my secretary?"

Jose was the beginning of the Free Government. His first important job was to take notes on the daily news broadcast from San Francisco and type a summary that was distributed under the name of *Victory News*. Copies passed from hand to hand throughout the province and were read even in towns garrisoned by Japanese troops.

A key distributor of *Victory News* was Mr. Arrieta, a Spanish friend of the Bells, who owned a plantation near Tanjay. Although threatened by Colonel Gador's lawless guerrillas, Arrieta did not seek help from the Japanese; instead he moved his family into the hills away from Tanjay. He kept up with the news by radio himself and eagerly circulated *Victory News* widely in his region with the help of his plantation workers.

After Jose Hernandez's departure from Villanueva's staff, his friends in the governor's office soon found out through the grapevine what Jose was doing at Malabo. They came to realize they were really working for the Japanese by staying with the governor. So Mr. Ibanez, Villanueva's auditor, and Fernando Fuentes, his clerk, both followed Hernandez's example and joined Roy's Free Government at Malabo. Likewise, Villanueva also lost Nicolas Teves, his tax clerk. Teves started keeping Free Government records and also was sent by Roy to check on conditions in various villages in Free Government territory.

Roy tried to recruit a fiery town official for the Free Government when Norberto Pareja, peacetime mayor of New Ayuquitan, asked Roy, "What can I do for the resistance?" Roy remembered Norberto as a strong student leader and a good scholar at Silliman; after graduation he had become a lawyer. Roy quickly answered, "You could help us a lot right now on my staff to help establish the judicial system for our free government."

But that was too tame a job for the ex-mayor. He burst out, "Mr. Bell, that's not what I had in mind. I have found a safe place for my family in the mountains of Cebu and have come back here to fight. I want to drive the Japs out of New Ayuquitan, where I used to be mayor."

Roy couldn't change Pareja's mind, so they finally decided that Pareja would stay in the hills as a guerrilla leader close to occupied New Ayuquitan. From there he could lead the harassment of the enemy inside and outside the town. This would be very feasible because the present puppet mayor was also a member of the resistance. In this way Pareja found a useful role in the resistance. In time the enemy became aware of his presence, but their raiding parties never could catch him—bolo men always warned him in time.

In the Free Government area, the mayors rather than Major Ausejo's staff supervised the supply of food from farmer to soldiers. As before, each farm household supported Ausejo's 75th Regiment with a weekly quota of rice, corn, fish, or meat, according to the family's main occupation. The bolo men collected and delivered the food.

Another Free Government project was education. From the time Edna Bell and Edith Carson had first moved their families to Malabo, they taught Sunday school and realized the need for regular schooling for Philippine children there. Feeling more settled in August 1942, Edna had hired Miss Felipe Hermoso to start an elementary school—there were thirty-six in her first class. Then, when Roy was establishing the Free Government, he realized that it should and could promote schools in the hills. It wasn't so difficult because schools were in great demand by mountain people—three hundred were established during 1942. The superintendent was Venancio Aldecoa.

Malabo now became a beehive of activity because of Ausejo's military staff and the staff of the Free Government. Roy had a loudspeaker set up outdoors to catch the daily news broadcast from San Francisco. The loudspeaker was a good excuse for the civilian and military workers at Malabo to take a break from their regular duties. They gathered daily to listen—a tranquil scene in the farming village on the shelf of a green mountain.

Roy turned over the house built for the Bell and Carson families to Ausejo for his regimental headquarters. The Bell family moved to a smaller house that was built nearby. Even though they had many guests, Edna Bell usually had plenty of food to serve—cornmeal mush, dried beef, sweet potatoes, bananas, coffee—and she could buy coffee beans most of the time to roast and grind. But the guerrillas' need for food sometimes limited variety for the Bell family because the farmers supplied the guerrillas first. Yet many guerrillas were former Silliman students or faculty members, and they shared what they had when the Bell family ran short. For Christmas dinner Kenneth Bell gave up one of the fat turkeys he had brought up from Dumaguete—he had continued with his hobby of raising turkeys.

While both military and civilian projects were succeeding, Roy continued to be disappointed by the failure of Ski's radio transmissions to arouse any response. Roy asked his U.S. Signal Corps officer, Lieutenant Louis Vail, "What can we do about Ski's failure to make any contact? We are both convinced he is a capable operator."

Vail answered, "Before I was captured on the other side of the island, I buried some good U.S. Army radio equipment. It should work for us if it's still there and I can get it over here. I would like to make the effort, and knowing my bride, she will insist on coming too." Roy could only admire the courage of Louis, his former Silliman student. And he was not surprised that both Louis and his new bride, Rosa, would go. They had both spurned the welcome Captain Tsuda promised if Louis agreed to stay in Dumaguete—should he be freed. Instead they had escaped and joined Roy at Malabo. Now Roy pointed out, "That equipment could be crucial for our work. You'll probably need one of the Norwegians to help carry the heavy components."

After Louis told Rosa about the two-day trip they were taking across the island, he brought up the question of which Norwegian they should take with them. Immediately they exclaimed together, "Arne Hansen would be best!" Rosa went on, "Arne is the youngest of them and loves to talk—he has at least one girl in every port. You don't have to believe his stories to be entertained." When approached, Arne was delighted, saying, "That will be nice break from my guard duty on the trail. I guess Mr. Bell will have a soldier replace me for a few days."

Even after Louis and Rosa had departed, Ski kept trying to contact another station. Ski had about finished a second day of futile efforts when an articulate voice responded in English, "I am the operator at the San Francisco military station, KFS. Who are you? We don't know your station." Ski provided his name and serial number, but to Ski's chagrin, the KFS operator demanded, "Spell out the names of your mother and father." Only after the names matched Ski's U.S. Army Signal Corps records was the San Francisco operator satisfied. Then he gave Ski the call sign and frequency of General MacArthur's Southwest Pacific Area (SWPA).[1] But subsequently Ski was unable to contact the SWPA.

When the usual group gathered that afternoon to hear the news broadcast, they burst into cheers upon learning of Ski's contact with KFS. Nevertheless the contact caused Roy to worry about security. He sternly warned the resistance workers who had cheered Ski's success: "We have had a wonderful transmitting breakthrough with our radio project, but it brings us acute danger if the Japanese down in Dumaguete find out about it. We are less than 15 miles from them, and they could mount an attack against us on short notice or try a small-unit foray to destroy our equipment. In talking to anyone—and there are collaborators or people who talk to collaborators all about—you must not give any indication of our transmitting success. Just talk about our news broadcasts." The men's serious attention satisfied Roy.

While Ski's unexpected success was taking place, the Vail party hiked across the island without incident. Lieutenant Vail found the buried transmitter untouched. But there was so much of it, they had to rethink how to get it back to Malabo. They could load up a mountain carrier with the tubes and lighter components and send him on the long trail back. But could he find his way on unfamiliar trails and turns and could he be trusted with the expensive equipment? Vail and Arne would be needed to get the heavy equipment on a boat. Then the passage down Tanon Strait along the eastern coast of Negros would be dangerous because of Japanese sea patrols. On the other hand, the hike through the mountains across the island had been uneventful.

Rosa, a Filipina, was the logical person to conduct the carrier back to Malabo, and she volunteered. Once the carrier was loaded, Rosa started down the trail with him. She waved a good-bye to her husband and Arne before a bend in the trail took her out of their sight.

Lieutenant Vail and Arne carried the heavy equipment down to a remote beach on Tanon Strait. There Roy had arranged with the Chinese merchants in Dumaguete to provide an outboard motorboat. Vail and Arne waited until dark to load the radio gear and during the night chugged down Tanon Strait to Sibulan. There local bolo men hauled the cargo into the brush for the day. After nightfall, Vail and Arne led the bolo men with the equipment up to Malabo. They woke up Roy Bell to show him the prized radio equipment. The delighted Roy told them that Rosa had safely returned on January 5, 1943, with the lighter parts. But Vail had already had a joyous reunion with Rosa.

Despite his late arrival, Vail slept lightly and woke up early the next morning, eager to install the new transmitter. By evening he told Ski to try to reach General MacArthur's SWPA with the call sign and frequency Ski had obtained from the military station in San Francisco. Ski contacted the SWPA on his first try and roughly described the situation at Malabo without revealing its location.

The following day MacArthur instructed the guerrilla leaders at Malabo: "The need for information comes first. Guerrilla military activity is desirable only if it provides safety for an intelligence network to operate." MacArthur would soon show his desire to use Negros for this project.

MacArthur was planning for his eventual return to the Philippines— a return that became a real prospect after the Battle of the Solomons ended on November 15, 1942. This decisive U.S. Navy victory halted the Japan's attempt to reinforce its soldiers on Guadalcanal. The next day MacArthur's drive north started with the landing of American soldiers at Buna on New Guinea.

Chapter 11

Roy Bell's Journey to Mindanao

January 1943

I n mid-January 1943 Ski—who had recently contacted General Mac-Arthur's SWPA command from Roy Bell's station at Malabo—had another success. While searching the frequencies, Ski got a screeching sound that hurt his ears. But he turned down his volume, responded to the noise, and got a barely understandable answer. With difficulty Ski learned that the transmission came from the large island of Mindanao, only thirty-five miles south of Negros at one point.

The sender was at the headquarters of a General Fertig, an American resistance leader there. The operators agreed to make contact the next day so their superiors could talk directly with each other. At the appointed time a scratchy message could be made out—General Fertig wanted Roy Bell to come to his camp and fix his transmitter. Fertig hoped to make his transmissions more effective; the communication with Malabo had been his first contact.

As soon as he could make out the substance of General Fertig's request, Roy replied, "I would be glad to come. I've been a ham radio operator for years and maybe I can help your scratchy transmission. I will plan to reach the Mindanao coast at Dipolog. Can somebody meet me there at dawn? I would like to come in the next few days." Fertig's operator said the general's men would meet Roy at Dipolog at dawn the day after next.

Roy hadn't needed time to consider whether to go or not. He immediately liked the idea of meeting with a high-ranking guerrilla officer—coordination between resistance forces on Negros and Mindanao could be useful even if only by adding prestige to organized forces on both large islands. Furthermore, everything was going smoothly in Major Ausejo's guerrilla forces and Roy's Free Government. So Roy felt free to enjoy the adventure of the trip. As usual, he was unconcerned about any danger.

Two members of the resistance volunteered to go with Roy—like Roy, they were looking forward to the adventure. His companions were William Lowry, an engineer who had worked at the manganese mine on Siquijor, the small island off Negros, and George Ghent, one of Roy's excellent physics students, who also did well in the required course World Religions. George had a calm nature. His being along lessened Edna's fears for the party's safety—Roy might be more cautious. Edna no longer tried to keep Roy from making his risky trips. But this time the risk would become all too real.

Roy's party first hiked twenty miles southwest through the jungle-covered hills of Negros, skirting the enemy-controlled coastal area. They descended to the coast at Zamboanguita to find a boat for the thirty-five-mile crossing to Dipolog on Mindanao. The travelers found a fisherman who had a large sailboat and was ready to cross and bring back a load of corn to Negros. Roy had once brought Mindanao grain back to Dumaguete before the town was occupied.

The fisherman wanted to make a daytime crossing, but Lowry strongly favored going at night to avoid Japanese sea patrols. Nevertheless, the fisherman insisted, saying, "I'm more worried about landing on a strange coast in darkness than the chance of meeting a patrol boat in the daytime." Roy and George Ghent shrugged their shoulders, and Roy said, "Even if our boat is spotted, it likely could be taken as engaged in fishing. The three of us could hunker down so as not to be seen—at least from a distance."

At 7:00 AM they were under way, with a strong wind from the north that caused rough seas but allowed the fisherman to sail directly for Dipolog without tacking. They disembarked in midafternoon.

Although the visitors were hours late, a few of Fertig's men were there, sitting in an old automobile that looked abandoned. One of them explained, "This car is for you to drive eastward along the coast. It runs well on alcohol we get from fermented coconut milk. We operate stills which produce tens of gallons daily." Roy asked, "Will it take us all the way to General Fertig's camp?"

The guerrilla answered, "You are to follow this road eastward until you come to a big river. We have a ferry there, but it can't handle the car so you leave it with the ferry people. The ferry takes you across where you'll find another car. There are more rivers, and eventually you'll be hiking. Our men will be giving you directions so you'll eventually reach General Fertig's camp."

After these instructions William Lowry drove their sputtering car eastward. He was just getting used to the car and rutty road when they reached the first river. They left the car and boarded the ferry. Thereafter, everything continued to work out as the guerrilla explained. Very late in the afternoon, they reached General Fertig's camp in Misamis Occidental Province, twenty miles inland and south of Oroquieta.

The next morning Roy faced General Fertig across a rough desk in a nipa hut. Fertig was lean and tanned, and looked fit. He was about fifty and had red hair and was balding somewhat. He looked like a general—and a silver star sewn on each shoulder of his tattered shirt indicated he held the rank of brigadier general. After greeting Roy, Fertig said, "I appreciate your coming over here, Mr. Bell. It was a long trip—I hope my men took good care of you after you landed. As you know my transmitter is not working well, and I need to establish communication with MacArthur's SWPAC." Roy replied, "I'll do my best to fix your transmitter. We're very impressed with your transportation system from Dipolog and your men who make it work. I'd like to know about your organization so we can communicate regularly and help each other."

Fertig smiled and began his story, "To start with I am Army Reserve Lt. Col. Wendel T. W. Fertig.¹ I've been in the Philippines for years as a mining engineer. When the Japs came, I just stayed away from them for a time until I witnessed a Death March on this island, Mindanao, of a column of American POWs tied together heading north from Lake Lanao. When two exhausted Americans were holding back the march, Jap guards untied them, motioned the column onward, and shot the laggards.² Safely hidden in the jungle myself, I was horrified. From then on I decided to wage war instead of just keeping free of the invaders in the interior of Mindanao."

Fertig went on to explain his rank. "A ferocious Filipino resistance leader, named Luis P. Morgan, came to me and wanted me to become his commanding officer to give him more prestige among his men and the Philippine population—of course my being a general would be more helpful to him than being a Lt. Col. so I had a couple stars sewed on my shoulders, as you see, to make me a brigadier general. I've asserted more control than Morgan expected and gathered a lot more Filipinos and some Americans into my force. Morgan himself sometimes is hard to handle, but I try to keep him busy at a distance with small unit attacks—at which he excels."

Roy Bell immediately understood Morgan's thinking about using Fertig's assumed rank. He asked, "How would you like to add Major Ausejo's 75th Regiment on Negros to your command? Also could you show that I continue to be Civil Affairs Officer of Oriental Negros Province as originally appointed by Governor Villanueva? These appointments would make

Ausejo's command and my free government more legitimate in the eyes of the Philippine people in our territory." Fertig was delighted to comply with Roy's requests—having a subordinate 75th Regiment on Negros Island would build up his own image on Mindanao.

Now it was time to look at Fertig's transmitter. Roy found that Fertig's equipment consisted of a conglomeration of old radio receivers and motion picture projector parts—these assembled on the walls of a nipa hut on a wooded hillside overlooking Panguil Bay. To construct this mess, Geraldo Almendres, a slight but determined high school boy, had followed the diagrams of an old International Correspondence Schools book. Roy Bell was bemused by the apparatus but praised the boy's efforts.

After Roy devised a new aerial, Geraldo's creation burst into its strongest signal yet. But the signal could not keep on one frequency because the set lacked crystals. After Roy left, Geraldo continued his daily transmissions but was greeted only with silence except for sporadic and difficult communication with Roy's station at Malabo.

Yet the military operator at KFS in San Francisco did hear Geraldo's erratic signals and could make out the words "General Fertig." But KFS did not reply—the station had queried the Army and found that no General Fertig existed. Geraldo's transmissions in an outdated U.S. code had to be a Japanese attempt to jam or confuse.

Finally the Japanese themselves verified General Fertig's existence in their news broadcast. It claimed that Major General Fertig's headquarters had been destroyed—a false report probably intended to provoke a response that would provide information. But back in the Pentagon, the Japanese broadcast triggered another search of U.S. Army records, which showed that Lieutenant Colonel Wendell W. Fertig, a reservist, had been called to active duty in the Philippines in 1941. There was no record of Fertig since the surrender. Now the Pentagon was interested and ordered KFS to contact General Fertig's station.

After finishing his business at Fertig's headquarters, Roy decided to try for a direct forty-mile sail to Negros. This was not much longer than the thirty-five-mile sail his party would face if they retraced their long journey by land and river crossings back to Dipolog. Ghent and Lowry agreed; but this choice brought frustration from the beginning. They could find no captain who would risk the direct crossing of that frequently patrolled part of the Mindanao Sea.

Then Roy talked to someone who was sailing to Bohol Island with a load of grain. On the way the boat was to deliver some grain to the island of

Siquijor, which lay just eleven miles east of Negros across Bohol Strait. From there Roy could hire a local fisherman to take them across the strait to their home island. Besides, Roy wanted to visit the guerrilla leader on Siquijor, Major Benito Cunanan, who had placed his battalion in Major Ausejo's 75th Regiment. All three restless travelers were eager to try the grain boat, so they boarded late one afternoon and sailed northward, favored by a mild south wind.

After watching the vivid colors of a spectacular sunset, the three passengers arranged themselves so they could lie down on the deck, which up to then barely gave space for all to sit—lanky William Lowry had to extend his feet over the side. Unbelievably they were able to fitfully sleep. At 3:00 AM excited chatter awakened them. A light on the horizon had stirred up the boat's crew. One declared, "That is Siquijor. We will soon be there." But another insisted, "That has to be a Japanese patrol boat." After more talk the crew decided to reverse course and sailed back toward Mindanao. The wind died, and by dawn the passengers and crew were all alone on the motionless sea. They were about halfway between Mindanao and Siquijor, twenty miles from either island.

Then a favoring breeze took them toward Siquijor for about an hour before it almost died and they were barely making headway. The impatient passengers noticed another sailboat overtaking them at a much better pace. Roy shouted to the other boat, "Come closer!" When the boat's captain could hear him, Roy asked, "Would you take the three of us aboard?" He added, "I have some money to make it worth your while." The captain answered, "The money sounds good, but I must tell you that my outrigger is broken." At a glance the passengers realized that the damaged outrigger could not achieve its purpose of stopping the boat from tipping over in heavy weather. They stayed where they were.

Around noon another sailboat overtook Roy's party and came within shouting distance. Roy offered some money right away. The passengers were increasingly worried about drifting on the open water for the rest of the day—there was no place to hide on the small boat if an enemy vessel came close to inspect it. The enemy could easily recognize Lowry and Bell as Americans and eagerly seize them. George Ghent looked like a Filipino, so could easily pass as a crew member—his mother was Philippine and father American.

Roy's offer brought the new boat alongside, but the captain wanted more money than Roy was willing to pay—he had to keep enough for the later passage from Siquijor to Negros. Roy kept on talking and finally reached an agreement for taking the three to Siquijor for slightly more than Roy's initial

Ragnvold Myhre, the singing Norwegian sailor.

Kenneth Bell, back in the United States, joined the Navy.

Roy and Edna Bell.

Donald Bell (right), his wife, and Ausejo Jr.

offer. Yet no sooner had the three passengers transferred to the faster boat than the wind died completely. The transfer to still another boat left them as helpless and more discouraged than before. With theirs sails slack, all three sailboats drifted slowly northward toward Siquijor, loaded with the grain that was needed for its people. Without wind, the current carried Roy's party about ten miles toward Negros Island by 5:00 PM.

When the reluctant wind did fill the sails, Roy Bell asked the captain if he would change course and take them to Negros before delivering his grain to Siquijor—Roy would add a little to the passage fee. The captain declared, "That is an uncertain landfall on Negros for me, the Japs control all the coast around Dumaguete and extend far to the north." Roy pointed out. "I know where the Japs are. I know of a number of safe landing spots. They are cautious and don't like to expose themselves at night."

Yet the captain still would not change his mind. The slight wind taking his boat toward Siquijor almost reversed, making an approach to that island possible only by time-consuming tacking. Instead the captain steered for a small, low, flat coral islet nearby, populated by only twenty to thirty fishing families. Passengers and crew stepped ashore at 9:00 PM. Apparently the islet had few visitors, because Roy's party and the boat crew were greeted by a score or more of islanders, eager to take a look at the newcomers. This boat especially rewarded their curiosity. They kept staring at Roy Bell and William Lowry. They had seldom seen such large men and never men with white skin. George Ghent escaped such notice—he looked like his Philippine mother.

Now Roy's party urgently asked for water—they had been on different boats for more than twenty-four hours without anything to drink. However, the islanders could not understand Roy's imperfect Philippine dialect—they used a quite diverse form of it. But George Ghent could communicate with them. George reported to Roy, "There's no water on the island. They use the sap from the Saba tree. They're getting some for us." After a taste of it, though, Roy exclaimed, "It tastes like carbolic acid!" Then someone noticed a coconut and broke it open. The milk tasted good after the saba tree sap. Luckily there were plenty of coconuts.

The islanders took the visitors to their leader, who feasted them with corn and chicken—a special treat for the unusual, white-skinned visitors. The islanders' common fare was dried flying fish. They caught them with very light nets that entangled the small fish.

The next day stormy weather and heavy seas followed the calm weather that had slowed the Bell party's passage from Mindanao. But the travelers were anxious to leave despite the mountainous waves. The islet, called

Salinog, was so small that it took only a half hour to walk all the way around it. Staying longer frightened them—there would be no escape if somehow the Japanese found them.

Yet the first owner of a fishing boat they asked to take them over to Negros exclaimed, "I wouldn't think of getting out on the water today. It's too rough. We could all lose our lives. I don't think you'll find anybody here on Salinog who will try to take you today!" Other boatmen gave Roy the same answer.

The following day Roy tried again, but everyone believed the weather was still too bad. By this time Roy had given up all thought of stopping at Siquijor Island to see Major Cunanan, the guerrilla leader. All three passengers were eager to return to the jungle-covered mountains of Negros, where the 75th Regiment held sway at Malabo and the Norwegian sailors mounted a watch well down the trail to give early warning of any enemy forays against resistance headquarters.

Only late in the afternoon did their gloom lessen. A fisherman told them, "I'll take you over to Negros on my boat tomorrow if the weather has let up some." Roy quickly said, "We'll be back in the morning." Later Roy tried to cheer up George Ghent and William Lowry, saying, "Maybe we'll get home tomorrow. In the meantime, we're safe from the Japs because they would never try to land here in this weather."

They awoke early the next morning, hoping for a calmer sea. But it was still very rough, and the fisherman who said he might try to take them said it was still too dangerous for him to go. But he added, "I know three young men who are not very good fishermen but will do most anything for money!"

The fisherman spoke the truth—the three young men were daring and also eager to make money. They charged the passengers 40 pesos—at least $500 in today's money—for crossing that day instead of the usual 10 pesos they charged in good weather. Luckily William Lowry had enough money for the extra charge. The young men's sailboat normally carried ten to twelve persons and cargo. But now, with no cargo and only the three passengers and the three-man crew, the sailboat rode high on the water.

Huge waves broke over the deck as soon as they were under way and drenched them all. It was a case of everyone having to keep busy to stay afloat. The youthful George Ghent volunteered for the most dangerous task. He stood on the boat's outrigger to keep the craft from tipping over. Roy and William Lowry had to bail continuously because of the waves breaking over the boat. The three-man crew had plenty to do with the sails and rudder but seemed unfazed. After five hours of pounding, they landed on the south coast of Negros, two miles south of Zamboanguita. Despite his exertion in constant bailing, William Lowry was so cold when they landed that he ran all the way to Zamboanguita to warm up.

Edna, Ken, and Don were greatly relieved to see Roy back. They had not had word of him for three weeks. Then worry had turned into anxiety when a typhoon struck Malabo. Fearing the worst—that the typhoon had caught the travelers on the water—Edna knelt down and prayed. But now safely home, Roy pointed out to her, "During the worst day of the typhoon, we had to stay on the tiny island because nobody would take his boat out." Yet unlike his accounts to Edna of earlier trips, Roy did not play down the peril of their final boat ride. He declared, "Never before have I or my friends been so anxious to reach dry land again . . . it was the wildest sailboat ride I've ever known or want to have." Edna exclaimed, "It looks like George on the outrigger saved all of you. I always liked his going with you, Roy—not knowing his being so brave."

That evening after supper, Roy and his companions entertained the Free Government staff and Major Ausejo and his officers with the story of their journey—but they downplayed their worries on Salinog and the danger they faced during the final stormy passage to Negros. President Arthur Carson was also an eager listener. He had come from the lake to be treated for malaria by Dr. Garcia, who served both guerrillas and civilians at Malabo.

Chapter 12

Major Villamor
Lands on Negros

January 14, 1943

On March 11, 1942, Washington had ordered General MacArthur to leave the Philippines and personally retreat to Australia to avoid being part of the impending surrender of his forces on the islands. Yet by early the next year, the situation in the Pacific had changed drastically. The Japanese no longer seemed invincible. The enemy drive on Australia had been blocked by the American landing on Guadalcanal. Two Japanese efforts to dislodge this force resulted in heavy enemy losses of their aircraft and ships. Earlier, at the Battle of Midway on June 3–6, 1942, the enemy drive toward Hawaii was turned back with the loss of four aircraft carriers and hundreds of skilled pilots.

Because of these Japanese setbacks, General MacArthur began to think about his promise to the Filipinos—to return to the Philippines. But first, as indicated in his initial message to Roy's radio station at Malabo, MacArthur planned to establish an intelligence network on the islands. The intelligence effort on Negros started after dark on January 14, 1943, when Major Jesus Villamor and five companions climbed off the U.S. submarine *Gudgeon* onto a rubber boat off Negros' western coast.[1]

But they didn't know exactly where they were. The *Gudgeon* had hovered off the fishing village of Tolong earlier in the day. But after viewing the number of fishing boats through the periscope, Villamor decided to look for a place where their landing would be less noticed or not noticed at all. Now, a few hours later, the major and his men headed for what seemed a deserted part of the dark shore. Here the palms overhung the narrow beach, and a thick jungle loomed beyond. After they landed, Villamor sent three of his men inland to find someone and learn where they were.

But Villamor's night landing was observed. The party he had sent to reconnoiter had no sooner stepped out of sight into the jungle than they were surrounded by local guerrillas who stuffed rags into the intruders' mouths to keep them from crying out. The captives were brought to the guerrilla chief, Captain Jose Madamba. A refined-looking man, Madamba listened to their cover stories and false names but didn't believe a word of what they said. Full of suspicion, Madamba sent a party to pick up Villamor and the other two men, who were still waiting for their companions to return. All six of Villamor's party were soon bound up and spent an anxious and uncomfortable night on the ground.

The next morning Madamba set his first three captives—already questioned—to digging their own graves. The rest of Villamor's party faced Madamba's questions, but he didn't believe what they said either. The captain thought about doing away with the whole party. He knew they were lying to him, so they had to be Filipino collaborators hired by the Japanese to infiltrate the guerrilla organization.

But while Madamba was considering what he should do, one of his soldiers reached out and touched a prominent scar on Villamor's face. Madamba then stared at the scar and looked at Villamor closely, wondering why Villamor seemed so familiar. Suddenly Madamba came to attention, saluted Villamor, and greeted him by his real name and rank.

The scar and face together had jogged Madamba's memory back to the first days of the war when pictures of Villamor, a fighter pilot, had appeared many times in Philippine newspapers because he had shot down a Zero, Japan's best fighter plane. What made Villamor's feat astounding was that he was flying an obsolete U.S. training plane, the P-26.

When MacArthur was ordered to retreat from the Philippines, Villamor, now a national hero, was also sent to Australia for safety. Ten months later, MacArthur assigned Villamor to an entirely different task—establishing the Philippine intelligence network. Yet he was well fitted for the work. As a young Philippine officer, Villamor could easily work with Filipinos, and at the same time he knew the intelligence requirements of the SWPA.

Major Villamor started his project on Negros right away by asking Captain Madamba, "What is the guerrilla situation around here? Are any other groups close by?" Madamba gladly covered what he knew about his own area and then advised, "You should talk with my boss, Major Salvador Abcede. He is the leader of all guerrillas in Occidental Negros Province, basically the western half of this island—Oriental Negros Province takes up the eastern half. Do you want me to arrange a meeting with Abcede?" Villamor answered, "That's what I want, but my identity and mission must not be revealed except to Abcede." Several days later a courier brought back a message from Abcede, calling for a meeting on a deserted beach that was a three-day hike north from Madamba's camp.

As Villamor and Madamba passed through villages on his way to meet Abcede, it was impossible for Villamor to hide his identity. He was recognized by his scar in the first village they passed through, and then word of his presence seemed to move ahead of them faster than they could travel. So people crowded around their heroic air ace and prodded him with questions and advice many times during their journey. Villamor did his best to be gracious while hiding the purpose for his being there.

Yet outside one village, Villamor stood entranced when a beautiful young woman walked toward him at dusk. The girl said, "My name is Maria. I'm the sister of your old Air Force friend, Captain Hernandez." Maria's smile drew him to her, and it was easy for him to turn around and accompany her back home to her parents. The next morning, after bidding Maria a fond farewell, Villamor rejoined Captain Madamba, who had passed the night with friends in the village.

Late the next day Villamor and Madamba saw ahead of them a dozen or so figures slouched on the beach. Coming closer, they noticed that the roughly clad guerrillas were heavily armed. Besides them stood a lean, erect young man of twenty-eight or twenty-nine in a neat Philippine Army officer's uniform. Villamor thought, *This must be Major Abcede. [SWPA] briefed me that he's a 1936 University of Philippine graduate with a reserve Army commission. He's certainly brought along a lot of protection for our meeting. Like Captain Madamba's men, these soldiers don't look or act like our old peacetime Army.*

Abcede saluted Villamor and greeted him warmly but a little diffidently, conscious of Villamor's status as a national hero. But Villamor's friendly response and first few words convinced Abcede that the war hero respected him and his guerrilla soldiers. And Villamor saw Abcede as a trustworthy resistance leader even though his men did not look like soldiers. So Villamor briefly outlined his project, then asked about the Negros resistance.

Abcede gave him an earful. "I am leading the guerrilla soldiers in the southern part of Occidental Province while Major [Ernesto S.] Mata leads them in the northern part of the province as part of my command. The Japanese number 2,000, deployed in Bacolod and outposts of about 80 men [in] each of 20 villages along the west coast of Negros. I would like to take over the rest of Negros, but the two main groups of the other province, Oriental Negros, will not join up with me. Lt. Col. Gador leads one group. He has promoted himself to Major General and claims command of all resistance forces in the Philippines. But he actually controls only a small area. The other group is directed by Major Ausejo from Malabo in southern Oriental Province. He does not have grandiose ideas like Gador, but he won't transfer his allegiance from 'General' Fertig, who has a large guerrilla force on Mindanao. Fertig infuriates me because joint operations with Ausejo are impossible since they are on different islands."

When Villamor asked about the neighboring island of Cebu, Abcede also had strong opinions. "Two Americans control the guerrillas there; but one of them, Harry Fenton, is not normal—he is a madman. He's insane with hatred of the Japs. Anyone with a Japanese yen in his pocket is executed. Any guerrilla soldier questioning Fenton can be called a collaborator and shot. His troops do not handle money but steal all their supplies. He rules the countryside by—"

An exasperated Villamor interrupted. "This is terrible and short-sighted. These farmers and villagers are going to side with the Japs when we come back to retake the Philippines—they haven't experienced any such bad treatment from the Japs. We cannot have resistance fighters extorting food and goods from farmers and villagers. Nor can we persecute anyone who has had any sort of contact with the enemy."

When Villamor paused after this outburst, Abcede quickly jumped in. "But Fenton's co-leader on Cebu is entirely different. Col. James [H.] Cushing capably leads military operations and has the goodwill of everyone around him. He handles guerrilla operations while Fenton stays in camp." Stunned by Abcede's report on Cebu, Villamor declared, "I must go see Cushing and resolve this mess. Fenton is a disgrace to the Philippine resistance movement."

The two men talked themselves out. Now they stood in silence, watching the mountains above the jungle catch the last daylight as the sun dipped behind the sea's horizon. After a supper of rice and some fish the soldiers had caught, the leaders and the soldiers wrapped themselves in palm leaves and lay down at the edge of the jungle for the night. Yet two of the soldiers stayed on their feet for a few hours before awaking two others to replace them, thus setting the pattern for the night.

On the journey back to Madamba's camp, Villamor didn't stop to spend time with Maria. Instead his mind was full of ideas for dealing with the crazy guerrilla command structure on the islands—a necessary step before he could establish an intelligence network. Keeping up with the guerrilla officer's brisk pace, Villamor remarked, "We have a peculiar situation in Oriental Negros Province, where Major Ausejo, the guerrilla chief, places his forces under the command of an officer on another island." Madamba replied, "Yes it is. Professor Bell, Ausejo's civilian partner, made a trip to Mindanao to fix the radio of the chief guerrilla on Mindanao, 'General' Fertig. Bell arranged to place Ausejo's forces in Fertig's command. I don't know why."

To this Villamor quickly responded, "At your camp, we'll send a messenger to Bell and Ausejo. I want them to come over for a talk, but the messenger should not mention my name. I'll just be an officer from SWPAC."

A few days later Roy and Major Ausejo were surprised when a guerrilla courier brought an invitation for them to meet a SWPA officer on the other side of the island. They eagerly undertook the long journey in response to this summons—the first indication of SWPA interest in their nonstrategic island. Roy and Ausejo were first to reach the remote beach that Villamor had chosen for the meeting.

Villamor soon arrived to face a robust, middle-aged American sipping coconut milk from its shell and an impressive-looking Filipino officer. The Malabo guerrilla leaders in turn recognized Villamor from the newspaper pictures of him as the courageous Filipino air ace during the early days of the war.

A few minutes of conversation brought mutual trust and respect. Roy and Major Ausejo saw Villamor as an effective leader, not just a skilled aviator. Villamor soon felt comfortable in telling Roy and Major Ausejo about his mission and talking about the confused command structure in Negros Oriental Province. Villamor began by saying, "General MacArthur has decided that the most effective resistance would result if there were individual commands on each major island. He is having me establish an intelligence network in the Philippines. I need a stable guerrilla organization on each island to coordinate with my agents and radio operators."

Villamor paused to see his words' effect. He saw serious faces and looks of understanding. Then Villamor continued bluntly, "Here on Negros we have a disjointed command structure. Major Abcede controls the west part of the island, which consists of Occidental Negros Province. But in the island's east part, consisting of Oriental Negros Province, your group controls the south portion and says it is under a 'General' Fertig on Mindanao. In the north portion of Oriental Negros, the situation is also odd. Lt. Col. Gador controls a limited area but claims to command all guerrillas on all Philippine islands."

Roy and Ausejo showed no resentment at Villamor's plain words. Roy answered, "We will support what you are trying to do in any way we can. Our relationship with Fertig never resulted in any military operations. In the early days of the occupation being part of a larger command structure added to the prestige of both groups in the eyes of ordinary Filipinos."

Villamor smiled and replied, "Don't let the enemy learn anything about command changes in your radio contacts. In fact, keep them going to show nothing has changed. I'll get word to Fertig that I am establishing separate island commands and that you are no longer part of his command. But that is no reason that the two of you cannot continue to exchange useful information."

As Roy and Major Ausejo hiked back to Malabo, Roy told his companion he was concerned that Villamor might find it difficult to fit Gador into the new organization of guerrilla units on Negros. Roy added that he still wanted to talk with Gador in the hope that together they could resolve the friction between the competing guerrilla factions in the Tanjay area.

But Ausejo was worried: "I don't trust Gador. We know he doesn't control his soldiers around Tanjay. His calling himself 'General' is crazy." Roy did not pursue the subject; he had confidence he could deal with Gador, person to person. Then Ausejo hit a happier note: "If anyone has the luck and leadership to make our guerrillas on Negros more effective and more respectable, I believe it will be Villamor."

Chapter 13

In the Hands
of Gador

February 2 to February 16, 1943

R oy Bell and Major Ausejo returned safely to Malabo after their conference with Major Villamor. They had been back about a week when
they received another invitation that required travel. General Gador
asked them to meet with him at Payabon, his camp in the northern part of
Negros Oriental Province. So Roy and Major Ausejo resumed their discussion of Gador, which had begun on their way back from seeing Villamor.

Now Ausejo fumed: "Even if I trusted Gador, it would make no sense for
us both to leave Malabo, where you are leading the Free Government and
I am responsible for my soldiers deployed over a wide area. And I would
hate for you to go after Gador has shown such quirky behavior—as when
he deployed 70 riflemen overlooking an expected passage of Japanese troops
and then failed to order his men to fire when the enemy appeared. Then a
few days later we had to send Rito Dominado to persuade a respectable
guerrilla officer, Captain [Herminigildo] Mercado, from attacking a Gador
unit, which had killed one of Mercado's soldiers. Also Gador may resent
the fact that a few months ago you traveled half way to his camp and then
turned back—you didn't need him anymore because I had already taken the
job he might have had. Not only those incidents but remember the petition
I received from the citizens of Tanjay asking for help against the looting and
worse inflicted on Tanjay citizens by Gador's men."

Roy cut in: "But the Tanjay problem is the reason I must go. We have our
troops operating up there close to Gador's men—a clash between the two
forces is a real danger. By meeting with Gador, I should be able to straighten
things out between our men and theirs and hopefully get Gador to restrain
his men from mistreating citizens there. I knew Gador slightly before the
war, and his reputation then was all right. I'm going to meet him now, but
I agree that you should stay here in command of our guerrilla force. Your

being here certainly will protect me from Gador." Ausejo accepted Roy's decision and pledged his support, saying, "We'll stand ready here if any rescue effort becomes necessary. I believe Captain Rito Dominado would be an outstanding companion for your trip. Besides being resourceful, Rito is fluent in Spanish and Philippine Dialect as well as English." Roy agreed: "I would like to have Rito with me—he was on my football team. Also I'm planning to take Captain Lamberto Macias—he is an attorney who recently joined the Free Government and wants to go."

As Roy's party readied themselves for the journey, they learned that Gador now claimed that the U.S. government had promoted him to the rank of major general. Gador declared further that he was taking command of all guerrilla forces in the Philippines.

On the trail to Gador's camp at Payabon, Roy remarked to Rito and Macias, "I don't believe Gador's claim of promotion, which had to be based on a radio transmission from SWPAC. I don't believe Gador could have established communication with Australia because he doesn't have the power supply to operate his 220-volt, 60-cycle transmitter. Also our station at Malabo is in daily contact with SWPAC, and we have not been informed of Gador's supposed promotion."

A day's hike from Gador's headquarters, Roy encountered one of Gador's units that was led by a former colleague at Silliman, whom we shall call Pedro. Roy had helped Pedro obtain a commission in the Philippine Army. After the surrender, Pedro had helped enlist former soldiers at Malabo. When Major Ausejo took charge of the guerrilla bands, Pedro sought to be Ausejo's administrative officer. But Ausejo did not choose him. A disappointed Pedro decided to join Gador's unit, and did so despite Roy's effort to dissuade him. That was a few months before, but Roy remembered that he and Pedro had parted on friendly terms.

Now, in what Roy felt was a friend-to-friend exchange, Roy said, "I doubt Gador's promotion to Major General and his claim that General Sharp—who surrendered all the Philippines south of Luzon—had assigned Gador to lead the guerrillas on Negros Island. In that case why had Gador waited until the guerrillas were already organized?" But Pedro did not say a word against or on behalf of Gador. The next morning Roy bade Pedro a friendly farewell before again taking the trail northward.

On the last day of travel, Roy and his companions stopped at the coastal village of Manyuod to have lunch with Major Ignacio Longa, an old friend of Roy's whose children had been Silliman students. Longa reported, "Around here Gador's men have been stealing rice and chickens from farmers and other stuff from villagers—using the old excuse that these things were needed to fight the Japs. But they seldom attack the enemy." Longa went on: "We have another guerrilla band around here—it acts responsibly. Its support comes from me and the Sycip family. The Sycip plantation donates the proceeds of its salt production. Our band protects us from Gador and discourages Japanese raids on the plantation."

At 5:00 PM on February 6, 1943, the Malabo party reached Gador's advance outpost at a small bridge. Several men guarded it with spears, shotguns, and rifles. Roy's party was ordered to halt and asked their business—despite Gador's invitation. Gador's officer barked, "Just wait there with my men until I've informed General Gador and get his permission for you to proceed." An hour passed before the officer came back and reported, "The general is ready to see you now. My men will take you to him."

While being escorted through the camp, Roy, Rito Dominado, and Lamberto Macias shouted and waved to several of Gador's officers who had been Silliman students. But the former students did not respond; surprisingly they turned away. Also disquieting was the fact that the guards did not lead the visitors to Gador. Instead Roy and his companions were taken to a rough but substantial house. At the door a well-dressed civilian, whom the escort introduced as Governor Alberto Furbeyre, greeted them.

Standing next to Furbeyre was a young officer who introduced himself as Lieutenant Longa, the son of Roy's old friend Major Longa, with whom Roy had lunched the day before. Roy remembered the father's disgust with his son for joining Gador's guerrilla band. Now the son drew Roy aside and warned, "You should not leave the house because you are being watched and actually are under confinement." Roy thanked the young man for the information and then to emphasize his civilian status, Roy ostentatiously removed his sidearm and laid it on a shelf. He was now totally unarmed for the first time in months. But Rito Dominado and Lamberto Macias kept their sidearms with them.

Then Alberto Furbeyre, a pleasant, scholarly looking man, asked Roy about conditions in Dumaguete and their trip up to Payabon. Then he explained his position: "General Gador has appointed me Governor of the guerrilla-held interior of Oriental Negros Province." Roy felt no need to mention his Free Government in Malabo. Roy was thinking he had said too much to Pedro on his way to Gador's camp. Now, as Gador's prisoner, Roy decided to rein in his sometimes outspoken self.

The next morning the prisoners hoped to see Gador, but the whole day dragged by without word from him. At the same time, Furbeyre did his best to be a gracious host. Night fell and still no word came from Gador. The following day was just the same. As he waited Roy realized how fortunate it was that Major Ausejo had not accompanied him; if he had, their two headquarters at Malabo would have been left leaderless. Roy now suspected Gador of having had that intent.

It was not until the third morning that a man came from Gador and said the general would see them. This time an actual meeting seemed possible because the messenger waited to guide them. Playing the part of a confident guest, Roy urged his friendly host, Alberto Furbeyre, to come with them. Roy's insistence finally overcame Furbeyre's hesitation. Guards appeared outside; they conducted Roy, his two companions, and Furbeyre up a nearby hill and into an empty schoolhouse.

The building contained one large room filled with children's seats except for a long table at one end, where the only chairs backed to the wall and faced the rest of the room. The wall to the right was empty except for three chairs. Roy took one look at the arrangement and walked calmly to the table, picked up a chair, and placed it along the wall next to the three chairs. Roy motioned for Furbeyre to sit along the wall with the three prisoners. Furbeyre hesitated, but Roy's gentle persuasion was again successful—just as when he persuaded Furbeyre to come along to the meeting. As Furbeyre joined the other three along the wall, the guards ordered them to sit down.

They waited ten minutes, but it seemed like an hour. Then there was a commotion outside. Expecting Gador, the four stood up. As the well-dressed "general" approached, Roy did not immediately recognize him from their earlier acquaintance. Gador wore large, colored glasses, and the sun at his back also made it difficult for Roy to get a good look at him. Even though Roy was quite sure who it was, he asked in a friendly tone, "Are you General Gador? I remember working with you before the war." Gador replied in a harsh voice, "Don't deceive yourself. I am now General." Roy realized that Gador had understood his friendly question to be an expression of his doubt about Gador's rank. Roy now believed his doubt about Gador's rank—spelled out to Pedro on the way to Gador's camp—had reached the guerrilla leader.

Yet it was not in Roy's nature to act like a prisoner. And he was a well-known educator who had lived in the province for twenty years. Surely Gador would stop short of physical mistreatment of him or his companions because prominent citizens on the island would find out. Furbeyre, Gador's puppet governor, was sitting next to Roy and would also probably be a restraint on Gador. Gador could also be concerned that Major Ausejo would send his guerrilla forces on a rescue effort.

Nevertheless, Gador was now clearly in charge, and Roy had to be careful not only for his own safety but for that of his companions. He would appear confident but not aggressive while facing Gador and his men.

Gador strode past his prisoners and took a seat at the center of the long table, followed by his officers, who sat on both sides of him. At the same time three new guards entered and took stations with fixed bayonets behind the three prisoners. Finally Gador's lower-ranking officers and men came in and filled the seats in the middle of the schoolroom. Everyone was quiet during the moments before Gador started the proceedings.

The general abruptly stood up and demanded, "Mr. Bell, why did you come here?" Roy answered, "General, I came here in response to two invitations from you." But Gador challenged this: "Then why did you delay so long in coming?" Roy explained, "I did not understand the invitations as commands or orders to come at once—but that I should come as soon as it was convenient." Now Gador demanded, "Why did you go to Mindanao before you came to see me?" Staying unruffled but courteous, Roy described General Fertig's urgent need for someone to fix his radio transmitter and his request for help.

By this time Roy was feeling impatient, but he quietly said, "General, could I ask a question?" Gador coughed and finally nodded. Then Roy addressed Gador matter-of-factly: "General, I don't quite understand this show. I came up here for a conference with you and I did not expect to have all of this fine audience. You have an excellent group of men here; many of them are my friends. But I don't quite understand whether this is a trial, or a court martial, or a conference. It has something of all of these. What is it?"

Gador coughed again, paused, and at last said, "I guess it's a conference." Feeling it was important for Gador not to lose face, Roy said, "Thank you, General. I feel relieved."

Gador continued to ask questions which seemed of little importance. Then Gador inquired in a hostile tone, "Why did you bring Attorney Macias with you?" Roy politely replied, "Lamberto asked if he could come because he wanted to see some of his friends in your command." But Gador was unconvinced. He muttered, "We understand you brought him along to cross-examine us." Gador's concern about being cross-examined seemed odd to Roy with scores of armed followers around him. The atmosphere remained tense as Gador challenged Roy about his other companion, Rito Dominado.

Gador demanded "Why have you brought Rito Dominado with you? To spy on us? He persuaded Captain Mercado not to lead his bandits into an ambush we had set so we could destroy his illegal force." Roy just calmly answered, "I personally vouch for Captain Dominado's good character and patriotism. He and all of Major Ausejo's forces seek cooperation with you against the Japs. That is the reason we are here. But General, I still do not understand your purpose, whether you are trying to humiliate us, or get us angry, or to scare us. So far, I do not feel afraid. And I do not feel humiliated or embarrassed."

Gador did not answer. By this time he was frustrated by his failure to shake Roy's composure or anger him. He turned Roy over to his adjutant officer for more questioning. That officer had been a lieutenant in the Philippine Constabulary force and had commanded the Silliman ROTC some years before. The school dismissed him because of improper and obscene language he used in instructing the cadets—language the Presbyterian university would not permit. Now he had suddenly jumped from his former Philippine Army rank to become a lieutenant colonel and been given the job of Gador's adjutant, or administrative, officer.

The adjutant first asked, "Mr. Bell, do you claim to be an American?" To Roy's answer that he had always considered himself an American, the adjutant declared, "You do not act like an American. You don't have any red blood in you." After some more wild remarks, Roy countered, "Colonel, all of these fine officers here have known you and me for the past 15 or 20 years. I shall be glad, and perfectly willing, to let them be the judges as to whether your charges are just or not."

Roy's challenge did not stop the stream of crazy charges. Only one charge had any truth—when the adjutant asserted, "You have been going about the province telling people that General Gador's rank was not legitimate." Again Roy was reminded that he had blundered in telling his former friend Pedro his doubts about Gador's rank of general. Pedro, loyal to the guerrilla leader, must have sent a runner ahead to report Roy's remarks about Gador's rank.

Roy couldn't rebut the charge about doubting Gador's rank, so he calmly declared instead, "I knew General Gador for several years before the war when he was stationed in this province. Now I would not have come up here to consult with the General about cooperation against the Japs unless I respected him."

Now the adjutant had a new charge against Rito Dominado, in addition to Gador's complaint about Rito saving Captain Mercado from ambush. The adjutant claimed, "Your companion there, Captain Rito Dominado, has been going around making unfortunate remarks about you." To this allegation, Roy raised his voice for the first time: "Colonel, I do not know that, or believe it, no matter what you might say." The adjutant just smirked and said he had finished with Mr. Bell.

Next, Gador's supply officer, who had a PhD from Cornell, took over the questioning. He continued the hostile remarks. Finally Roy tired of the game and asserted, "Major, I am not too much surprised at some part of this show, but I am surprised that a Ph.D. from Cornell would enter into and take part in this kind of proceeding."

After this comment by Roy, the supply officer had nothing more to say. He turned out to be the last person to question Roy. With Roy out of the firing line, Gador had his adjutant and supply officer take over the interrogations. First up, Captain Rito Dominado. Rito's brother, Juan, had been a double agent in Dumaguete and had repeatedly hoodwinked Captain Tsuda, the enemy garrison commander. Now, in Payabon, Rito showed the same coolness under pressure by frustrating Gador's interrogators. They could arouse no fear, confusion, or outward anger in him. Roy thought Rito remained as calm as a crystal.

Finally it was the turn of Lamberto Macias. He looked the most worried of the three prisoners. He kept his hands folded in front of him all of the time he was being questioned. He feared that any casual move of his hands would seem like he was drawing his sidearm and thus arouse the guard who stood behind him with a fixed bayonet. The tormentors fired questions at the slightly built Macias much like those asked of Roy and Rito. But Macias said nothing to which Gador could take offense. When they were finished with him at last, Macias pulled out his handkerchief to wipe off his eyebrows, worried that perspiration would trickle into his eyes. He relaxed even more when Roy bent over and whispered, "You did an excellent job, Lamberto!"

Now Gador stated that the prisoners' answers had "partially satisfied" his command and adjourned the meeting. The three soldiers with bayonets left their station behind the three visitor-prisoners. Nearby officers came over to converse with Roy's party. In a few minutes, Gador walked over and said he was sorry to have subjected the visitors to the questioning, but his command had been aggravated. Then he invited Roy and his companions to his headquarters for lunch. While they ate, Gador and his officers engaged them in friendly conversation as though the morning of interrogation had never happened.

After lunch Gador took Roy aside and abruptly declared, "I plan to take command of all resistance forces in the Philippines. You have the experience and prestige to be the national food director in my resistance organization. You would gain great stature in postwar Philippines by having this job. Right now we could build a strong national resistance organization."

By now Roy had too many doubts about Gador's policies and ability to even consider the offer. So he thought fast for a diplomatic way to decline. "I appreciate your offer very much but my qualification for that job is poor. I would recommend Vicente Furbeyre, a trained scientist, to be your food director. He is the brother of Alberto Furbeyre, your senior civilian here, and is equally capable. More important, Vicente is much better acquainted with the Philippines than I. And Vicente's language skills are far better than mine. He speaks English, Spanish, and the Philippine Dialect."

Gador was not very happy with Roy's polite refusal. Nevertheless, Roy decided he had better bring up the strife between Gador's and Ausejo's guerrilla soldiers—the reason he had made the trip. It might be the only time when Gador could speak outside the hearing of his officers and hopefully be more open to a reasonable solution.

First Roy suggested, "Your soldiers and Major Ausejo's could be more effective in the Tanjay area if we coordinated so our forces had separate targets most of the time but could combine for larger operations." But Gador quickly nixed the idea: "No! No! That would be too complicated for me to manage my officers so far away from here." Then Roy tried another idea: "We could avoid that complication and keep our soldiers from getting in each other's way by simply drawing a line there that would separate our areas of operation." At that, Gador bristled. He said, "That idea makes no sense because before he surrendered to the Japs, General Sharp ordered me to take charge of all guerrilla forces in the Philippines. I don't recognize your forces as legitimate."

Roy knew Gador's claim of such authority was invalid. He had become well aware of MacArthur's plan to have separate resistance commands for each main Philippine island through his talks with Major Villamor. But instead of pointlessly challenging the scope of Gador's authority, Roy had something else to bring up that would probably also annoy the "general."

In low tones but firmly, Roy told Gador, "Recently, Major Ausejo received a petition signed by citizens of Tanjay that complained of your men's behavior there—such as taking food and other supplies without paying and sometimes brutally treating civilians. You ought to correct those officers and men who are taking orders from you." But Gador only remarked, "Some of that may have happened some time ago, but now is not the time to correct our men."

After this reply, a discouraged Roy gave up and announced with a confidence he did not feel, "We must return to Malabo now. All three of us have important duties there." But Gador insisted in a friendly tone, "No, no. You stay a few days longer. You must not go yet." The three visitor-prisoners had no choice but to return to Furbeyre's house. The next day Roy sent Gador a note again explaining the need for the visitors to return to Malabo. Roy thought he had hidden his disgust for Gador, but something he said probably was keeping his party from being released—now if ever by Gador's consent. But neither Rito nor Macias ever said anything then or later about what Roy could have done differently. The three refrained from saying anything adverse about Gador for fear that they might be overheard by the guards, who entered Furbeyre's house at will. Recognizing their predicament, Furbeyre was probably sympathetic, but he kept quiet.

By the third day Roy began to worry about a possible rescue effort by Major Ausejo that could lead to futile bloodshed. But late in the morning a note came from Gador that granted their release. He had had Roy and his companions in his control for almost a week but had gained no advantage. To keep them longer might upset those of Gador's officers who had been Silliman students. In his note releasing Roy and his party, Gador warned, "Be careful of what you say or do on the way back over my area."

The next morning Roy's group thought they were free of Gador after covering a few miles. But then a sharp turn in the trail brought them face-to-face with a lone guerrilla. His manner was not unfriendly, and he simply urged them, "Don't go back the way you came. You will be passing by a band that Gador claims is his. But it does what it wants—including stopping and robbing passersby." Before Roy could ask something about the bandit group and find out the messenger's allegiance, the man turned aside and vanished into the jungle.

Roy and his companions were left not knowing whether this warning was a final sally by Gador or a sincere warning from someone else. In either case the encounter with the lone guerrilla convinced Roy that they should seek a water route on the way back to Malabo. Hoping Major Longa would help them get a boat, Roy's party stopped by his friend's home.

First Roy told the major about the encounter with the lone guerrilla and then shared his idea about returning much of the way by water. Longa answered, "I'm as puzzled as you about that man and his warning. But it should be safer anyway to go south by boat. I'll arrange for your party's passage down Tanon Strait."

Roy's party waited until late afternoon to hike over to the coast at Manyuod. Benedict, a Catholic priest and a friend of Major Longa's, walked along with them. Benedict had met Roy at Major Longa's home the week before when Roy was heading for Gador's camp. Now Benedict told Roy, "I am greatly relieved that you and your party are back from Gador's camp safe and sound. My parishioners have been robbed by Gador's men, and there was little I could do about it."

Roy answered, "You have the difficult task of helping and protecting your people as best you can here very close to Gador's camp. Your staying with them shows wonderful faithfulness. But these conditions here will not last forever. We are establishing an island-wide resistance organization that treats citizens with respect. In the longer run, the Philippines will be freed. I hear American news broadcasts that report both Germany and Japan are suffering important military setbacks." Somewhat cheered up, Benedict replied, "That is great news! I learn nothing of the outside world except Japanese claims of great victories."

At the beach a fierce wind had stirred up Tanon Strait and was driving black clouds across the moonlit sky. Benedict pointed out a house where they could wait out the foul weather and then bade them a fond farewell. After Roy's party had taken shelter in the house, they were joined by a few others waiting for the storm to let up. They all stood around for two hours, but still the wind blew at full strength. So the three found sporadic sleep on the bamboo floor alongside twenty-five others who had gathered inside to wait for the storm to end but had given up for the night.

The weather wasn't much better in the morning. A look at the disturbed water and the palms arching toward the ground caused Roy to think again about their route south. He remembered the frightening time he had spent on the sailboat on the last day of his return journey from Mindanao. Waiting for good weather here might cause days of delay and put them in danger—they were still in Gador's neighborhood.

So that morning they headed south along the trail they had previously taken to see Gador. Despite their concerns, they didn't meet any of Gador's guerrillas on their four-day hike home. Before they reached Malabo on February 16, 1943, Major Ausejo had learned that Gador was holding Roy and his companions as prisoners. Ausejo had already organized a rescue mission when Roy's party arrived and made it unnecessary.

Chapter 14

Checking on the Cebu Guerrillas

Late February and Early March 1943

R oy had been home in Malabo for only a few days, relaxing from his frustrations with Gador, when another request came from Villamor. The major wanted Roy and Major Ausejo to visit him again. It was a week's trip across the southern end of Negros and back, but neither Roy nor Ausejo hesitated—both believed in Villamor's aim of strengthening the resistance. After an uneventful journey, they reached the isolated beach Villamor had chosen for the meeting. Villamor soon arrived, not apologizing for asking them to make a second long trip to see him so soon after the first.

The first time they met, Villamor had criticized Ausejo and Roy for the allegiance of Ausejo's 75th Regiment to General Fertig on Mindanao Island, which ran contrary to Villamor's objective of a unified Negros Island command. Roy and Ausejo had readily dropped the connection. At the earlier meeting, Villamor had been so impressed by the two that he now sought their help.

He began by saying, "I am bothered by what I have learned about the guerrilla situation on Cebu—the guerrillas treat the civilians harshly and even kill some in areas of guerrilla control. I understand you have tried twice to send your men to Cebu to gather information, but they were imprisoned and then sent back without learning much of anything. I want to correct the situation on Cebu. At first I thought I would like to try to go myself, but thought better of it after considering what happened when my party first landed on Negros. Then Captain Madamba's guerrillas were about to do away with us until a soldier recognized me by the prominent scar on my face—he had seen my picture in Manila newspapers because I shot down a Jap plane. What do you know about the situation there on Cebu, Mr. Bell?"

In answer, Roy explained, "In peacetime I was casually acquainted with Harry Fenton, one of the two joint leaders of the Cebu guerrillas. Before the surrender he was a radio announcer on the radio station at Cebu City. Then just before the surrender, the U.S. Army commissioned Fenton and Charles Cushing, a mining engineer, as Lieutenants—in the belief they might be treated better as officers by the conquering Japanese. But instead of being captured, the two of them organized guerrilla forces on Cebu and promoted each other to the rank of Colonel."

Villamor listened carefully to Roy's sketchy account of the Cebu guerrillas. He later recalled, "For a while I toyed with the idea of going to Cebu myself . . ." But Villamor had heard that "any non-Cebueno who managed somehow to reach the Fenton-Cushing headquarters risked the chance of being ordered shot on the spot by Fenton. I believed that a non-Filipino, an American, would stand the best chance; and so for the job I selected Dr. Harold [*sic*] Roy Bell . . . who I had heard was active in the resistance movement."[1]

After mulling over his options, Villamor asked Roy directly, "Professor Bell, I believe you are the one who can make this trip successfully. You are widely known not only as a prominent teacher but since the war as a responsible resistance leader. You should be safe. But no one could ever question your patriotism if you don't want to risk it. You have good reason not to go because of your family and the blow to the free government's operation at Malabo if you didn't come back."

In answering Villamor, Roy turned to his companion as he spoke. "Major Ausejo understands our civilian administrative setup at Malabo, and if necessary, he could find a replacement for me." Ausejo nodded and said, "Of course we could manage somehow and keep the free government going. But I hate to see Mr. Bell go on still another risky mission. You already know of his experience with Gador and before that—the trip to see Fertig—"

Roy interrupted: "I need to do this as an American citizen in its war against Japan. Yet I would like to delay a day or two by going back to Malabo and picking out some companions for the trip." To which Villamor replied, "Of course, take a few days to get ready, but whatever you do, come back!"

Villamor later wrote, "I smiled to myself at Bell's request for a short delay in starting. His nonchalant tone gave no indication that he foresaw any danger in sailing over Japanese-patrolled water on a journey that would take two weeks at least. And he apologetically asked two days to get ready."[2]

Before they headed back the next morning, Major Villamor gave Roy a password to use in dealing with Fenton, the Cebu guerrilla leader. Villamor explained, "On my way to Australia just before the surrender, I ran into Harry Fenton in Cebu City. We worked out a password for later use in retaking the Philippines." Until they parted and he was alone with Ausejo, Roy hid his surprise at Villamor's previous contact with Fenton. But on the trail, Roy remarked, "I had thought Villamor did not wish to go himself because he was unknown by the guerrillas on Cebu and could be considered a traitor." Ausejo replied, "Perhaps Villamor, a Filipino, feels you, an American, would be more successful in dealing with Fenton, another American, who may have to be criticized. Yet, as Villamor said, you would be justified in not going. You have a family to take care of as well as resistance responsibilities. But of course I would take care of your family." Roy knew Ausejo's offer was sincere but believed it would never be necessary to carry out. Roy had no doubt he would return, just as he already had after the other dangerous journeys he had undertaken for the resistance.

Back at Malabo, Roy found he wasn't the only one who wanted to take an adventurous journey. Lieutenant Juan Dominado, who had duped Captain Tsuda so that he could bring Lieutenant Vail up to Malabo, and Vail himself were happy volunteers, as well as William Lowry, the mining engineer who had shared the terrifying boat ride with Roy on the way back from Mindanao. Finally Arne, the gregarious Norwegian sailor, was eager for another trip. He had helped Vail transport radio equipment needed for Roy's radio station down Tanon Strait. The weather looked promising in the early afternoon when Roy's party set out for the shore of Tanon Strait to make the crossing to Cebu.

They hoped to get under way in the late afternoon, after the last enemy patrol for the day but before it was dark. However, halfway there a sudden heavy squall forced them to take shelter in a small house. There they waited impatiently for two hours before the rain finally stopped. It was already dark by the time they reached the beach. There Lieutenant Vail and Arne had hidden the motorboat they had used to transport the heavy equipment for Roy's radio station a few weeks before. But they had hidden the outboard motor separately and too well. By the time the motor was found and the boat launched, the travelers did not feel up to crossing the strait that very dark night. The five-mile hike and getting the boat ready had worn them down.

By good fortune Juan and Louis Vail had some friends living close by, who treated the travelers to a tasty dinner and good lodging for the night. Early the next morning a Japanese motorboat woke Roy up. It was cruising close to the shore, but Roy was not much concerned because Japanese boats patrolled this stretch of the coast, four miles north of Dumaguete, several times a day. A half hour later Roy walked down to the beach and found the patrol boat to be out of sight. Back at the hospitable house, Roy joined his companions, who were already having their breakfast. Their hosts had risen before daybreak so the visitors could eat before an early departure.

It seemed like a lucky day when the small motor started all right after not being used for some weeks. Then it began to cough, but it did not die completely. Nobody knew much about small motors except William Lowry, the mining engineer. He fiddled with it for ten minutes or so without much success. Yet finally it seemed to turn over better, so they slowly chugged away from the shore of Negros, heading for Cebu—five miles away across Tanon Strait.

There had been no enemy craft in sight from the beach, but away from shore they could see smoke on the northern horizon, coming apparently from a slow-moving craft. Confident that their motor, now running smoothly, could take them across before the slow boat came very close, Roy decided to keep on going. But when they were about halfway across, the supposedly slow-moving boat had come close enough for them to see it was a Japanese patrol craft. Suddenly it changed to a pursuit course and belched more smoke, but it didn't move much faster. William Lowry exclaimed, "That boat has gotten too close. We aren't halfway there so let's turn back. If the motor conks out before we reach the other shore we've had it! There would be no time to tinker with it."

Roy looked at both shores and decided for the party. "We're at least halfway there," he said. "We might as well continue." Then Roy sat down with his back to the pursuing craft. He donned a straw hat to shield him from the glaring sun and fixed his gaze on the Cebu shore. But Lowry couldn't take his eyes off the pursuers. As his face became whiter and whiter, his companions unkindly joked about his appearance. Yet the little motor kept taking them toward the island.

The pursuing craft was still not moving very fast and was a half mile away when Roy's boat chugged behind a little jut in the Cebu coastline and suddenly became invisible to the pursuers. On the Cebu shore, a couple of fishermen's wives had been watching the chase. Now they hastened across the narrow neck of land to the inlet where Roy's boat had taken refuge. The women urgently motioned the boat's party to come ashore even as Roy's men were shouting for help. Once the men were ashore, the women helped them pull the boat out of the water and conceal it behind the mangroves. The travelers had just hidden themselves when the Japanese patrol craft passed by them as close as the shallow water would permit.

But the pursuers could not spot the well-hidden boat or Roy's party hovering farther back behind the mangrove thicket that lined the beach. So the enemy craft slid slowly beyond the hiding places through the narrow waters close to shore for a half mile. The Japanese must have sighted something that looked suspicious then because four shots rang out. Apparently satisfied they could do nothing more, the Japanese turned their craft about, reentered Tanon Strait, and continued their patrol.

Roy's party was safe on Cebu, but upon hearing the firing, their friendly hosts back on Negros feared the worst—they had been watching the pursuit from the Negros shore and could not see what had happened behind the jut of land. Word of the chase and shots soon reached Malabo and left Roy's wife full of worry and praying for his safety. But Major Ausejo was less concerned—he simply believed Roy led a charmed life after seeing him survive so many perilous situations.

On Cebu Roy's party felt relieved for only a short time. After entering a small village to seek information about reaching the Fenton-Cushing camp, they were immediately surrounded by guerrillas who took their weapons. Jose, their leader, harshly explained, "We have standing orders from our leaders to disarm everyone reaching Cebu." But Roy calmly announced, "I have come from the Southwest Pacific Command to confer with Colonels Fenton and Cushing. Please tell me how to reach them and let them know I am coming."

Jose looked dubious, but then he got a message off to Fenton on a telegraph line that the guerrillas had strung along most of Cebu's western coast to their headquarters. By evening the same day, Fenton answered, "You should not try to come up here. It is too dangerous, and we can't spare the men to protect you during your two- to three-day journey up here." Meanwhile Roy's party had found hospitality nearby in the modest quarters of Father Francisco, a Philippine priest who had stayed with his flock, much to Roy's admiration. They stayed with Father Francisco for two nights before Fenton gave in to Roy's persistent messages.

Fenton even directed Jose to furnish the visitors with an old car for much of the journey. But when they reached the vicinity of Toledo, Roy's party had to turn inland by foot to avoid the large Japanese garrison there. To save their shoes, they waded barefoot across stream after swift-flowing stream. In so doing, they often sank eight to ten inches through mud to a harder bottom, where upright edges of coral stuck in the sand sometimes cut their bare feet. Everyone was glad when they reached higher ground in the northern forests of Cebu.

The party was just moving along more comfortably when a dozen or so guerrillas suddenly emerged from the jungle and surrounded them in much the same way as Jose's unit had when Roy's group came ashore on Cebu. This time the enforcers insisted that only Roy could go forward and meet Colonel Fenton. So Roy proceeded alone for a mile or so before another guard took him to the guerrilla headquarters. Besides the assorted rough buildings scattered about a jungle clearing, Roy was dismayed to notice what he could only identify as a gallows in the center of the camp. When Roy asked the guard about the structure, the man boasted, "Oh yes, we finished off all of the mayors on Cebu who stayed in office for any time after the surrender of American forces on May 7, 1942."

Roy was appalled by this bloodbath of natural leaders on Cebu during an uncertain period. In Roy's hometown of Dumaguete, Mayor Perdices had stayed in office after the Japanese had taken over—but he had secretly helped the resistance and persuaded the hospital to return to town, where it could serve more people than in the hills. But Roy kept his thoughts to himself as he was led to Fenton's office, a sturdy hut with a nipa roof.

While remaining seated, Fenton challenged Roy: "Mr. Bell, why did you come here?" Roy, ignoring Fenton's self-assumed rank of colonel, answered brusquely, "I did not come here to ask any favors, Harry. I came to get information about your organization on orders from General MacArthur's Southwest Pacific Command. I would not have needed to come if you had received two delegations from our command on Negros and given them the information we requested. Instead, you imprisoned them and sent them back without any information. So now I have had to come myself at the request of Major Villamor of General MacArthur's command. I have a password that should assure you of my authority to request and receive information."

Upon hearing the password, Fenton rose from his chair and demanded, "How do you happen to know that password?" Roy explained, "Major Villamor gave it to me when I set out to see you and gain an assessment of the guerrilla situation here." Fenton responded, "I would not have believed anything you have said without your having that password. Now I will have your companions brought into camp, and here at headquarters we will try to furnish you with answers to your questions." Roy said, "Fine! Lt. Dominado will be asking questions about what you know of enemy strength and operations while Lt. Vail will try to arrange for radio contact between your command and ours on Negros."

Thereafter the information gathering went smoothly. Lieutenant Juan Dominado's queries confirmed the execution of the mayors of Cebu. Like Roy, he was repelled by the mass executions and also kept quiet. Yet the guerrilla officers convinced Juan that their men had killed many enemy soldiers.

In fact, the three to seven thousand Japanese troops seldom ventured out of Cebu City and Toledo except in large detachments. Lieutenant Vail succeeded in arranging for radio contact between the Cebu guerrilla command and Roy's station at Malabo on Negros.

But besides seeking information from the Cebu guerrilla command, Villamor had relayed through Roy an important offer from the SWPA to the Cebu guerrilla leaders. Their command was to be given full recognition by the U.S. Army—which meant pay for officers and men as well as weapons and food when it became practicable. But the SWPA would like to have a single commander, just as it was requesting for each major island. Unbelievably, Fenton looked unhappy and wanted to think it over until the next day. The next morning even Roy Bell was shaken when he heard Fenton declare, "To hell with that stuff. We don't want recognition or anything like that from MacArthur or anybody else until the American flag is flying over here once again." Fenton added, "Col. Cushing and I know how to fight the Japs here better than they do. We shall remain a joint command—I handle the paper and organization work, and Cushing is doing the fighting." Roy decided to wait to broach the second topic requested by Villamor.

The next morning, hoping Fenton was in a better mood, Roy informed him, "Villamor also wants you and several of your officers to come back to Negros with me to report on conditions here directly to him." Fenton answered, "I cannot go now. The Japanese are pressing my men too hard for me to leave. Maybe one of my officers can get away." But when Roy and Lieutenant Dominado suggested several different officers, Fenton found one reason or another to reject them. That was how matters still stood when Roy and Harry Fenton said their farewells the evening before Roy's departure. Fenton was in the habit of working late at night and sleeping late in the morning.

The following morning Roy and his men ate breakfast with Fenton's officers before leaving. While eating, Roy struck up a conversation with the prewar governor of Cebu, Hilario Abellana. He told Roy, "I stayed in office for a time after the Japs took over, but I was a complete figurehead with no chance to help the people in Cebu City. The Japs have thousands of troops there—it is the largest city in the Philippines after Manila. I could not stop the brutal treatment of the people so I fled into guerrilla territory." Roy figured that Abellana had escaped the guerrilla vendetta that took the lives of the mayors who had stayed in office because unlike them he was protected by the large Japanese garrison in Cebu City. Then later Fenton may have invited Abellana to join the guerrillas, believing he might be useful.

In any case, Roy saw Abellana as a knowledgeable person who could provide Major Villamor with information about Cebu. But before asking him, Roy first explained, "General MacArthur needs information on Cebu. Major Villamor has come to Negros as his agent—Villamor would be radioing the information directly to General MacArthur's headquarters in Australia. It seems to me you are the ideal man to go with me because of your knowledge of the situation here on Cebu." Abellana was willing but first wanted to get Fenton's permission.

Roy rose and headed for the sleeping Fenton, intent on getting permission to take Abellana with him and heedless of Fenton's habitual late-morning sleeping. Roy woke Fenton up and asked if Abellana could go back to see Villamor. The sleepy Fenton hemmed and hawed for a time before coming up with an excuse to keep him there: "I don't think Abellana has been with us long enough to speak on our behalf." But Roy pressed Fenton to provide someone else to go. Finally, eager to get rid of Roy, Fenton said, "I'll send one of my sergeants back with you."

Now unhappily awake, Fenton got dressed and joined Colonel Cushing, his co-commander, in walking down the trail for a short distance with Roy's party. When Fenton turned back, his words were not in keeping with the friendly cooperation given Roy's party the last few days, with the exception of Fenton's disdainful rejection of the SWPA's offer of pay and recognition for his officers and men. Reverting to that mood, Fenton now said to Roy, "Tell Villamor next time not to expect the return of anyone he decides to send—if he is going to be crazy enough to do so."

At these words, Colonel Cushing winced but said nothing. However, he did not join Fenton in heading back to their camp. Instead he walked on with Roy's party. Roy had not had a chance to talk with Cushing because he had just returned from operations the day before. Roy sensed that Cushing had something serious to say, but they just chatted about the weather for a half mile or so. Then Cushing drew Roy aside, out of the hearing of Roy's men.

Cushing, a tall, powerfully built Mexican-American, pleaded, "I hope your report about us to Villamor won't be all bad. We've been rough in our dealings with many people but Villamor must try to understand why—there are many collaborators in and around Cebu City. It has been difficult to identify them there—the largest city outside Manila." Cushing paused and lowered his voice to add, "But I cannot go on like this much longer." Abruptly he headed back to the guerrilla camp.

As Roy and his party continued on their way, Roy pondered Cushing's remarks. Cushing's admission of treating people roughly around Cebu City probably hinted at another bloodbath in addition to the execution of most of the island's mayors for not leaving office right away after the surrender. But Roy was nonplussed by Cushing's final despairing remark.

Depressed by all the bloodshed and Fenton's attitude, Roy tried to be cheerful. He remarked to his companions, "Well, we're lucky to be safe and well. We should be back home in a few days. At least we have some information to report to Major Villamor."

Meantime, back at Malabo, two weeks had passed, and Edna and the boys, as well as the relatives and friends of Roy's companions, were becoming resigned to the loss of Roy's party. But Major Ausejo was still optimistic, even though nothing had been learned of the party's fate since the enemy craft had fired several shots after chasing Roy's boat behind a jut of land on Cebu. So the major was not too surprised one afternoon when he heard Roy's exuberant shout to Edna, who was washing clothes at the spring. Edna's gloom vanished as Roy hurried over toward her from the top of the trail that ended on the Malabo plateau. Juan and Louis soon found their young brides and William Lowry his wife. Arne was welcomed by his buddy Tore. To the curious people who soon gathered, Roy reported, "All of us are safe and sound. We'll have some stories to tell after setting a good time for Major Ausejo's staff and the Free Government workers to listen."

Only later did Roy find out the reason for Cushing's parting words of distress. A few weeks before Roy's visit, Fenton had left camp for a few days and returned to see Cushing wearing the insignia of a real colonel and learned that the U.S. Army had sent it along with a valid promotion. Consumed with jealousy, Fenton stuck a gun in Cushing's back. The frightened Cushing managed to explain before Fenton could shoot him, "Your promotion to full Colonel came with the same messenger." Successful operations against the Japanese did not survive that incident.

Through the summer of 1943, Fenton became more irrational while the guerrillas were being pushed by large Japanese reinforcements. Food and ammunition shortages resulted. Yet Fenton still refused U.S. Army recognition, which would have provided weapons, pay, and eventually food for the guerrilla soldiers. This support was now possible because more submarines were making clandestine deliveries of supplies and men to the Philippines since Villamor and his party arrived on the USS *Gudgeon* in January 1943.[3] Receipt of American pay by the guerrilla soldiers would not only improve their morale but also make Japanese currency less acceptable and hinder Japanese efforts to bolster their hold in the Philippines.

By late August 1943 Cushing lost patience with Fenton and his refusal to embrace recognition, so he journeyed to Negros to deal with Major Villamor without interference from Fenton. While gone, however, Cushing was concerned as to what Fenton might do. A worse situation would result if Cushing failed to return—Fenton would be left in complete charge of Cebu's guerrillas. Therefore Cushing instructed a few of his top officers, "Don't tell Fenton what I am saying now—but if necessary, stop him from undertaking anything that would endanger our soldiers. I don't trust his ability. If I don't come back, you, Lt. Col. Estrella, should take charge and keep Fenton only if he wants to stay."

After giving these instructions, Cushing proceeded safely to his meeting with Major Villamor on Negros. He gained U.S. Army recognition and pay for his troops, who became soldiers of the Philippine 8th Military District, encompassing Cebu and commanded by Cushing.

On his return to Cebu, Cushing found that while he was gone, Lieutenant Colonel Ricardo Estrella had taken the opportunity to deal with Fenton in his own way. Estrella had arrested him and conducted a trial that resulted in Fenton's execution. Quickly Cushing put Estrella on trial, which resulted in the subordinate officer suffering the same fate as Fenton.

Chapter 15

Problems in
Negros Oriental

ecause of the disturbing situation on Cebu, Roy rested only a few days after his April 10 return to Malabo before hiking across Negros for the third time to report to Major Villamor. Roy reached the meeting site ahead of Villamor and plopped down on the ground, tired from the long hike from Malabo only a few days after his hazardous trip to Cebu and the tense encounters with Fenton and Cushing. Villamor soon arrived and thanked Roy profusely "for your dangerous Cebu journey"—an accurate description of what he was about to hear.

Villamor became angry when Roy told him of Fenton's disdain for recognition—that is, receiving pay and direction from the U.S. Army. Villamor declared, "This is insane. If the guerrillas don't get the recognition they deserve, they will lay down their arms and go over to the Japs. It would be one of the bleakest days in Philippine history." He went on: "Without recognition of the guerrillas as U.S. soldiers, we play into Japanese propaganda that the guerrillas are nothing but bandits out to raid and rape. Some people, including guerrillas, are listening carefully to that line."

Then, changing the subject, Villamor informed Roy, "Here on Negros I'm planning to take temporary control of all the guerrilla groups to establish the stable situation necessary for the intelligence network I'm establishing. In conjunction with the guerrilla command, I want to establish a counterpart civilian government as you, Roy, have already done in southern Oriental Negros. Would you be interested in continuing to act as Governor of Oriental Negros Province? I have learned of your success in establishing schools in the hills and your recruitment of puppet Governor Villanueva's staff, who left their jobs in Dumaguete for Malabo to help you administer the civilian government in Major Ausejo's guerrilla territory."

Roy quickly answered, "I would much prefer that a Filipino would be appointed as Governor if one could be found who had the right experience." Villamor responded, "Well, think it over and give me someone you think qualified tomorrow. I have to send recommendations to General MacArthur, who is to send them on to President Quezon in Washington for decision."[1]

Roy had always thought that a Filipino should have his job, but no one had ever popped into his mind. For the rest of the day Roy could think of no suitable Filipino. Finally, before going to sleep, Roy decided to recommend a fellow faculty member and an American, Robert B. Silliman, a history professor.

Silliman had not been active in the resistance, but was well known and liked by Major Ausejo and other guerrilla leaders. His wife, Metta, had written a daily sheet of anti-Japanese news before and after the occupation that had circulated throughout much of Negros Island. Roy thought Silliman would make a good interim civilian chief because of his personal leadership qualities; he also had no political ambition, and would be seen that way by Filipinos. Accordingly Villamor forwarded Bob Silliman's name for approval as resistance governor of the province.

As to Roy, Villamor did not consider him for a lesser job in the belief Roy wanted more time with his family. Yet as their meeting ended, Villamor, wanting to keep Roy's experience, asked him, "Is there any other job you would like in the new resistance organization?"

Villamor did not realize how eager Roy was to give up the tedious, stay-at-home part of his current governor-like job as civilian counterpart to Major Abcede, the guerrilla leader in Negros Oriental. Even with that responsibility, Roy had been happiest in going to new places and meeting new people—such as his Fertig, Gador and Cebu adventures. So Villamor was surprised when a pleased Roy answered him by suggesting, "I think I might help the resistance by going to different places to encourage farmers to produce more to feed the guerrilla soldiers and help others speed up production of alcohol from coconut sap, which can be used as fuel for vehicles and smaller motors."

Villamor was enthusiastic in answering, "I think that is a splendid idea. I'll discuss it with Col. Abcede in due course. He will take charge of the island's guerrillas after I leave. I believe you'll need the clout of a military rank to make your work effective. I'll let you know after your replacement as head of the Free Government at Malabo has been worked out. It will take some time."

Roy returned to Malabo, hoping he would be on his new job sooner rather than later. Meantime he was looking forward to a little quiet while waiting to be replaced by his old colleague Bob Silliman. Yet problems kept arising.

A few days after his return from seeing Villamor, Roy's chief assistant, Rodrigo Tugade, reported that an armed Japanese merchant ship was sinking close to the southern shore of Negros between the coastal towns of Siaton and Tolong. Tugade urged Roy to hasten there, but for once Roy was reluctant to make a trip. He replied, "I would like to go and see what happens, but I don't think it would be wise." Later Roy explained his thoughts at that time: "The people and guerrilla units there will handle the ship's survivors in their own fashion—probably in ways that would not seem appropriate to me."

Roy eventually learned that the Filipinos on the shore had been watching the sinking merchant ship with interest because Japanese ships had sent parties ashore there to seize supplies and even young men to use as forced labor elsewhere. Now, as the Filipinos waited, two more explosions shook the ship, causing it to list and sink more rapidly—to the wild cheers of the crowd on shore. When eighty survivors pulled away in lifeboats, the American submarine that had attacked the enemy ship surfaced and fired on the lifeboats. The Japanese in the lifeboats jumped into the water, but many of them were dispatched by angry Filipinos who had pushed away from shore in small fishing boats.

The nearby guerrilla unit temporarily saved twenty of them, only to execute eighteen of those the next day. The other two were sent to General Fertig on Mindanao for interrogation. Roy believed there were no final survivors who could report to Japanese forces what had happened. Otherwise, there would have been bloody reprisals on the Filipinos in that area and blanket destruction of their homes. Roy remarked later, "However brutal the submarine and local Filipinos had been the setback to the Japanese raised morale in southern Negros to a new level."

In this period while waiting to be replaced as de facto governor, Roy received a message from a trusted guerrilla leader near Tanjay, Lieutenant Galicano Sibala. Tanjay had long been a trouble spot because it was where Gador's guerrilla territory impinged on that of Major Ausejo's. Sibala's unit, located in mangrove swamps also close to Tanjay, kept being a thorn in the side of the Japanese garrison in the town.

Now Sibala wrote Roy, "I fear a serious food shortage here. People may die for lack of food. The planters and farmers here have decided to quit planting because their rice, corn, and sweet potatoes are being taken by Jap raiders or by Gador's undisciplined guerrillas. The producers say, 'What's the use of growing anything if we can't sell it?'" Then Sibala gave an example. "A man who believed he was a target for a Japanese raid recently killed all his stock and sold as much as he could. But he had too much to sell at once so he and his neighbors gorged themselves on the meat of unsold stock. The result was a permanent reduction in future production." Sibala concluded, "Mr. Bell, would you come up here and talk to these planters and farmers? I'll gather some of them together for you. I hope we can prevent the strong possibility of starvation around here."

Roy was soon on his way north to meet with the food producers. He had planned to take along a guerrilla officer, but no one happened to be available that day. So Roy set off alone on a small horse he borrowed. He felt safe riding down on the provincial road rather than hiking through the hills as in the past. Increased guerrilla ambushes had forced enemy soldiers stationed in Dumaguete and Tanjay to stay in town most of the time. They seldom roamed out into the countryside except in large numbers and sometimes moved troops by water between coastal garrisons to avoid the guerrillas. But Roy was to discover that decreased danger from the Japanese on the road had been replaced by a different but familiar danger.

Roy's actual route passed through the farm village of New Ayuquitan, where the ex-mayor, Roy's friend Norberto Pareja, told him, "Captain Asis has been robbing civilians here in my village and close by. He says he operates under 'General' Gador's authority and says he takes food and supplies only to fight the Japs." Roy listened carefully and said, "We'll talk later about Asis on my way back from meeting with the planters."

As Roy rode on, he thought, *I remember Fernando Asis before the war as a friend who was a regular Army sergeant. Since the war, Sgt. Asis led a guerrilla unit, which cooperated with Major Ausejo's command. Now he seems to have joined Gador and been promoted to Captain. Maybe, I can have a friendly talk with him about improving conditions in this area.*

With these ideas in mind, Roy entered the neighboring village of Amblan, where a couple of Captain Asis' soldiers greeted Roy and wanted to visit. Roy got off his horse and, after a friendly chat, told them, "I hope to come back through Amblan tomorrow and talk with my old friend, Captain Asis. I don't have time now because I'm due to meet with the planters and other main food producers around Tanjay today. Tell your Captain I hope to see him tomorrow."

Roy was on time for the meeting with the planters, which Sibala had arranged. He needed little introduction. Some of the planters were friends, and the others knew him by reputation from both his university job and his resistance activity. They hated their current losses to both Gador's guerrillas and the Japanese but were willing to listen. Not an accomplished speaker, Roy found his voice. He urged, "Plant to produce as much food as possible. Otherwise, a famine could result to add to the troubles of having the Japs on top of you. But they won't be here forever. They have been stalled short of Australia and suffered severe naval losses at the Battle of Midway last year. Our respectable resistance forces on Negros are already receiving arms and ammunition by American submarines—Gador's units do not have access to this assistance."

As he rode back to Lietuenant Sibala's guerrilla camp, Roy felt that the good war news had helped some of the planters to respond to his plea to keep on producing crops, thus forestalling the danger of widespread hunger and starvation in the region. At Sibala's camp, Roy reported that the meeting had gone well. He stayed at the camp all night. The next morning Roy skipped having breakfast with Sibala so that he could get an early start and avoid some of the tropical heat on the provincial road. A few miles down the road, Roy entered Amblan, where he hoped he would meet Captain Asis for a friendly conversation.

As Roy approached the market area, he noticed people running from the road and away from the area; it was totally unlike the peaceful scene of two days before. Roy knew that something was amiss, so he slowed down. He rode on that way for a few minutes. A fruitful talk with Asis did not seem likely now. The only figure Roy could see not running away was one of Captain Asis' soldiers, who stood in the middle of the street ahead of him. Since the soldier looked calm enough, Roy resumed his normal pace and rode down the street toward him.

Coming nearer to the soldier, Roy saw some good-looking bananas for sale in a small store and wanted some. But the woman tending the store had taken off and was running through a coconut grove. Roy called to the soldier, "Won't you please call that woman and tell her I would like to buy some of her bananas?" The soldier's yell brought her reluctantly back, and Roy bought some bananas.

But when Roy began to mount his horse, the soldier said, "Mr. Bell, wait!" To Roy's "What for?" the soldier explained uneasily, "Captain Asis wants to see you." Roy replied, "All right. Where is the Captain?" When the only answer was that Asis would be coming "by and by," Roy retorted, "Captain Asis knew that I was coming through here this morning. If he wanted to see me, he should have been here. I have made a date to meet the

Mayor down the road at 8 o'clock so I must be going." But the soldier just repeated Captain Asis' request that Roy meet with him.

Roy then climbed on his horse, saying, "I am sorry, but I told you I was going on." As Roy started down the road, he heard the click of the soldier's rifle as though he were loading it. Then the soldier cried, "Halt!" Yet Roy rode on, thinking that the soldier was bluffing. But when Roy was about thirty-five yards away, the soldier fired in his general direction. Roy at first thought it was a bluff shot. However, after riding on for a few more yards, Roy decided to take the soldier more seriously. He turned his horse to the side so he could look back as he climbed off. But the soldier was running through the coconut grove in headlong flight. The soldier did not heed Roy's call for him to come back.

Roy stood where he was for a few minutes and then walked the horse back down the street and stopped in front of the store where the woman had sold him the bananas. For a few moments, he wondered what he should do as he looked around the area, still empty of people.

Then Roy saw a man on a bicycle about a hundred yards away, coming toward him on the road Roy had used to enter the village. As the man calmly rode nearer, Roy noted a rifle across his handlebar. Roy recognized him as a one of Major Ausejo's soldiers. Finally the man got off his bike and asked Roy, "What is going on here? I heard a shot and came to find out."

While Roy explained to the soldier what had happened, the shopkeepers and their customers came out of their various hiding places. Apparently they had feared bloodshed and danger if Roy's soldiers had suddenly appeared to save him from Captain Asis. But Roy's early arrival upset Asis' plans. Asis had only one soldier available to stop him, and that man could not handle Roy. So when Roy's protection arrived, people resumed their normal business or errands.

But some gathered around Roy to see if he had anything to say. Among them was a Chinese boy he knew. Roy motioned the boy to come close and whispered, "Go down the road and tell Mayor Pareja what is happening." Then Louis Flores, one of Roy's former football players at Silliman University, joined the group and decided to stay after learning what had happened. Flores had previously complained to Roy about mistreatment of civilians by Captain Asis' men.

Within a few minutes, a panting and excited Captain Asis appeared himself. Roy greeted him: "Good morning, Captain. You seem to be excited about something." Asis, struggling for breath, answered, "I've been hurrying because I wanted to be sure and see you. Let's go over here to one of these houses to get away from the people. I wish to talk with you privately." Roy countered: "I have nothing to say to you but what I wish these people to hear." Then Roy motioned to the gathering crowd to come nearer, calling to them, "Come up closer to hear this. It might be interesting."

As the people pressed closer, Captain Asis and his companion, Lieutenant Norberto Emilio, who had studied law at Silliman, became uneasy but started to question Roy and charged him with criticizing General Gador for taking that rank and for claiming that Gador's men robbed and mistreated civilians. Roy challenged them: "Who told you this? I want to see him." His questioner quickly produced one of the soldiers Roy had talked with in that village a couple days before on his way to his meeting with the planters. But Roy had made no such criticisms of Gador to the sergeant and only talked about his meeting with the planters and his plan to return that way. Now the soldier looked at Roy and bravely declared in answer to Emilio's question about Roy's recent remarks, "I am sorry, but I did not hear Mr. Bell say these things."

At that statement, Asis turned to Emilio and used the Philippine dialect to say, "This is useless. We can't get anywhere without the cooperation of this man, and we can't make him suffer much after so many people have heard and watched this questioning." Asis did not know that Roy understood the dialect. Roy thought, *I knew I wanted the crowd to hear this meeting with Asis, and now it looks like it helped the soldier do a brave thing by telling the truth. But he should be safe from Asis because the crowd heard everything.*

Then Asis asked Roy, "Why did you go see the planters? Were you planning to protect their crops from Gador by using your bandits? We use that food to support our fight against the Japs!" Roy answered, "On the contrary, I urged the planters and farmers to produce as much as possible to avoid a famine in this area. The producers had planned to drastically cut production because you Gador men and the Japs were taking most of it away from them. I advised them to produce as much as possible to avoid a famine here that would be far worse than the present shortage." The villagers, who had pressed close to hear, believed Roy and became disgusted with Asis and Emilio. Louis Flores, Roy's football player, wanted to manhandle Asis and Emilio, even though the two had sidearms and a couple of Asis' armed guerrillas were standing by. However, Roy was able to restrain Louis. Now, with great aplomb, Captain Asis changed the tone of his remarks and brought up matters of common interest with Roy while laughing and joking as if the whole procedure had been a joke. He invited Roy to his headquarters for breakfast, but Roy replied, "No thanks. I have promised to meet Mayor Pareja about now."

Then Roy proceeded down the road with Louis Flores and the friendly guerrilla who had first come out and stood by Roy in his uncertain situation in the middle of the scared village. Roy's arrival in the village had been too soon for Asis' plan to work as he had arranged. It had not been possible to seize Roy in front of unfriendly witnesses. Then the interrogation before the unwelcome crowd had brought only embarrassment to Asis.

While riding on to see Pareja, Roy asked himself, *Why was Captain Asis so hostile? We had been good friends before the war. But now in the eyes of Asis and Emilio, my meeting with the planters and farmers had a different purpose than combating famine—they thought I was meeting with these food producers to plan ways to restrain Asis' men from taking their crops.*

A few days after Roy's return to Malabo, Roy's intelligence agent in Amblan, a man named Juan, sheepishly reported, "I found out that Captain Asis and Lt. Emilio planned to apprehend you that day. I thought I was on the road going into the village early enough to warn you, but you had already passed. Then I followed you at a distance but made no contact because Captain Asis or his men would notice us getting together, and then my usefulness as an agent there would be over." Roy smiled and said, "Keep up the good work, Juan. I'm counting on you to keep track of Captain Asis and his men—just as you already were able to do."

Besides Juan in Amblan, Roy had a female intelligence agent who socialized with the Japanese officers stationed in Dumaguete. She was Nora, a recent graduate of Negros Oriental Provincial High School. She was a tiny, curly haired girl who lived in the hills with the Ridad family—Frederico Ridad, a prewar, quiet Silliman college student, had formed a guerrilla band after his frail father had been beaten up by Captain Tsuda's bodyguard. Now Nora regularly and fearlessly went into Dumaguete to play Mahjongg with the Japanese officers. They did not know Nora understood Japanese, so they talked quite unguardedly about military matters. The next day Nora returned to the hills and reported to Captain Ridad what she had learned. The information quickly reached Roy Bell, who praised her work.

Ridad often celebrated Nora's return with a dance at his camp. His invitation brought enough girls from families in the hills to dance with his young soldiers to the music of an old Victrola.

Rev. James McKinley, a Silliman faculty member, met Nora at "daredevil" Captain Ridad's camp. He termed her "the famous spy girl" and described her as "quite good-looking even in blue denim slacks and a shirt."[2] But Roy wasn't sure of Nora's complete loyalty until the enemy officers suspected her and Nora had to go into hiding. Yet Angela, an equally courageous young woman, volunteered to replace Nora. A relative of Mr. Ridad, she also liked to play Mahjongg and so keep tabs on the Japanese garrison in Dumaguete for Roy. Angela often rode Roy's gray horse, Peanut, into Dumaguete. She would leave the horse with friends while visiting the officers.

The calm situation at Malabo in May 1943 was little affected by Roy's trip to meet the planters near Tanjay or his confrontation with Captain Asis on the way back. During that month Roy's Free Government operated smoothly in most of southern Negros Oriental Province, while Major Ausejo's guerrilla soldiers kept the Japanese forces mostly inside their garrison towns of Dumaguete and Tanjay.

Chapter 16

Villamor Gathers
Island Leaders

W hile Roy Bell was trying to maintain agricultural production around Tanjay and was coping with Captain Asis, Major
Villamor was attempting to establish a unified guerrilla command on Negros Island.[1] Villamor had come in January to establish an intelligence network for the American Southwest Pacific Area (SWPA), but its
operations would require reliable guerrilla support.

However, Villamor had been appalled by the disjointed and inconsis-
tent nature of guerrilla operations on Negros—there had even been fighting between Colonel Abcede's guerrilla soldiers and those of Colonel Gador.
Villamor had persuaded Roy Bell and Major Ausejo's 75th Regiment to
give up its connection with General Fertig's forces on a different island,
Mindanao. But that was a minor problem compared to the overall situation.
Villamor decided on a drastic solution that had been approved by the SWPA
command—he would assume personal command of all guerrilla groups on
Negros. When Villamor saw fit, he would turn over the island command to
a qualified guerrilla officer.

Now all he had to do was assert that authority over a group of guerrilla leaders who had been depending on themselves to make decisions. He
started by calling for all guerrilla leaders on Negros to meet with him on
May 28 near Cartagena on the southwestern coast of the island. Most of
them were unhappy with the summons—they were worried that Villamor
might try to reduce their guerrilla ranks or interfere with the operations of
their bands. Yet dozens came and lounged on a grassy plateau overlooking
the sea. These guerrilla leaders already knew Villamor from his early celeb-
rity for shooting down one of Japan's formidable Zero fighter planes while
flying an obsolete P-26 American plane. But now Villamor wasn't actively
fighting the Japanese like they were. They wanted to know what General

MacArthur's representative would say and hopefully protect their interests. However, one prominent leader was missing—Colonel Gador.

Villamor sat at a plain wooden table with his back to the sea and a body-guard standing at his side. He knew that many of these leaders had formed bands from ex-soldiers and volunteers and led them to success against the enemy, but those capabilities would make it difficult to organize them into an island-wide command. He drew a .45-caliber pistol from his holster and placed it on the table with its barrel pointing toward the guerrilla leaders. His fingers closed on the pistol, and he declared, "I'll use this. I'll use this if I don't get a pledge of cooperation from every one of you."

He proceeded to berate them: "The Japs are drinking toasts to us for fighting among ourselves, for not making severe trouble for them . . . right now you are nothing but a disorganized group of fighting men." Villamor went on to declare that he was taking over command of all guerrillas on Negros for the time being until he found a suitable replacement. Good results could happen soon, as in the case of the unified commands on the islands of Mindanao and Panay. Their guerrilla forces were receiving quantities of arms, ammunition, and medicines from American submarines. Furthermore, Villamor told the motley group in front of him, "As part of the island command, you and your soldiers will be paid and have status like other members of America's armed forces."

After scolding them and then showing them the advantage of the new command, Villamor felt "completely drained" but believed his talk was working. Just then, however, there was scuffling in the rear, and someone exclaimed, "It's Gador." Villamor saw someone "push himself forward," surrounded by companions and a large number of guards. When some of Villamor's own small group tried to keep the newcomers to the side, "Gador and his men, like a mob, shoved their way to the front, seeming bent on making trouble." Yet once Gador's group got close to Villamor, they settled down and the meeting proceeded.

But Villamor didn't repeat anything for Gador's party. He continued by declaring that in the new organization all former officers would keep the rank they held before the surrender and all noncommissioned officers who had become guerrilla officers would take the rank of acting third lieutenant. All officers would be given new names to protect them and their families from Japanese atrocities. This proposal formed a friendly bond among the officers, who all had relatives or known of others who had experienced Japanese cruelty. But suddenly there was shouting as Gador again stood up and demanded attention.

His face filled with rage, Gador angrily asserted, "I am the senior officer on Negros so I, and no one else, should command our troops here." Getting more excited, Gador screamed, "In fact, I should be corps commander of the entire Visayas!" (This island group includes all of the major Philippine islands except Luzon, the northernmost, and Mindanao, the southernmost.)

Villamor quietly answered, "You will be the executive officer in the island command while Col. Abcede will command the troops." Before Gador could say anything more, Villamor adjourned the meeting. Gador's intrusion had not dampened the rising spirits of the other guerrillas, which Villamor had noticed during the day. But they were happy to be finished for the day and headed for their camping sites to start fires for the evening meal.

The next morning Villamor presided over friendly discussions about unified attacks on the enemy, intelligence collection, and supply by submarine. But further discussions had hardly begun after lunch when a guerrilla coast watcher signaled that Japanese troops were landing from motor launches close to where Villamor had originally planned to hold the meeting.

Even so, the enemy was so close that Villamor had time only to order the leaders and the few soldiers present to station themselves in the thick jungle on hills in a rough semicircle above the landing Japanese. Villamor watched his officers scatter to form the rough battle line above the enemy and station themselves at reasonable distances from each other. Their speedy deployment impressed Villamor, but at the same time it made him wonder if he "had done right in bringing together in one place almost every guerrilla leader on the island." But the heat of battle distracted him from further worry. The guerrilla leaders worked effectively side by side as they had in the past fought beside their own guerrilla soldiers. They used the jungle to keep out of sight and set ambushes. The intruding Japanese also faced the jungle's leeches, rattan needles, mosquitoes, and monkeys, which screeched their anger at the invasion of their territory. After four hours, the Japanese withdrew in the dusk to their boats and returned to the safety of their ships. The guerrillas had suffered no casualties; the next day Villamor's men found the bodies of eight enemy soldiers. As the action began, someone had noticed Gador and his men slipping away—Gador was the only leader not to engage the enemy. His flight convinced Villamor that Gador would not be suitable as executive officer of his new island command. Instead Villamor selected Colonel Abcede to take that position.

Yet Gador still wanted weaponry just weeks after the Villamor gathering when he learned that the U.S. submarine *Thresher* on July 9 had delivered 5,000 pounds of stores, 20,000 rounds of .30-caliber ammunition, and the same amount of .45 ammunition. Gador sent Lieutenant Julian Aspilla and a party to pick up arms and a million or two pesos. But Villamor sent Aspilla back empty-handed with a message, "The existence of your unit as a separate organization in the 7th Military District is [an] obstacle to the consolidation of Negros."

Turning to civilian resistance that summer, Villamor helped establish an island-wide government under Alfred Montelibano and a common currency to pay the troops that was based on Philippine government reserves in Washington.

Villamor achieved these successes after coming down with a high fever a few days after meeting with the guerrilla leaders. By chance Maria, whom he had met early in the year soon after coming to Negros, arrived for a visit just when he needed her. She nursed him back to health and made him happy with her presence. Learning that the Japanese had put a price on his head, Villamor began to feel every day might be his last. On an impulse he proposed to Maria, and she accepted. Montelibano, the resistance governor of Negros Occidental Province, performed the civil ceremony. Because of his fever and his feeling of vulnerability, Villamor decided to replace himself as island commander with Colonel Abcede sooner than planned. On October 20, 1943, Villamor boarded the U.S. submarine *Cabrilla* for passage to Australia after nine months on Negros.

Lieutenant Aspilla, whom Gador had sent to obtain arms from Villamor, had been so impressed with the efficiency of the new island-wide organization that he tried to persuade his boss to become part of it, but to no avail. Then, in September and October, Aspilla induced two of Gador's major units to join Colonel Abcede's new island command. Finally, on December 1, 1943, under cover of night, Gador sailed away to Cebu, and later continued to the island of Bohol.

Yet not only Lieutenant Aspilla had been impressed by Major Villamor's well-organized 7th Military District with its better-armed guerrilla soldiers. The Japanese had probably also become more aware of the new situation after Villamor's first general order to his soldiers on May 14, 1943. In June the enemy brought in large reinforcements and launched new operations on Negros. The military and civilian headquarters at Malabo—long neglected by the Japanese—now came under attack.

Chapter 17

The Destruction
of Malabo

June 10 to July 1943

ormer Silliman professor Bob Silliman arrived at Malabo on June 10, 1943, to take over Roy Bell's duties as head of the Free Government in southern Negros Province. He was greeted by Roy, who was to familiarize Silliman with his new job and introduce him to the trusty Filipino staff members who had helped Roy start the Free Government and were staying on the job. Roy had recommended Bob for the position to Major Villamor in mid-April.

This replacement was part of Major Villamor's organization of island-wide control of Negros resistance. Another part of Villamor's plan happened at the same time at Malabo—Major Rito Dominado replaced Major Ausejo as commander of the guerrilla forces for roughly the same area covered by the Free Government. Ausejo moved to the staff of Major Villamor's island command as his operations officer.

To help Roy Bell carry out his new assignment within the Negros Island resistance, he was made a major in the island guerrilla forces. The military rank was to give him standing with Filipinos in carrying out his responsibilities, which were to promote and maintain production of useful commodities in the large areas of Negros that were free from Japanese control. These commodities included alcohol made from coconut sap, which was used to make the popular drink *tuba* and to fuel autos and other motors, and cloth woven from abaca and hemp.

This was a big change for Roy. But he had suggested it after telling Major Villamor in April that he would prefer not to continue as head of the Free Government, a decision reflecting Roy's preference to travel on resistance missions over staying at Malabo to administer the Free Government. And he felt relaxed about leaving the job to his colleague and friend Bob Silliman, because Roy's competent staff was staying—they had left the puppet governor, Guillermo Villanueva, to help at Malabo. Now Roy looked forward the job of promoting civilian production—it would certainly involve lots of travel.

In regard to his family, Roy thought, *They will continue to be safe here at the guerrilla headquarters at Malabo and now commanded by Major Rito Dominado—my former athlete at Silliman, who has become an excellent guerrilla officer.*

But Roy's presumption that Malabo was a safe haven for his family would not last long. A couple days after the change of jobs took place, Roy had just stepped out of the house first thing in the morning when Angela suddenly appeared. She usually came up Sunday afternoons with whatever she had found out from playing Mahjongg with the Japanese officers in Dumaguete. The pretty, self-possessed girl had always kept calm, even when she had something of interest to report.

Yet now she was out of breath and had an anxious look on her face. Roy beckoned her to sit down beside him outdoors, where they could not be overheard, and said, "Angela, thank you for coming up here in such a hurry. You must have some news. Tell me about it carefully and [as] slowly as you wish. We have lots of time." Angela sat quietly while she caught her breath, then reported, "Last night I was playing Mahjongg with them as I often do when I heard a slightly-drunk officer brag, 'It won't be long before we have reinforcements, and then we'll wipe out these pesky guerrillas and pretence government up at Malabo. Then we'll head for Siaton and Tolong.'"

Roy believed Angela's report and the officer's statement, but he still didn't know when the reinforcements were coming. He thanked Angela and suggested, "If you feel comfortable doing it, keep playing Mahjongg with the officers. But don't hesitate to stop if anything doesn't seem right. For now though, come in and have breakfast with us."

Later Angela headed back down the trail toward Dumaguete. She was pleased to be continuing her spy job and duping the Japanese—she was related to Mr. Ridad, the surveyor who had been beaten up by the Japs when he refused to return to his profession in Dumaguete. Angela had volunteered to replace Nora—Roy's earlier Mahjongg agent—after the Japanese became suspicious of her.

Now, as Angela came out of the mountains near Palimpinon, a figure coming out of the bushes not far ahead jolted her out of her musings. But her anxiety soon turned to relief when she recognized Georgio, one of her high school friends at Silliman. Georgio exclaimed, "I'm glad I found you soon enough! The Japs have taken your horse and are waiting for you to come and look for it. I believe they think you are a spy. Are you?" Angela didn't answer that. Instead she asked, "Georgio, would you help me find my uncle's retreat cabin in the hills? I've been there, but I've forgotten its exact location."

The next day, June 14, a Sunday, Roy, Edna, their boys, and forty mostly Silliman faculty families listened to a sermon by young Rev. Alvin Scaff. Scaff was a former Silliman professor in the theology department. Alvin had taken his wife and baby to the hills after helping Roy dig up buried Mission Hospital funds that Roy then used to pay Silliman faculty members who had settled inland.

Scaff called upon his audience, who had all evacuated from Dumaguete to avoid the Japanese, to look for God's help in their new locations. The young minister declared, "Besides finding food and freedom in the hills, we should cling to our convictions of justice and right all wrongs for love of mercy." After the sermon, the Bell family and Bob Silliman dined with the Scaffs and enjoyed a tasty meal of corn pudding, baked camotes, and a cassava cake with sliced mangoes.

Just as they were finishing dinner, one of Roy's male agents in Dumaguete burst in upon them. He took Roy outside and reported, "About three hundred Japanese troops landed this morning. I'm afraid they'll be coming up here soon. There's nothing else nearby to attack that would need that many men." Roy thanked his agent for coming up promptly with his report. The agent headed back to keep up with developments in Dumaguete and left Roy to ponder by himself why the Japanese were suddenly so interested in Dumaguete, which they had been content to garrison with about forty soldiers since the American surrender of the Philippines. Through listening to American news reports, Roy knew of the serious setback suffered by the Japanese ground forces at Guadalcanal—after the war it was learned they had withdrawn the 13,000 troops from Guadalcanal who had survived of the 36,000 who had tried to prevent American capture of the island. Now Roy wondered if the enemy was already beginning to bolster its control of Negros in the face of a future American offensive in the Philippines.

The next day over a hundred enemy troops did head for Malabo. Moving slowly, they covered five miles to the edge of the coastal plain at Palimpinon, then followed the Ocoy River inland a few miles and crossed it. There they faced the presence of the first guerrilla outpost and halted for the night.

On June 16, 1943, the new governor, Bob Silliman, heard gunfire down the trail from Malabo. He had already arranged for the government's records to be moved south through the hills toward his evacuation house and excused his new staff for the week—they needed to take care of their families. Bob soon followed his records. He took a little-used mountain trail southward to join his family at their evacuation home in the hills back of Siaton on the southern coast of Negros.

Roy Bell, now free of government responsibility, helped Edna, Ken, Don, and Nelly, the stranded college student, scatter their household goods in various hiding places as they had done in the early days of the resistance. But it was not until two days later that the cautious Japanese, uncertain of the guerrilla strength, got close enough for Roy to have his family load up their wandering horse, Peanut.

The horse had luckily escaped the Japs after Angela had to abandon him in Dumaguete to keep herself safe from capture. So instead of becoming horse-meat, Peanut had climbed up the steep trail to Malabo, hoping for some hay. Now the loaded-down Peanut joined the procession—consisting of the Bell family, Nelly, and George Ghent, as well as Ole and Tore, the Norwegians, and Ski, the radio operator—heading for the old Bell-Carson evacuation house by the lake. After climbing up the trail just a few miles above Malabo, the group stopped for the night with Major Ben Viloria at his evacuation house, confident that the enemy would keep on moving slowly. Viloria and his wife did not have enough beds, but those sleeping on the floor were still grateful to be inside, safe from hungry insects and prowling pythons.

Roy was awake at dawn, ready to continue their withdrawal. But far below them, he could see the distant group of village dwellings, looking quiet and undisturbed. To investigate more closely, Roy took Kenneth, Ski, George Ghent, and the two Norwegians back toward Malabo. They were armed with an assortment of loaded weapons. Edna and Donald waited with the Vilorias until Roy had decided what to do.

Roy's party soon reached a rock outcropping that gave a clear view of the threatened cottages. But when no enemy had appeared by noon, they went down into the deserted village. They were looking around for somebody to talk to when a young villager, named Pablo, suddenly appeared at the top of the trail that led down toward Palimpinon and Dumaguete.

He hurried over to Roy's party and exclaimed, "I've been watching the enemy's approach to Malabo from a safe distance. Yesterday they caught a couple guerrilla soldiers, and, seemingly satisfied, headed back down the trail." When Pablo volunteered to take a message to Edna, Roy said, "Please tell her to stay with the Vilorias for the time being. We're staying down in Malabo for a couple days." Then Roy added, "If you would like to come back here and keep watch on the trail up here from Palimpinon, it could help us a lot." Pablo delivered the message to Edna and returned to Malabo for guard duty.

Two days passed uneventfully. But in the middle of the third night, Pablo banged on Roy's door and shouted, "The Japs have sneaked up the trail and are now less than a mile away!" Roy stepped outside. The full moon lit up the dark landscape. Perhaps the moonlight had emboldened the Japs, who usually didn't operate at night. Roy didn't believe the enemy was as close as Pablo reported, but he woke up everyone anyway and told them, "In case they're really that close, we'll watch from a few hundred yards up the side of the mountain from the house."

They had hardly settled in their hideout when some mortar shells flew over them and changed Roy's plan. Shaken up, they all dropped their heavy packs in the bushes and scrambled toward the nearest forest. On the way they were partially hidden by the foliage of overhanging abaca. Inside the forest they hastened along a trail to where a beaten path crossed. But they kept on the main trail until they reached another trail crossing. Again Roy did not make a turn. He was following a strategy based on the common wisdom that the Japanese usually pursued and captured enemies by coming from two directions. Thus Roy thought his party had moved beyond the normal two-pronged pursuit by moving past two entering trails.

Using this analysis may have saved them. Later Roy's party received machine-gun fire from behind while crossing a small cornfield. The Japanese were still pursuing but had not succeeded in getting on two sides of their quarry—a possibility, had Roy had chosen any side trail.

The sudden fire from behind them startled Roy's son Kenneth and George Ghent into ducking behind a large stone. A few days before, Roy had taken his party down to Malabo with loaded guns, as though he wanted to take some shots at the Japanese. But now he shouted to Kenneth and George, "Get up and keep on running!" Whether the two armed boys had been scared or had wanted to get a good shot at the enemy didn't matter to Roy now—he just wanted to keep them safe. Roy's urgent command brought them to their feet. The whole group ran all out for the thicker forest ahead of them.

They plunged into the dark jungle and kept pushing through the brush until they were so out of breath they had to stop. But now there was no sign of pursuit. The Japanese may have feared ambush in the dense jungle. Roy was so relieved that he didn't say anything about the loaded shotgun George Ghent had left behind the big stone.

Higher up the mountain a half hour later, they reached an open hill from which the village of Malabo could be easily seen in daylight. But now, even with the strong moonlight, they could see only moving spots of light in the distant dark landscape down below.

Then flames shot up in several places, showing buildings on fire. The spots of light had been flashlights the enemy had used while starting the fires. Before the watchers' horrified eyes, the Japanese soldiers set fire to Roy's Free Government headquarters, the guerrilla headquarters, and the whole village for harboring the resistance activity. All of the villagers had fled to safety sooner than Roy and his group, choosing not to court the danger Roy's short-lived boldness had brought his party. Among the fleeing villagers were Rev. Alvin Scaff, his wife, and their infant child. They had first moved higher in the mountains, but like the Bell family had found the weather wet and gloomy, so they had settled finally in the sunnier climate at Malabo.

Despite the destruction of their village because two headquarters of the resistance were located there, the fleeing villagers never blamed Roy or Major Ausejo for what had happened. In the next few weeks, the villagers moved a mile or two farther up the mountain and built small, crude houses among the trees after foraging through the ruins of their cabins to see if anything useful remained.

After watching the village go up in flames, Roy's discouraged party headed for the safety of the lake evacuation house, which the Bell and Carson families had constructed and shared earlier in the war. The Carson family was still there. Roy's party trudged out of the jungle near the lake at 10:00 AM. They were thoroughly tired, and their clothes had been torn among the stones, thorns, and bushes during their flight through the forest in their off-trail escape. Roy's Edna, son Donald, and Nelly were already there. They and the Carson family rejoiced that none of them had been captured or shot.

Edna thanked God in a fervent prayer. She had so prayed several times before after Roy had survived dangerous situations. But Edna's spirits hit a new low this time—even though Roy, Ken, and the others had again returned safely. Now Edna broke away in the middle of Rev. Scaff's Sunday service at the lake house and went outside to weep. Edith Carson quickly followed to comfort her.

Edna explained her feelings to Edith: "The Japs are always after our family because of the radio station and our guerrilla activity. I believe they'll capture us sooner or later." Edith pointed out, "We can be thankful to the Filipinos and the guerrillas, who have let us stay in their mountains and kept us safe with warnings so far. They will continue to do so even though there are more enemy troops now. There are miles of empty forest here where we can hide." Then Edna smiled a small smile as Edith patted her back.

Early in the war, when the two families first stayed at the lake house, there had been an enemy garrison of forty in Dumaguete, and the Japanese had never ventured into the hills. But now at least a hundred enemy soldiers were stationed in Dumaguete, and they had boldly advanced into the hills to Malabo and burned the whole village, along with the headquarters of the military and civilian resistance organizations. And the stronger Japanese garrison also offered a bounty for information that would lead to Roy's capture.

A rumor reached the now-large group at the lake that the Japanese were preparing rubber boats to use on the water to seek out Roy. He and Arthur Carson already believed the enemy knew of their lake hideout. To forestall the enemy, Roy organized a rotation of household males, including the four resolute Norwegians, to stand watch from spots where they could observe the trails leading to the lake retreat as well as the lake itself. Their posts were far enough away to give them time to bring warning of intruders so that the large household could scatter.

Arthur and Edith Carson never mentioned the increased danger that Roy's presence brought to their family. But Roy himself realized that his being there endangered the whole group. Neither the Carsons nor the Scaffs had been active in the resistance, so they might well remain safe—so far the enemy had made no attempt to seek out families just because they were American.

With these thoughts, Roy decided to seek a new evacuation site for his family in the mountainous area south and west of Malabo—at higher elevations, closer to the center of the island, and more thinly populated than the Bell family's previous location. When Tore learned about Roy's search, he eagerly volunteered to go along. Tore loved to travel even if there were no girls at the end of the journey—unlike when he had been a sailor, traveling from port to port. On the first afternoon, Roy and Tore came upon a deserted house higher on the mountain and deeper in the forest than Malabo. When the owner offered to repair the house, Roy gave him 20 pesos to start.

But on the way back, Roy talked with some people in the neighborhood who had heard of the Bell family and the destruction of Malabo. They deplored the end of the village and were glad that everyone had escaped. But one man added, "Perhaps your family could settle farther away. We might not be so lucky in getting safely away as the people in Malabo. We have learned of earlier random shooting of Filipinos. We don't want the Japs to come around here." That was enough for Roy to look elsewhere.

Two days later Roy found a suitable spot still higher in the mountains and beyond where anyone was living. A spring bubbled a constant stream of water. Nearby was an opening in the forest from where they could see the lowlands and the interisland sea. The following day, feeling that his presence at the lake could be a danger at any time to the group there, Roy moved his family from the lake house to a deserted bamboo hut in the vicinity of the spot chosen for the new house.

The hut sat on a small open hill in the middle of a field of tall corn. Although dense forest stretched away in all directions from the clearing, Edna worried aloud about the hut being in such plain view. Then she declared, "During the night when we're all asleep we could all be captured. We don't have any Norwegians here. I wish Tore would stay with us. We've heard of Japanese night raids in which the enemy soldiers carried torches to move along the trails."

The next evening, as it grew dark, Edna noticed a group of moving torches at a lower altitude some distance away. However, Roy explained the torches as "mountain people returning from their fields of work. They won't be coming up here because nobody lives this far up the mountain. Since we don't have any candles, let's turn in." They were all so tired that the dry floor seemed comfortable, and they quickly fell asleep.

But Kenneth's sleep was brief. At about 8:00 PM he got up and looked out over the cornfield. Several spots of light were moving in the forest, not far from the edge of the corn. While moving randomly about each other, the cluster of lights headed straight for the bamboo shelter. Ken yelled, "The Japs are coming! We have to get out of here!" After one look Roy shouted, "Everyone grab something and hide in the cornfield." Soon Edna, Don, and Nelly were hidden in the tall corn while Roy and Ken stood behind coconut trees close to the hut. The lights came steadily toward them. Then they could make out the friendly faces of three Filipino boys carrying flickering torches.

When Roy asked what they wanted, one answered, "Mrs. Bell asked us to bring you some vegetables a couple days ago and we found you had moved here." Roy took the vegetables, thanked the boys, and asked them to come again. The boys happily headed back down the trail, waving their torches around as they had in coming.

Roy and Ken then tried to persuade the rest of the family to come out of hiding, but Edna and Nelly said, "We feel safer here in this thick corn." Edna explained, "I didn't know where we were going to be when I ordered the vegetables a few days ago. I don't know how the boys found out where we were so fast. Now the Japs might be waiting a little way back for the three boys to report they've found us." But when nothing happened after a time, Edna and Nelly came out of the corn, and the whole family went back into the hut and slept without interruption for the rest of the night.

This surprise food delivery at the cornfield led Roy to seek still another location for a cabin. Since a remote location had not hidden the family, Roy decided to settle in the mountains just above Malabo—close to the farmers who had been providing the family with food and near the friendly villagers, who seemed to blame the Japanese for burning their homes, rather than Roy Bell's resistance operations at Malabo that made the village the target of the raid. Roy decided on a spot in the forest near several springs. There, with the help of Macario, a loyal mountaineer, and his boys, the Bell family built a dwelling and cleared enough land for a large garden.

Meanwhile the Scaff family had again become unhappy with the dampness at their lake location after the new rainy season set in. So they followed the Bell family to the new location, and Macario helped them build a small cabin across the clearing from the Bell's dwelling. There was plenty of sunshine and space for both families to plant fast-growing tropical vegetables such as sweet potatoes. Their new homes were in an area the Filipinos called Manalanco.

Chapter 18

Manalanco and Flight

July 1943 to January 1944

T he destruction of the Bells' home and household goods in Malabo brought a flood of assistance from their longtime neighbors and friends in Dumaguete. Mountain carriers brought bedding, bundles of clothes, and food to the Bells' new cabin at Manalanco, high in the forests above Malabo, despite Roy's concern about revealing their location. Yet he had decided to move closer to friendly Filipinos. The remoteness of their previous area did not seem to have any advantage—friendly Filipinos had soon found them, and so could collaborators who would then report their location to the Japanese. The family's real protection was to be warned of enemy raids by friendly Filipinos living near Manalanco.

The new house was smaller than the family's previous dwellings in the hills because three longtime members of the household were about to leave. Ski, Roy's radio operator, had been requested by General Fertig, the guerrilla commander on Mindanao. Ski had become available after Ray's station was taken away by Colonel Abcede's Negros Island command to save it from the Japanese destruction of Malabo. Ski was eager to go; he wanted to keep on helping the resistance.

Two of the Norwegians, Ole and Arne, decided to go along with Ski, expecting to fit into Fertig's command. Besides liking the Norwegians, the Bell family was grateful to them for guarding the trail up to Malabo in the early days of the resistance. And losing Ski was like losing one of the family. Now Edna and Nelly were close to tears as they waved to the three as they became visible for the last time through the trees down the trail. Soon Nelly also risked the crossing to Mindanao to reach her parents. Then the other two Norwegians likewise headed south.

Once the Bell family had settled at Manalanco, Roy began his new island-wide duties, which took him to distant parts of Negros to increase useful production. Roy's constant companion was George Ghent, who had shared some tight situations with Roy before. Many trips took Roy away for two weeks, leaving Edna and the boys feeling much more vulnerable than they had during Roy's absences from Malabo, when the family was next door to Major Ausejo's guerrilla command. Instead of that protection, Rev. Scaff and his family had settled on the same clearing in the forest.

The Scaff family had also become targets because of a new policy pursued by the enlarged Japanese garrison in Dumaguete. The Japanese were scouring the hills to find and bring in to Dumaguete for questioning all Silliman faculty members. Then American faculty families were sent on to the Santo Tomas Civilian Internment Camp near Manila.

For now, Edna was left alone with her boys and the neighboring Scaff family. She kept the boys busy in the family's thriving garden during the day. In the evening she and the boys read to each other, hoping to keep their minds turned to other times and places. But Edna dreaded moonlit nights because the Japanese had chosen those times to find the hideouts of other faculty members.

Every night before she fell asleep, Edna became worried whenever a limb fell or the howling monkeys chattered—they sounded the same whether they were just talking or sounding a warning of human intruders. Then she would pray herself to sleep, putting herself and her family in God's safekeeping since she was powerless herself.

When Roy was home, Edna easily fell asleep. But during one of the nights Roy was there, the whole family was abruptly awakened by the loud squawking of the chickens in the coop next to the house. The whole family followed Roy outside. He had grabbed a shotgun and lit a kerosene lamp, which he held up for them to look into the coop. A young black python was crushing a chicken in its coils, undisturbed by the protests of the other fowl. While Ken held the lamp, Roy blasted the snake with his shotgun. It was already six feet long and its body the size of a man's wrist—a full-grown python can stretch twenty feet. The coop being only a few yards from the forest's edge, the chickens were convenient prey for a hungry snake.

Having heard that python meat was tasty, Edna cooked some of it the next day, but nobody thought it was a treat. But there were happy distractions. Edna admired the majestic trees, orchids, ferns, and beautiful birds in the surrounding jungle. The family watched three kinds of bright-colored woodpeckers tap holes in dead trees and pull out worms. Edna liked to visit with the Scaffs, who lived on the other side of the clearing. She was entranced by the Scaff's three-year-old boy, Larry, who thrived on native oranges and the tomatoes grown in the clearing.

The only expected visitors were one or two friendly guerrilla soldiers who had the duty of stopping by now and then. Craving solitude, Edna had Pedro, a neighboring boy, go out marketing three days a week. The family just stayed at their cabin clearing all the time at first, but soon they missed the regular broadcast of world news at Malabo—especially news of American operations against the Japanese. So once a week Ken or Don took a hike to listen to the radio at the lake house or the Fleischers' evacuation house. Paul and Paz Fleischer were former Silliman students who had fled from their plantation near Tanjay with their four children.

Edna and the boys could hardly wait for the latest Pacific war news, hoping for American advances toward the Philippines. But such advances seemed very slow. In reality, after the Japanese were driven from Guadalcanal, General MacArthur's strategy of island hopping would move American forces steadily toward the Philippines. In the process U.S. soldiers skipped past strongly held enemy islands and landed on islands farther on. Thus they stranded hundreds of thousands of Japanese troops at Rabaul on New Britain and elsewhere—their war had ended.

While Roy spent most of his time on increasing production in resistance territory, he still kept in touch with Mariano Perdices, who was seemingly the puppet mayor of Dumaguete but actually an ally of the resistance. One day Perdices sought Roy's help with these words: "Roy, our director of the Mission Hospital here, Dr. Ponce, says he can't stand the Japs anymore so he and his wife are about to take to the hills."

Perdices explained further: "A Jap officer forced Dr. Ponce to fix his flat tire outside the hospital. While the officer coolly watched, Ponce dripped with perspiration. As you know, he is a small man; and besides wearing him out physically, this was a bad emotional experience. To top it off, the next day Ponce's wife was forced to sit on the pavement in the sweltering sun for two hours because she had not bowed properly to a Jap sentry. But you know, Mr. Bell, that is the only hospital in the province and we need Ponce there. Would you talk to him?"

Roy answered, "The Japs' behavior is unbelievable if they care about an effective hospital. We persuaded Dr. Ponce to bring the hospital back from Pamplona in the early days of the occupation. I hope he'll still realize how much the people need him in Dumaguete and the province. I'm going to arrange a meeting with him. Victor Jornales, one of our earliest guerrilla leaders here, will join me."

At the meeting, Roy diplomatically explained the need for Ponce's leadership at the hospital, especially in the unsettled conditions of the war and occupation. Then Victor Jornales—a proven guerrilla officer before finishing college—bluntly addressed Dr. Ponce: "We shouldn't let our anger at the Japs prevent us from treating our people the best way we can! They need an effective hospital here to go to when they are sick. You are the one who makes it effective!"

Dr. Ponce's admiration for Roy and Jornales helped him to swallow his pride. He answered, "I believe I can persuade my wife to stay. As you have said to me, Roy, the Japs won't be here forever." And then Ponce turned to Victor and said, "You and others, Victor, run risks every day against the enemy. My wife and I will stick it out at the hospital."

During this period the new Japanese leader in Dumaguete, Captain Kamoto, was just as trusting of Mayor Perdices as his predecessors had been. He confided to Perdices, "Even though we destroyed Roy Bell's headquarters in Malabo, I believe that he is still nearby and causing most of our problems around here. So I'm going to raise the reward from 500 to 9,000 pesos to anyone whose information helps us capture him." Perdices forwarded this information to Roy. Even as Kamoto worried about Roy being in the area, Roy found a new ally in Dumaguete. This came about after the Japanese organized their own version of the prewar Philippine Bureau of Constabulary (BC), which had been formed years before to keep order at the provincial level. Now the Japanese established their own BC with former Filipino soldiers, who were persuaded to join by the prospect of pay and food. The head of the BC unit at Dumaguete was Lieutenant Ceferino Galvez. The Japanese had not made a good choice—Galvez had been assistant commander of the ROTC at Silliman before the war and was a brother-in-law of the fierce young guerrilla leader Frederico Ridad.

Galvez soon was secretly corresponding with Ridad and then with Roy. Galvez proposed to Roy a plan to retake Dumaguete. It involved a strong guerrilla attack on the town, supported by Galvez's Constabulary group, which was stationed at the former women's dormitory at Silliman University. The Japanese troops were garrisoned at the men's dormitory. But Roy answered, "We will welcome you and any or all of your soldiers to come out into the hills to join us. But for now, it is too risky for us to count on the complete loyalty of your men."

In coming months, Lieutenant Galvez and many of his men followed Roy's suggestion and broke away from the BC to join the guerrillas. But one of the BC soldiers—not known by the Bell family—showed up at Manalanco about November 15, 1943, while Roy was on a trip to southern Negros.

Edna had been watching a woodpecker and the boys were working in the garden that morning when a group of four or five people appeared on the far side of the clearing and came toward her. Edna tensed because no such group was expected and its size was unusual. She was only able to relax when she recognized a former student, now a young wife, who was accompanied by her family and a man who was introduced as a recently escaped BC soldier.

Then Edna enjoyed a pleasant chat with the visitors. As the party left, Edna said to the young wife, "Please do not talk to anyone about where we are living. Our safety depends on our location [not being] widely known." The woman answered, "We will do our best to keep your presence here unknown and will help you in any way we can since we already know where you are." Edna welcomed these words from somebody she and Roy had long known and trusted, but the ex-BC soldier who had come with the family did not say a word.

The following week Roy returned from his trip but soon was in bed with pleurisy. He brought with him two guerrilla soldiers, one of whom, a man named Amut, had been held prisoner at a guerrilla camp Roy had visited. The guerrilla in charge there, a Lieutenant Gonzalez, had explained, "This man is responsible for the death of a fellow soldier. We'll have a trial for him." Roy had not quite followed Gonzalez's account of what had happened but did not inquire further.

Yet as Roy had left the camp, a young soldier strolled beside him until the trail turned and made them invisible from the guerrilla camp. Roy then remembered the boy as Henri, a conscientious member of his physics class. Roy asked, "What is it, Henri?" Henri explained in a low voice, "The prisoner Amut is not guilty of killing the man. He caused his death, but it was entirely accidental." Roy knew and trusted Henri, so he had returned to Lieutenant Gonzalez and suggested, "Let me take the prisoner off your hands. You won't have to feed and guard him. I'll see that justice is done." Gonzalez had readily agreed to Major Bell's suggestion. A grateful Amut began to serve as Roy's orderly.

On November 21, back at Manalanco, Roy was still in bed when a courier brought him a coded message from Wendell Fertig, commander of the guerrillas on Mindanao. Roy and Fertig had worked out a code to communicate with each other when Roy had visited the general months before.

But now Roy was so weakened by pleurisy that he didn't have energy to find out what Fertig had to say, even though the dispatch of a courier for the long trip was a sure sign of its importance. But Roy's usually nonassertive son Donald had both energy and curiosity. After two days of Don's asking what the message said, Roy relented and Don broke out the message on the afternoon of September 23. It read: "Would the American Silliman faculty and other Americans on Negros be interested in coming to the northern coast of Mindanao with a view to being repatriated by submarine to the U.S.?"

That evening the Bell and Scaff families were ecstatic about the prospect of getting back to America. Hitherto they saw only a prolonged wait before going home—until American forces recaptured the Philippines. Roy, suddenly feeling better, and Alvin Scaff planned to notify the other Americans in the hills and join them in planning a final Thanksgiving celebration two days hence.

The next morning Edna and Roy woke up early because Roy had to write a couple of messages to guerrilla headquarters. They were to be taken by Amut and the other guerrilla soldier, who were waiting outside and planning to leave at dawn. At 5:00 AM Edna was sitting on Roy's bed—he still had fever—scribbling the messages. Suddenly they were startled by shouts of "Japs!" from the guerrilla soldiers. Shots followed, apparently aimed at the soldiers fleeing into the jungle.

The shots instantly awakened Ken and Don in the cabin's loft. They looked out the small attic window to see Japanese soldiers moving in single file among large boulders and clambering over the fallen trees that were left in the center of the clearing after the two cabins were built. The boys hurtled down the loft's crude ladder and out the door without a word. They rushed up the few yards of slope and into the forest. Like the fleeing guerrillas, they drew a few shots but scurried out of sight unscathed.

In the cabin Edna cried out, "What shall we do?" Roy yelled, "Run!" He had gotten out of bed and grabbed the rifle above his cot. They started up the few yards to the forest, but Edna stumbled and fell halfway up the short slope. Roy turned to see if she had been wounded by the bullets flying around their legs—apparently the Japanese were aiming low so that they could be captured. As Edna got up, Roy took a bullet a little above his right knee. He hardly noticed it or his pleurisy as they plunged into the forest. Shots from an automatic weapon now came, but after a few rounds the weapon apparently jammed. Barefoot and in pajamas, they hurried upward in the thick forest. At Edna's insistence they kept going through the brush rather than turning off on a couple of beaten paths they crossed. Instead they proceeded toward a little mountain hut, where they had stored a few provisions in case they needed to escape quickly.

Back at the clearing, the Scaff family had made no attempt to escape because of their three-year-old son, Larry, so they were watching the flight of the Bell family. But the raiders paused at the edge of the forest, not knowing which of two rough trails to take, obviously hoping to cut off the Bells' off-trail flight. Mrs. Scaff noticed their uncertainty. When they started up the trail toward the Fleischer's hideout, Mrs. Scaff appeared to act the part of the compliant prisoner—the Scaffs had not participated in the resistance, nor had they tried now to escape capture. She cried out, "No! No! That way," while pointing toward Malabo. The raiding party—tired and disoriented after a long early morning climb from sea level—followed her advice.

So Edna and Roy were actually safe for the time being even though they thought the Japanese were close behind them. After a while, though, they had to stop to catch their breath. Hoping to calm Edna, Roy remarked, "I bet the Japanese soldiers were worn out after climbing in the dark from Dumaguete up to reach our clearing at 3,000 ft just before dawn. Their shots were pretty wild and they didn't fire their automatic rifle until after we were in the forest. And their shots seemed low as though they wanted to hit our legs and take us alive so they could have some prisoners to parade on the streets of Dumaguete. After we entered the forest, we don't know that the Japs followed us. Maybe they feared an ambush because of my rifle and our two armed guerrilla friends, who could still be around here."

Edna, partly convinced by Roy that they were in no immediate danger, answered, "That all may be true, Roy, but right now we need to find the boys. Maybe they're at our little hut up here where we stored some food and old clothes by good fortune." In about an hour, they reached the hut, but the boys were not in sight. However, the parents were soon relieved by shouts of "We're here!" The boys came out of the bushes, even more relieved than their parents because of the multiple shots they had heard after they had fled into the forest.

After they all found some rough clothing to replace their pajamas, Edna picked up a can of milk and a little brown sugar and insisted that they keep on moving. When they came to a small brook, the family followed it upstream for some time among tangles of low-growing brush. After leaving the brook, they climbed up a good-sized ridge and on the far side found shelter from the gentle rain under large, drooping tree ferns. Then they thought of the can of milk—they hadn't had anything to eat since awakening. But they had no knife or tool to open the can. Finally they punctured it with a belt buckle.

Yet sharing a small can of milk and a few pinches of brown sugar apiece did little to satisfy their hunger. Worse, the damp mountain air under an overcast sky chilled them—they were at an altitude of four thousand feet, more than a thousand feet higher than Manalanco, where their flight started. They had matches but feared to light a fire because of its telltale smoke.

After staying a couple hours, dry but getting colder, the Bell family realized they couldn't stay there for the night. So they followed the top of the ridge until they came to a little-used path that descended in the direction of the Carsons' lake house as well as the Fleischers' retreat. Roy examined the overgrown trail carefully but saw no signs that it had been recently used. So they moved faster and more confidently until 4:00 PM, when they came to a fork in the rough trail. One path led to the Carsons' lake house and the other to the Fleischers' place.

At the fork Roy sent Ken to warn the Carsons of the enemy raiding party and get some clothes for the family. Roy warned him, "The Japanese may have taken the Carsons so watch from the edge of the clearing to see that they're okay before you make yourself known." At the lake house Ken quietly approached the open door and saw the Carson family all sitting quietly with glum faces and not saying a word.

As he stepped in, Ken asked with a smile, "What's wrong here? Why are you all so sad?" Mr. Carson replied, "Where is the rest of your family? Did you all get away? Amut came by this morning and reported that all of you almost certainly had been taken by the Jap raiding party."

Ken quickly reassured the Carsons: "We all escaped and without injury except Dad has a slight leg wound. They are headed for the Fleischer's hideout rather than coming here and putting you in danger. Dad says the Japs are little interested in the Fleischers because they're not part of the resistance and their place is less known than yours."

Meanwhile the rest of the Bell family took the fork toward the Fleischers' evacuation home. Outside the house, nobody was in sight and they heard nothing. They couldn't see inside because the house stood on stilts, so Roy had to climb up the ladder to the main floor to see if anyone was inside. At the top he found Paul and Paz Fleischer and their four children sitting around, looking stunned and morose. But as with Ken's entrance and report at the Carson's house, Roy's appearance and story brought relief and joy. Amut had also reported to them the Bells' probable capture.

Thus a day that started with near disaster ended in at least temporary safety for the Bells. They enjoyed a delicious dinner with the Fleischers, and Paul treated Roy's wound with sulfanilamide. As the Bell family looked back over the day's events, Edna declared, "We have to be grateful to God for our miraculous good fortune in being safe after barely escaping capture this morning. I'm thinking our trouble started when that supposed BC deserter visited the clearing while you were away." Roy agreed: "Yes. He probably told the Japs our location because of the reward Captain Kamoto offered for help in capturing me. Since Kamoto realized I wasn't there then, he waited a few days or else found out I had returned before sending out the raid."

Then Roy turned to Paul Fleischer and said, "We're concerned about the threat our being here brings to you. While we're here we must keep our presence absolutely secret. Whenever it is possible for you to know ahead of time that visitors are coming, let us know so we can keep out of sight. For unexpected visitors, we'll be alert all the time so we can get out of the way. As soon as I am physically capable, we will try to move away from you."

As Roy and Edna expected, Paul assured them, "Paz and I want you to stay here as long as it is best for you. We'll cooperate completely in keeping your presence unknown." So when the mountain people or the Fleischers' former plantation hands brought supplies or food to the cabin, the Bell family stayed out of sight before, during, and a while after the visit.

Chapter 19

Staying with the Fleischers

November 1943 to mid-January 1944

On November 24, when the Bell family moved into the evacuation house of the Fleischers, their friends were already providing a temporary home for Leland Archer and Peter Buchanan. Archer had been a Caltex representative on Cebu before the war. He had sought to keep away from the invaders by moving to thinly populated Negros. Buchanan, a former Silliman student, his wife, Mary, and their children were living on Negros and had evacuated to the general area of Manalanco, where the Bell family had settled. A few weeks earlier, an enemy raid had captured Buchanan's family while he was away.

To make more room for the Bell family, Archer and Buchanan started to build a hut for themselves higher up the rocky mountain stream that rushed around boulders beside the Fleischers' house. In a day or two, Ken and Don Bell went up to help expand the bamboo shelter to accommodate Roy as well. Roy needed the greatest seclusion possible because he was confined with his leg wound and pleurisy, and so could not flee the enemy. In a week or so Roy's sons carried him up along the rocky stream to the new hut.

During the day Roy contentedly basked in the sun by himself, and in the evenings he enjoyed visiting with Peter Buchanan. In a couple of days, Roy cheered up when Dr. Jose Garcia came to see him—the faithful Amut had learned of Roy's thigh wound and informed Garcia. The busy doctor assured Roy, "That .25 slug in your leg will do no harm. The pleurisy will mend, but you must stay off your feet for a month or more."

A couple of days later, while Roy was resting in the clearing, he noticed the top of a giant tree at the edge of the clearing teeter, tilt, and then topple ponderously toward the ground. As it gained momentum, Roy saw with horror that one of the Fleischers' young servants was standing petrified where the tree would fall, praying but too frightened to move. The tree hit

145

the ground with a thunderous crash, but Roy could hardly believe what he then saw—the young man was standing unharmed in the fork made by the tree's huge trunk and a major branch.

Now the Fleischers felt more vulnerable where they were because of a rumor—reported by a loyal employee—that they had become a Japanese target. So Paul Fleischer, Archer, Buchanan, Ken, and Don built another hut for the Fleischers in the secluded area where Roy had settled. With the completion of the second bamboo hut, everyone was together again.

As Roy relaxed in the new bamboo hut, he realized he had to do something about the message from Fertig regarding a possible evacuation by submarine. It was too late for the departure from Mindanao, as Fertig had suggested. Yet an evacuation was more urgent than ever. Roy had learned of the execution of a group of Baptist missionaries on the island of Panay, just ten miles north of Negros, and the Scaffs had been taken prisoner. Would the Japanese find the three other Silliman faculty members in the Dumaguete area?

The Japanese found the Magdamos first. But Mr. Magdamo assured the enemy soldiers, "There are no Americans around here. They fled farther into the hills weeks ago." However, the Japanese soon found the other two American families. Being Americans, they would be shipped to the Santo Tomas internment camp for American civilians near Manila—where the Scaffs had been sent.

But being Filipinos, the Magdamos faced an unknown and worrisome future—possibly more perilous because of the false information given to the Japanese by Mr. Magdamo, who had already suffered a painful beating. George Ghent, who had been Roy's frequent travel companion, was particularly worried about the Magdamos' fate—he planned to marry the Magdamos' daughter, Martha.

In despair George turned to Frederico Ridad, the Silliman student who had formed one of the first and most fierce guerrilla bands in the area. The Japanese had temporarily confined the Magdamos in Dumaguete. Always eager to harass the enemy, Ridad confidently planned a rescue.

On the first moonless night, Ridad sent a trusted officer into Dumaguete to meet with a few guerrilla soldiers at the jail. They were probably unnecessary. Recent successes had relaxed the new large Japanese garrison. It had destroyed Malabo, captured most of the Silliman faculty, and almost snared Roy. Inside Dumaguete the size of the garrison had greatly reduced resistance activity. So the Japanese command had become confident in the Bureau of Constabulary (BC) unit, composed of young Filipinos, it had established to keep order in Dumaguete. Being in the BC involved pay and food and, hopefully, gave the recruits a stake in local security. The BC Filipinos were given the job of manning the Dumaguete provincial jail. But the BC soldiers there were so knowingly unalert that they fired no shots as the guerrillas escorted the Magdamos out of the jail. Then Ridad's officer led the surprised Magdamo family along deserted streets and down to the water's edge. There a good-sized outrigger canoe was drawn up on the beach.

The escaping family sailed with a light but favoring and steady wind southward toward the Southern Cross—the prominent constellation on the southern horizon was spectacular that night. Its four stars shone so brightly that the Magdamos felt all would be well. But they did not know then the threats to their survival that lay ahead.

The Magdamos put ashore and stayed hidden the next day. Then, moving by night, they reached Zamboanguita, twenty miles south of Dumaguete. There they took assumed names but were recognized anyway. George Ghent learned about their problem and arranged for their transport to guerrilla headquarters at Basay, where they stayed until the war's end. George Ghent and Martha Magdamo were then married and eventually settled in the United States.

While his fellow faculty members were being picked up by the Japanese or still fleeing, Roy and his family remained safe in the high forests of Negros. In pondering an evacuation, Roy thought that a getaway from Negros would in all probability be safer than having first to make the dangerous sea crossing to Mindanao before meeting a submarine off Mindanao—the pickup opportunity Fertig had reported and the Bells had missed. A getaway from Negros would also be safer for President Carson and his family for the same reason.

If Roy found a way to evacuate his family, he was determined not to leave the Carsons behind. Roy had worked closely with President Carson in building up Silliman University before the war; since then, the two families had bonded in their joint flight into the hills to escape the invaders. So now Roy would try for another joint flight for the two families—by submarine from Negros. It should be possible because the USS *Gudgeon* had brought Major Villamor to Negros in January 1943, and Villamor had eventually been taken off by submarine on October 20, 1943.

Villamor's departure had left Colonel Abcede in charge of the Negros guerrillas, so it seemed he should be contacted about arranging for the submarine. But his headquarters was located near the far southwestern corner of the island. Messages on paper could well endanger the Bells, the guerrillas, and the submarine traffic if the messenger were captured. Roy didn't have the strength to make the trip himself, so someone else would have to take and bring back verbal messages.

This task would require someone hardy and intelligent enough to handle the long hike and also accurately transmit verbal messages. In addition the messenger would have to be resourceful—if captured, he would have to conceal the nature of his journey from his interrogators, especially anything about the submarine. Roy knew there was a qualified person right at hand.

During his recovery Roy had been enjoying long talks with Peter Buchanan, who had also found a temporary home with the Fleischers. Peter seemed well qualified for the long journey, but Roy didn't feel like he knew Peter well enough to ask him to undertake such a mission. Yet Peter had become well aware of Roy's problem from general conversation in the Fleischer household.

One day, while Roy and Peter were enjoying a lazy afternoon, Peter said, "I know that you need to get word to Col. Abcede about meeting a submarine since you aren't well enough to take a message yourself. I've been on Negros almost as long as you have and know the best trails to Basay. I would like to take the message to Abcede for you and return with the reply. The Japs captured my wife and child so I would like to help save yours." Roy knew Peter was sincere and gratefully accepted his offer. Peter took Frank Boylan, an American soldier who had escaped from the Japanese, as a companion. Frank had slipped away from his captors while being used as a truck driver.

A few days after Peter's departure, Roy's son Don came down with malaria. Upon learning of Don's illness, Arthur Carson made the long hike from the lake house with the quinine needed for treating the disease. Then Roy told Arthur of his effort to get the Americans out by submarine. But Arthur surprised Roy by his reply: "I don't believe it will be possible to connect with a submarine. Besides[,] reaching a meeting place along the coast would be too dangerous. We've stayed by the lake without intrusion so far. I believe we'll take our chances staying right where we are." Roy, concerned about his old friend and boss, countered by saying, "If I can arrange something, you must try. It will be a long time before American forces reach the Philippines, and you don't have the guerrilla contacts that have always helped me. And my information from the guerrillas has helped me keep you safe." Then Roy dropped the subject, hoping he had been persuasive.

Needing to stay hidden and being under Dr. Garcia's orders to stay quiet was an unwelcome experience for Roy. But he brightened at Christmas when the Carson family came over from the lake to celebrate with the Fleischers and the Bells. They all enjoyed eating and socializing as though they had no cares in the world. Roy felt still better after Arthur Carson told him, "Roy[,] we're going to join you to make a try for the submarine if you can arrange it." Arthur remembered that on that Christmas evening, "Our little group of hunted Americans . . . far back in the jungle heard President Roosevelt speak over the radio. We all stood for the 'Star-Spangled Banner,' which followed the President's speech."[1]

On the day before New Year's Day 1944, the two families at the Fleischers' house became concerned when they heard dogs barking not far down the mountain. Paul Fleischer grabbed his double-barreled shotgun and said, "I'm going down there and scare off the mountain people who must be hanging around with the dogs." Despite his wife's objections, Paul headed down the mountain. In a few minutes, everyone heard a shot. Paz rushed after her husband, not knowing what or whom he had shot. But she was soon back and reported, "Paul shot a deer swimming in a sizable stream—the dogs were barking at it. He wants us to bring a bamboo pole and help him bring it up here—we've been short of meat for sometime [*sic*]."

In mid-January 1944 Roy became apprehensive when Frank Boylan returned without Roy's emissary, Peter Buchanan, and wanted to speak privately with him. But once they were alone, Frank quickly explained: "Buchanan is okay and had some other business so he sent me. Col. Abcede gave us both the information that Silliman faculty members should gather at Basay near the southeast corner of the island to meet a submarine in early February. Peter will return here soon. He wants to lead you and the Carsons on the hike over to Basay."

Roy then had to explain to the Fleischers that they were not included because they were not Silliman faculty members. Paul Fleischer answered bravely and graciously: "We do not feel particularly threatened since we have not been part of the resistance or dealt with the guerrillas. We're happy you have the chance to get away." And both Paul and Roy realized the Fleischers would be safer once Roy was gone. The Japanese command had offered a sizable bounty to anyone who helped capture Roy.

Chapter 20

Basay Rendezvous

January and February 1944

In the middle of January 1944, Peter Buchanan came back to the Fleischer hideout, as Frank Boylan reported he would. Peter explained to Roy the route he planned to follow to the submarine rendezvous point: "Instead of the southern route following the coast but staying in the hills close to the enemy-controlled lowlands, we will first proceed north in the hills to the vicinity of Tanjay. From there we will follow an ancient trail directly westward, cross the island's central ridge and descend to the village of Amio. That trail is said to lead through deep jungle that is inhabited by hostile pygmies or Negritos, but I believe the danger from them is less than we might face on the southern route where we would be close to the Japs for a longer time. But it will take at least seven days to reach Amio, our destination." Roy agreed: "Yes, let's take the longer route. We have been going barefooted for months except for wife Edna and Edith Carson, and they have rubber shoes—a longer route is best."

On the afternoon of January 21, 1944, the Carsons arrived at the Fleischers' place to join the Bells and Leland Archer for the trek, which would begin the next morning. They brought along a half-dozen mountain carriers with their household goods. Peter Buchanan remarked, "You won't be able to take anything much on the submarine but yourselves." But Arthur Carson pointed out, "If we don't make connection with a submarine right away, we'll need these things while we wait there in guerrilla territory." Buchanan dropped the subject—he considered his main job was to deliver his motley group to the guerrilla command at Amio. Now he also had some carriers to bring along.

The Carsons' plentitude of belongings—they had not moved from the lake house since the war's early days—contrasted with the Bells' meager personal possessions. The Bells had made multiple moves related to Roy's resistance effort, leaving behind some goods every time they moved.

Early in the war, however, Edna Bell had stored some of the family's better clothing with their loyal Spanish friends, the Arretas. At that time Mr. Arreta was using his plantation employees to distribute the Free Government's *Victory News* to counter Japanese propaganda. Now, in preparation for the family's long trek across the island, Edna Bell requested some of the clothes. Mrs. Arreta gladly complied—but, to Roy Bell's consternation, she included a note with the items saying, "Why do you need the clothes? We're afraid you're leaving. We'll miss you."

Despite Roy's worries, the first day's hike went smoothly enough. The party stayed in the hills and met few people. The next day they continued north, staying in the hills but passing through thinner forest than they were accustomed to, making everyone uneasy. Nevertheless, they reached the saw-mill town of Kangiete safely and spent a comfortable night with old friends.

On the third day the travelers ventured onto the plain in a no-man's-land that was patrolled by both Japanese and guerrillas of uncertain loyalty. Here many houses were deserted, and the skeletons of dead trees dotted the cutover timberland. The few people they met stared at them and hurried on. The exception was a bystander who warned them while they were crossing a stream, "The Japanese have spies who watch this ford." Late that afternoon the group's mood changed when a farmer offered them some roast pig, which some of them ate heartily.

The weary group reached the ancient trail across Negros that evening. Close by they found a large-enough hut to stay in overnight. But it was located only a few miles from the Japanese garrison at Tanjay. Tanjay's citizens had once sought help from Roy against lawless guerrillas. Now, before the party could settle in, a farmer came by and told them, "A Japanese patrol used that hut several nights ago before taking the trail across the island next morning." The travelers were too tired to let that news worry them, however. After a brief and scanty supper, Peter Buchanan explained, "We need all the rest we can get. Tomorrow I hope we can reach the empty schoolhouse at Amio, which is over fifteen miles from here and across the island's central ridge." Then they collapsed on the bamboo floor, but it was too uncomfortable for sound sleep. At 4:00 AM practically everyone was awakened when Leland Archer was overcome with nausea. But when the party left at daybreak, Leland seemed better—he had eaten a light breakfast.

After they crossed a river and climbed the first steep hill, however, eighteen-year-old Bob Carson suddenly turned into some bushes to vomit.

Bob had eaten some of the roast pig the day before, as had Leland Archer. Arthur Carson said, "I'll stay with Bob and Leland—-they both still need to wait. The rest of you must keep going. We'll come along when we can."

An hour later Arthur started out with his charges, but it was too soon. After a couple of miles, they had to stop because the exhausted Bob had become dehydrated. They couldn't find any water, nor was any bamboo—an emergency source of water—growing there. Occasional passersby hurried on without stopping. Arthur and the boys were feeling helpless when they heard a cheerful call from up the trail. They soon recognized Amut, Roy's faithful guerrilla soldier. He had joined the group the day before to help Roy, if necessary. Now Roy had sent him back with food and water for the stragglers.

The revived Carson group continued onward to the bank of a wide river, which was a jumble of rapids and boulders. Then they heard a shout. It was Roy Bell, waving from an island in the middle of the river. Fully recovered from pleurisy and not having eaten the roast pig, Roy stood with a resigned air among the prone cargo carriers.

Once Arthur was on the island, Roy told him, "The rest of the party has gone ahead, but you can see the condition of these carriers. We'll all make camp here and hope everybody feels better tomorrow." Arthur asked, "Will the others get through to Amio by nightfall?" Roy could only answer, "I don't know." Then Arthur inquired, "What will happen to them if they don't get there by dark?" Roy tried to allay Arthur's worries: "I have a lot of confidence in Peter Buchanan. He should be able to take care of them if something unusual happens." Still uneasy, Arthur helped Roy make a shelter of palm branches on a smooth sandbar on the island. After those who were well enough to eat had some food, the whole group stretched out on the sandbar, hoping sleep would revive the still nauseous ones.

Meanwhile Peter Buchanan's advance party also faced roast-pig problems. First, Jean, the Carsons' daughter, became so weak she had to be carried. Ken Bell and one of the carriers took turns lugging the chubby girl for the rest of the day. Then Edna Bell needed Edith Carson at one side to keep going. The sun had already set when they reached the last river to cross before getting to the schoolhouse.

On his other trips that way, Peter Buchanan had readily found the ford needed for crossing. But now, in the darkness, he could not find the shallow water of the ford—the water was uniformly black along the river's edge. Edna sank down on the sandy bank, feeling nauseated and too weary to fight off the clouds of mosquitoes thirsting for human blood. But her friend Edith sat down beside her to fight off the fierce insects. On Edith's other side sat her daughter, who likewise was under attack. Meanwhile Peter Buchanan and the Bell sons made torches, but even then it took Peter an hour to find the ford. Then they waded across—Ken Bell carried Jean and others supported Edna on each side.

The party then pushed onward until they reached the Amio schoolhouse at 11:00 PM. They soon sank into sleep, grateful for the school's level floor and avoiding some wet spots where a few holes in the roof had let rain in. The next morning a woman from the village of Amio told them, "Japanese bombs made holes in the roof, and killed several people. But we haven't been bothered for awhile."

The woman's report worried Peter Buchanan. He had understood that someone from Colonel Abcede's command would meet them at Amio. Peter didn't believe it was safe to linger there—word of their presence could easily reach the Japanese by way of collaborators. The result could be another bombing of the schoolhouse or an enemy raid by land. Peter hoped Roy's lagging party would arrive soon so they could all move on and find Abcede's men.

That same morning, back on the sandy island in the river, everyone in Roy's group was able to walk, so they finished crossing the river. Then they hiked through a region where recent rains had left large mudholes bottomed with sharp coral edges. Such coral shards also lurked in the small streams they crossed. The Japanese had been in the vicinity recently. Roy and Arthur could see the fallen tree that marked a new trail that stretched through the jungle in a straight line, making for steep ups and downs across the deep ravines. By afternoon the party had crossed the central ridge. Soon they heard a rifle shot. A little farther along, they came upon Ken Bell with a duck over his shoulder. That night the reunited party feasted on duck at the Amio schoolhouse, and each group found out what had happened to the other.

Now Peter Buchanan brought up his worry about the safety of the party. He explained to Roy Bell, "Col. Abcede told me that his men would take care of you if I brought you this far. But I don't see anybody here to meet us. I think it would be a good idea if you and Mr. Carson went ahead to contact the guerrillas while I wait here with the women and children in case they need me. When you have returned with satisfactory directions, I will head back across the island and rejoin the Fleischers." So Peter stayed at Amio for the day while the rest of the party rested, ate, and slept. The travelers had come to feel secure in Peter's presence.

Roy and Arthur found a young man in the village who knew the trails down to the coast and was confident they could find someone in the guerrilla organization. By afternoon they were slogging through muddy rice fields near the coastal town of Tolong. Yet they had found no guerrillas and few people. Finally they came upon a rice farmer who was ready to take a break from his work. Arthur, the scholarly Silliman president, tried his best Philippine dialect to ask him, "Are there any guerrilla soldiers nearby?" But the farmer was a former Silliman student, so answered in good English, "Right across that field"—he pointed—"is the local guerrilla headquarters in the village of Candalaga. The guerrillas are operating a rice mill I use, and are building housing for a training course."

After Roy and Arthur told the guerrilla leader in the village about their group, he replied, "We thought you'd be coming about now. You must move on from Amio at once. I'm sending one of my men back with you to conduct your party onward. Attract as little attention as possible as you move along." These words echoed Peter Buchanan's concerns, so Roy and Arthur, along with the guerrilla who was to guide the party, hurried back to Amio.

On January 29, 1944, the whole party began its journey toward the southwestern coast of Negros Island. On the second day, they reached the swift-flowing Socopon River, where the guide greeted four sturdy mountain men. They stood by two long bamboo rafts. The guide helped the party settle on the rafts, and then the mountain men boarded. There were two of them per raft, with each man holding a stout pole. They were barely under way when the current whirled them toward a huge boulder in the middle of the river. But the unperturbed raftsmen thrust their poles into the riverbed just in time to swerve around the rock. Then a series of rapids kept the passengers anxious, but these did not faze the raftsmen.

In other places they floated quietly along deep and calm stretches of the river. Edna, now feeling much better and sensing that all would turn out well, enjoyed the glorious mountain vegetation—thick and feathery bamboo clumps, tree fern, and flowering orchids all along the riverbanks with vivid-blue kingfishers flitting in and out of sight throughout the sun-flecked forest. These beauties of God's nature took Edna's mind away from fears of enemy patrols. And the party seemed free of the enemy for the time being. That night they enjoyed the luxury of dinner and beds at the home of Don Juan Vicente, a Spanish plantation owner.

The party waited at the Vicente plantation until evening of the next day to proceed to the coast. There Major Ben Viloria, Roy's old friend and colleague at Silliman, greeted them. He exclaimed, "We're as eager as you are to meet the submarine. We expect it to unload the most ammunition and guns that have ever been landed on Negros." The submarine was the USS

Narwhal, one of the Navy's two 300-foot boats, the largest size in its submarine fleet. Viloria explained further: "To protect the delivery, we have concentrated our men along the 25-mile stretch of coast that lies between us and the rendezvous planned at Basay. Right now we're going to hike along that beach—the easiest and safest route to Basay because of our sentries along the way. We have a couple horses, not too vigorous, for anyone who needs to rest."

They started out under a pale moon, moving very quietly. Edna felt leery of the shadows cast by the taller trees in the jungle that lined the beach. The only sound was made by the horses' hooves squishing into and out of the wet sand. Each shadow made Edna nervous until they passed by it. Suddenly a loud challenge came out of the jungle: "Halt! Who goes there?" Viloria shouted back, "Pablo, it is me, Major Viloria. I'm heading for Basay with the Americans we expected." A smiling Pablo stepped out of the jungle and waved to them. Thereafter sentries stopped them several times, but these encounters were welcome, impressing the families with the guerrilla organization on which their rescue depended.

The Bells and the Carsons reached the guerrilla camp near Tolong late that night. The next morning they rested, washed clothes, and swam in a clear, deep pool. Around noon the two families were amazed when Bob and Metta Silliman and Metta's sister, Abby Jacobs, their old friends from the university, suddenly appeared. They had been given up for lost, perhaps captured by the Japanese. Instead, the emaciated Silliman family fell into the arms of the Bells and the Carsons, who had not seen them since the Japanese had destroyed Malabo. They had just won a frightening race with enemy pursuers.

In the next few days, Roy and Edna gradually pieced together the story of the Sillimans' harrowing flight. Just before the destruction of Malabo, the Sillimans had returned safely enough to their hideout back of the coastal town of Siaton and stayed there undisturbed until recent days. But the message from Colonel Abcede about the expected submarine stop had not reached them. However, Dr. Garcia, ever responsive to people's medical needs, now determined to get word of the submarine pickup to the Sillimans.

To find them, Garcia sought the help of Lieutenant Joaquin Funda, a Silliman student, who commanded the guerrillas in the Siaton area and had shared for a long time the Sillimans' hideout. Funda and Garcia came in sight of the hideout just as the Sillimans' bodyguard, Cornelio, shouted, "The Japs are here. The Japs are here." But a pouring rain made possible successful escapes by the three resistance members, who fled in different directions.

Cornelio had with him documents relating to Silliman's term as resistance governor. The ensuing retreat toward guerrilla territory was touch-and-go for several days. Bob Silliman likened the relentless Japanese pursuit to a football game in which one team with many substitutes tries to wear down a determined team that has no replacements. Nevertheless, the Silliman team escaped defeat, but they looked terrible after their ordeal.

The party, now consisting of three families, continued by sea because there was no road leading westward to Basay. But Japanese patrol boats were active during the day, so the party waited until dark to board large outrigger canoes, manned by guerrilla paddlers. Heavy seas exhausted the paddlers after they rounded the southwestern corner of Negros Island and turned north. At 11:00 PM they brought their passengers into the Tayabanan River. The boats rode easily now in the river's calmer waters, but the moonlight showed that the way to shore was cluttered with floating logs. After a pause the tired paddlers carefully took the passengers toward shore, maneuvering their way through the maze of logs.

At first only a small, empty dock loomed at the river's edge, but when they were about fifty feet from shore, Rev. James McKinley stepped out from behind a palm tree and shouted, "Welcome to Basay, my old Silliman friends!" Roy answered from the water: "Yes! All of our three families are here safe and well!" Roy was the first to come ashore and embrace McKinley, but he was quickly followed by the other husbands and their families. They had not seen the McKinleys since the spring of 1942, when McKinley, a member of the faculty, his wife, their three daughters, and two students evacuated to the sawmill settlement of A-si-a, far around the trackless southern end of Negros.

Close behind, Major Ausejo, who had taken over Roy's early guerrilla bands, and Ausejo's grown daughters greeted the group. They had fixed a midnight snack for them of hot rice, fried eggs, and carabao milk at a nearby cottage. While feasting, they caught up on all their different experiences during the previous two years. Finally conversation dwindled, and Ausejo directed the families to three different cottages for them to stay in until the submarine came.

The Bell family followed Manuel Utzurrum, Silliman University's treasurer, who proudly showed them his first evacuation house, which the Bells were to use while waiting for the sub. It was located around a sharp bend in the river and behind a steep hill. Their water flowed through a bamboo pipe that extended several hundred feet up the hill. Manuel promised, "My wife and I will see that you have a supply of food while you're waiting for the sub. We don't live very far from here."

Behind the hill and by the river, Roy's family was some distance from the other two families who had arrived with them. It went through Roy's mind that in case of an enemy raid, Colonel Abcede wanted to give Roy's family a better chance to escape because of the price on Roy's head. However, like the others, Roy and his family settled down to an unusual period of sleep and relaxation for a couple days.

But the family's period of peace and quiet soon ended. An hour after dawn on February 5, 1944, Bob Silliman pounded on their door. Bob could hardly wait for Roy to get dressed and come outside. An excited Bob asked Roy, "Didn't you hear the explosions and shelling at dawn?" Roy answered, "No, Bob. We didn't hear a thing. Maybe our location behind this hill shut out the sound. Tell me what's going on. Maybe we should get out of here." Bob answered, "I'm afraid the Japs have landed at Tolong and are driving on our guerrilla headquarters here." Roy pointed out, "But Tolong is too far away for firing there to have awakened anyone here—the noise probably came from closer."

Then an officer from Colonel Abcede came up and broke in: "Major Torres reports that an enemy destroyer shelled the coast close to here this morning with the intent of landing.[1] But the fire completely missed Torres' guerrilla soldiers, who were waiting for the landing behind rocks and coconut trees."

The officer paused for fitting words to end his account. But Bob Silliman couldn't wait. "So what happened?" he demanded. The officer happily continued: "Torres' men watched as the Japs climbed down the side of the destroyer into two boats and headed directly toward them. They held fire even after the enemy boats grounded about fifty feet from shore. But once the enemy soldiers had scrambled out of their boats and begun to wade ashore, Torres gave the order to fire. None of the Japanese got back to the destroyer, and it sailed away."

Colonel Abcede was dismayed by the appearance of the enemy destroyer, even though he was delighted by the annihilation of the Japanese landing party. Later in the morning, Abcede was still edgy. He was worried about a second landing in the vicinity, which might not be so easily handled. So when the *Narwhal* looked at the shore through its periscope that morning for a go-ahead sign for the rendezvous in the evening as planned, Major Viloria gave no sign.

By late afternoon, however, no enemy landing had been reported along the miles of coast and no enemy ship had appeared. So Viloria was able to persuade Abcede to go ahead with the rendezvous the next day. Accordingly, Viloria contacted the submarine, and its commander agreed to the twenty-four-hour delay. That evening, a messenger from Colonel Abcede told each of the American families, "The submarine will surface at sunset tomorrow unless the Japanese ships arrive sooner and occupy the whole coastal area."

But the Americans had another scare the next morning when Japanese planes roared along the coast. Bob Silliman told his wife and sister-in-law, "Our escape would have been nice if it could have happened." Nevertheless, at noon Abcede's messenger gave instructions to the four families: "You are to assemble at the river bank at 4 p.m."

The group that waited at the river was considerably larger than the Bells, the Carsons, the Sillimans, and the McKinleys—all Silliman faculty. Roy explained, "I have learned that more of us are going because of a recent Japanese decree calling for the execution of all Americans found in the Philippines after January 1, 1944 so SWPAC now calls for the *Narwhal* to take all Americans."[2] The passengers now totaled twenty-three. The non-faculty Americans included Emma Vail, sister of Lieutenant Louis Vail, who had been Roy's frequent companion on guerrilla trips. Everyone was there early, and all had followed instructions to bring just one small suitcase.

Right at 4:00 PM a large sailboat came alongside the dock, and all clambered aboard. There was just enough space for the passengers, seven crewmen, and Major Viloria, who stationed himself at the boat's prow. During the thirty-minute ride down the river, the passengers noticed that numerous small sailboats and other craft pushed out into the current from hiding places in the brush along the shore. Major Viloria explained, "We have the boats hidden up all the streams in this area, to go out after the ammunition and guns. The fishermen have made carts under our supervision, and we've corralled all the carabaos for miles around to cart the boxes into the hills as far as we can, then soldiers will carry them the rest of the way. Major Torres has men posted at all probable landing places, to hold off the Japs if they try to surprise us. We've waited a long time for this ammunition. And you know how much is coming? Tons of it. These fellows on boats will die before they'll let the Japs get any of it."

Bob Silliman and others were still doubtful that the *Narwhal* would appear, but Roy insisted, "It will show up for certain. We're about to leave." Roy was so sure because Major Viloria had told him, "We arranged the rendezvous details today by coded messages with the *Narwhal* skipper."

At the mouth of the Tayabanan River, Major Torres—whose guerrilla unit had wiped out the Japanese landing party—was pacing the beach, scanning the shore and ocean for any untoward movement. The contrast of his commanding figure with his simple attire only enhanced his air of authority. He wore blue denim trousers, a gray shirt, and a straw hat.

As the Americans' boat began to pitch in the ocean swells, the twenty-five smaller sailboats coming down the river with them took stations behind. A small, bobbing boat moved ahead of them to lead the fleet. It carried only a fisherman and Colonel Abcede. The commanding officer of all guerrilla forces on Negros was eager to receive the arms and ammunition for his soldiers.

On the blue-gray mountains behind them, seemingly discrete patches of smoke drifted toward the faint half-moon low in the sky—to Edna they looked like guerrilla signals rather than natural cogon-grass fires. She admired the golden hue of the western sky in front of them as the boats headed toward the setting sun. As the sun sank lower, the sky took on more subdued pinks, violets, and grays.

But Edna forgot about the beauty of the sky when the huge submarine *Narwhal* suddenly began to emerge from the sea right in front of them with water streaming off her shiny sides. Upon seeing the American flag being raised by the sailors, the Americans shouted and cried with joy. Sixteen-year-old Emma Vail jumped up so energetically she rocked the boat and fell into the ocean, but Rev. McKinley jumped in after her. In a few minutes the rest of the passengers dragged them both back on the boat. Then everyone stepped carefully aboard the submarine, and all except Roy, Edna, and Bob Silliman climbed down the permanent ladder into the living quarters of the sub. In the officers' wardroom they enjoyed real bread and butter, hot coffee and cream, and big mugs of tomato juice.

Meantime the fleet of twenty-five small sailboats came alongside, one by one, to be loaded with forty tons of small arms, ammunition, and radio equipment. Nobody had to encourage the guerrillas and sailors to hurry the job. Their furious work was completed in less than an hour. U.S. Navy records showed the *Narwhal* delivered 1,500 carbines, 10 cases of tommy guns, Browning automatic rifles, 375,000 rounds of ammunition, and various medical supplies that night.

After the arms cargo was temporarily stored ashore, a guard discovered to his dismay a medium-sized python, about fifteen feet long, coiled among the ammunition boxes. That was a sign that the ammunition was struck with ill fortune. So even though Filipinos found pythons tasty, unlike the Bell family, this particular snake was spared to lessen the chance of bad luck following the arms.

As Bob Silliman took a last look at the rapid unloading of arms and supplies, he remembered the dramatic boost in resistance morale that Major Villamor's arrival had brought—Villamor was a national hero after shooting down one of the highly respected enemy Zero fighter planes early in the war. After the U.S. submarine *Gudgeon* landed Villamor on January 14, 1943, he stayed until October 20, 1943. In that period he established a single guerrilla command for the island to make his island-wide intelligence network feasible. To arm the new command, the submarine *Thresher* also had delivered weapons, medicine, radio equipment, and supplies to the guerrilla soldiers.

As Edna and Roy stood watching the loading of the guerrilla boats, Roy had the lingering feeling that he should stay with his guerrilla comrades now that his family was on its way to safety. On the other hand, solid reasons for leaving came to mind. The efficiency of the rendezvous with the submarine had demonstrated the guerrilla organization's capability without him. The guerrillas really didn't need him now that a chain of command had been established after Major Villamor's arrival from General MacArthur's SWPA. Villamor had taken temporary command of the island's guerrillas himself.

Roy knew he was not needed like in the early days when local guerrilla leaders recognized no superior officer and had difficulty cooperating with each other. Roy and Major Ausejo had stabilized the situation in their area. However, they could not handle Colonel Gador, whose men preyed on civilians. But Villamor had come and organized the various guerrilla groups on the island in a single command. Gador would not join it, so he left Negros.

Besides not being needed as much, Roy would be in great danger by staying and continuing his job of encouraging civilian production useful to the resistance. He had already been wounded and almost captured—probably betrayed by a collaborator. As a well-known target for the enemy, Roy would endanger civilians and guerrillas wherever he went on his production job.

Edna knew that if Roy thought staying would be enough of a challenge, he might not go. Edna sensed Roy's feelings and blurted out, "If you have any idea of not going on this submarine, I'll stay here with you!" That stopped Roy's pondering. He bade a final farewell and shook hands with Colonel Abcede and Major Viloria before they climbed on the last boat headed for shore.

Epilogue
Traveling Home

February 7 to May 1, 1944

Note: The following first-person narrative is based on Edna Bell's account of the family's journey back to the United States, which appears in Roy and Edna Bell's unpublished manuscript "Trails of Freedom: World War II Story." The spelling, grammar, and usage of the original have not been altered.

We were still eating in the wardroom when the voice of *Narwhal*'s skipper, Commander Latta, boomed through the squawkbox, "Men, I want to congratulate you on tonight's work. In forty-five minutes you have unloaded 45 tons of supplies. We have accomplished our mission. Good work, men!"

Then the *Narwhal*'s engines throbbed, and we began our long southward journey to Australia. On our first day aboard, the sailors in the torpedo rooms loaded the torpedoes in feverish haste—making us believe an enemy ship had been sighted, but it was a drill and often repeated with a similar sense of urgency.

We were haggard and barefoot, and our clothes were limited for the most part to what we had on our backs. But we were the happiest bunch in the world even though our living quarters were cramped—all husbands, wives, and children were put in the forward torpedo room and the single men, Bob Carson, and our boys slept in the aft torpedo room. We readily complied with the officers' insistence that the passage ways be kept clear at all times—so the crew could reach their battle stations as quickly as possible. Our meals were wonderful—everything we had dreamed of eating again we ate on the *Narwhal*. Much of the time we traveled on the surface to make better time, but one morning we dove and stayed down all day. That was our hardest day because the air got pretty stuffy and warm. On other days,

161

we went down for shorter periods—sometimes when aircraft approached. Usually at night we moved on the surface.

Days passed quickly in spite of being cramped. Mr. Bell found a job for the wives when he noticed a sailor try to lengthen a pair of trousers. He suggested that I do it for him. Then several of the wives went to the wardroom where there was space to sew—we soon found ourselves very busy. When one job was done, there was always another sailor with something to mend. We worked all day and after supper until 10:00 PM. It was great getting to know those grand boys—I thought of their mothers worrying about them. Some proudly brought pictures of their girls to show us, and one sailor went to the galley and made us a delicious plate of fudge.

On the morning of the eighth day, the engines shut down and we came up on deck for the first time since leaving Negros. The sunlight delighted us as we looked around the harbor of Darwin on the north coast of Australia. But we were thrilled when the sailors raised "Old Glory" to wave in the breeze. I have never considered myself a very patriotic person, but I was thrilled to the soul. Some of us wept for pride and joy.

A small boat came alongside and took us ashore. My first night in Australia I slept the sleep of the unafraid—the consciousness of safety gave me a feeling of perfect relaxation.

Next day we boarded two C-47 Army transport planes—flown by Army Air Corps pilots who had been flying troops to New Guinea and bringing back the wounded. Soaring above fleshy-white clouds, we headed south over the vast interior of Australia. A one-day flight had been planned, but bad weather forced us to land at Alice Springs and spend the night there. The second day we landed for lunch in the sheep country and then flew onward and arrived at Brisbane in late afternoon. There the Red Cross installed us at the seaside resort of Caloundra.

During our stay of two months, General MacArthur met with the Silliman faculty members. Knowing of the Japanese execution of missionaries on the Philippine island of Panay, MacArthur first asked the group, "How does it feel to be raised from the dead?" Our President Carson did not remember the replies but later wrote, "In our thinking, we had not been dead so much as living intensely in another existence. We had lived in a different world—a crude and primitive one."

Mr. Bell handed General MacArthur a list of Americans still on Negros. This information was critical because of the Japanese decree that ordered the execution of all Americans in the Philippines after January 1, 1944. On the list were our friends the Fleischers and Mrs. Viola Winn and her three children. Viola and children had survived alone in the hills for two years under the protection of Bolo men and her Christian congregation. She was alone because the Japs had informed her husband Gardner that unless he surrendered, they would execute a Filipino friend—that Filipino had once sheltered the Winn family. When the Fleischers and Mrs. Winn and children reached Australia on May 11, 1944, General MacArthur informed Mr. Bell of their safe arrival with the message, "All deposits safe in the bank." Husband Gardner Winn survived captivity and eventually joined his family in the U.S.

Meanwhile at Caloundra, our appearance was changing. After a few weeks, President Carson remarked, "Good food, rest, and sunlight have brought color into haggard faces and sparkle into haunted eyes." Carson cabled the Presbyterian Board of Foreign Missions of the groups' safety but gave no indication of our means of escape—being very conscious of protecting the *Narwhal* and other U.S. submarines in the Far East. The news of our safety, however, brought a flood of letters from relatives and friends—overjoyed, having been doubtful we had survived Japanese occupation of the Philippines.

But the unaccustomed quiet of our life at Caloundra was not natural. Each day of waiting to start toward home took longer to pass than the day before. Yet the monotony was broken when two of our Norwegians, Arne Hansen and Ragnvald Myhre, arrived. Always entertaining, Arne described the Norwegians' adventures after they left Negros to join General Fertig's guerrillas on Mindanao.

Finally, after almost two months in Australia, we boarded the Army transport ship *Fred C. Ainsworth* on April 14, 1944. Our ship stayed blacked out for 17 days as it sailed eastward across the Pacific. We kept our life belts on at all times except when asleep.

Only on the 17th day were we told our destination. Then at midday on May 1, the very tip of the Golden Gate Bridge could be barely made out on the horizon. As the *Ainsworth* steamed around the Earth's curve, more of the graceful bridge came into sight. At last it towered above us as we passed underneath into the quiet waters of San Francisco Bay.

Passenger traffic on trains was so heavy we had to stay with friends a few days while waiting for reservations. Then a long ride eastward took us to Kansas City, where relatives met us. They drove us westward through the beautiful landscape of a Kansas spring. At our home farms more relatives and friends greeted us during a summer of relaxation.

We had come back in time for commencement at Emporia College that spring. Roy gave the main address, and his alma mater awarded him an honorary Ph.D. in recognition of his leadership in the Philippines.

Acknowledgments

My friend Don Bell surprised me one day when he presented me with his father and mother's description of the family's experiences in the Philippines during World War II. After reading it, I was captivated by the story of the family's adventures and dangers during almost two years of staying free on the Japanese-occupied island of Negros. While the rest of the family avoided capture, Don's father, Roy, organized resistance to the invaders.

Don and I had been fellow graduate students at the Johns Hopkins School of Advanced International Studies in Washington, D.C., in the late 1940s. Years later, when he asked me to write about his family's adventures in narrative form, I eagerly assented.

Adding to my interest in the story itself, I have enjoyed writing this book because while the Bell family was coping with the Japanese on their island, I was contending with the enemy in relative safety aboard a Navy landing ship that eventually took part in the invasion of Okinawa and the occupation of Japan. I appreciate my neighbor Paul Robbins' astute comments on the narrative's continuity. Don Bell's wife, Aili, has given me wholehearted help since Don's death. Also, Jim Gullickson, my copy editor, helped me make some important improvements.

Last, and most important, I am grateful to my wife, Betty, for her patience and her encouragement when I ran into obstacles.

Appendix A

Silliman Participants in the Resistance

U.S. Army records show 10,811 officers and men in the resistance forces on Negros Island. The officers numbered 960, of whom roughly one-fourth had been Silliman students, alumni, faculty members, or ROTC officers. Commanding the island forces, organized as the 7th Military District, was Lieutenant Colonel Salvador Abcede, who had commanded the ROTC at Silliman when war broke out. Of the five regiments on Negros, Silliman men commanded four of them at one time or another.

Edilberto K. Tiempo, Silliman fictionist and historian of the 7th Military District, listed many of the Silliman officers in 1946, as well as a few of the Silliman women who did office work for the resistance. Part of Tiempo's list has been lost, but he provides 150 of the names herein. Other names came from former Silliman president Arthur Carson's account of his experiences in his book *Silliman University, 1901–1959*. Other sources were Alvin Scaff, Proculo Rodriguez, Paul Lindholm, and James McKinley, Silliman theology professors. They conscientiously carried on pastoral and teaching duties for resistance soldiers and civilians in guerrilla-dominated territory.

The following list is regrettably incomplete—it includes few of the Silliman enlisted men and leaves out many officers in the resistance forces. But it does show the pervasive participation of Silliman people in the resistance effort on Negros Island.

Abcede, Salvador	Ausejo, Luz
Alba, Louis*	Ausejo, Placido A.
Almagro, Guillermo	Baldado, Isidro
Alviola, Demetrio	Baldado, Rodello
Antiquera, Arturo	Banares, Leopoldo
Antonio, Eugenio	Bandoquillo, Pedro
Artes, Santiago B.	Bandoquillo, Venancio
Aspilla, Julian	Banogon, Ericarnacion

Bell, Henry Roy
Bell, Kenneth E. (U.S. Navy)
Blanco, Eduardo*
Bolongaita, Manuel
Cabili, Tomas
Cabrera, Wadel
Caliston, Edwin
Campoy, Angel
Chuachipgcon, Clemente
Colina, Elaine
Corsino, Benjamin
Corsino, Eliseo
Corsino, Pablo
Damasco, Paz*
De Asis, Emilia
De Asis, Josefa
De Asis, Lilar
Decena, Sergio
Dionio, Jose A.
Dizon, Emilio
Dominado, Juan
Dominado, Rito
Estacio, Alfredo
Ellorin, Nemesio
Figueroa, Alfredo
Flores, Asuncion
Flores, Cecilio
Flores, Eduardo
Flores, Leon
Fonda, Fortugaleza
Funda, Joaquin
Gadiane, Asterio
Galicano, Francisco
Galvez, Ceferino
Ganaban, Georgenia
Garcia, Jose
Gargantiel, Celso
Gargantiel, Consolacion
Ghent, George

Guanzon, Jose
Guanzon, Leopoldo
Habawel, Francisco
Heceta, Jose
Heflin, Robert Dean* (European theater)
Hernandez, Jose
Hernandez (first name unknown; brother of Jose, Roy Bell's secretary)
Jacobs, Abby R. (sister-in-law of Robert Silliman)
Jalandoon, Manuel
Jason, Arturo
Johns, Jimmy
Jornales, Victor
Jurika, Thomas (European theater)
Kaindoy, Alberto
Lagrito, Felix
Layague, Aquilino
Layague, Keling
Lindholm, Paul
Llera, Jovenal
Locsin, Protasio
Lumbro, Fructuoso
Macaraya, Batua
Macias, Lamberto
Madrid, Marcelino
Magdamo, Guillermo
Magdamo, Majaracon Narciso (Guillermo's son)
Malahay, Enrique
Mananquil, Antonio
Maravilla, Eustaquio
Maypa, Horacio
McKinley, James F.
Mercado, Herminigildo
Mondigo, Antonio
Moralde, Socorro

Naval, Leonardo
Nazareno, Alejandro (Bataan)**
Oracion, Timoteo
Orendain, Juan
Ozoa, Pedro
Paralejas, Rustico
Plotena, Loreto
Presbitero, Jaime
Ramos, Lulabandis*
Ratunil, Alfredo
Ravello, Jose
Real, Samuel
Real, Vicente
Regalado, Felix
Remollo, Jose
Reyes, Teodorico
Ridad, Frederico
Ridad, Honorario
Rivera, Catalino
Rivera, Ramon
Rodriguez, Proculo A.
Romero, Cristita
Samson, Jose
Santa Cruz, Santiago
Scaff, Alvin
Siao, Melchor*
Sibala, Galicano
Sibala, Justo
Sienes, Segundino
Silliman, Robert B.
Somera, Francisco
Suasin, Pedro

Sumcad, Ricardo
Tale, Illuminado
Tatel, Frederico
Tayko, Telesforo
Teves, Lorenzo
Teves, Manuel
Tiangha, Cirila
Tiempo, Edilberto K.
Tiempo, Leonila
Timbal, Ancieto
Torres, Paterno
Tugade, Rodrigo
Tumbagahan, Tiburcia
Uytengsu, Tirso
Uytengsu, Wentworth*
Utzurrum, Jose
Utzurrum, Manuel
Utzurrum, Santiago
Vail, Louis
Vailoces, Isabel
Valde, Felipe
Valente, Rosalia S.
Valente, Taopisto
Venturanza, Gregorio
Vilario, Lope
Villadelgado, Manuel
Villaluz, Esperanza
Villanueva, Oscar
Villarin, Fructuoso
Viloria, Benjamin N.
Yam, Johnman
Yonalaga, Emilio

---

*Died in resistance service.
**Died in 1947, probably from effects of Japanese torture.

Appendix B

Capture of
Rev. Alvin Scaff's Family

Claremont, California
August 1, 1998

Mr. Scott Mills and Don Bell:

Of course, I am glad to write about the war years and especially about Roy whom I liked very much. I was very glad that he escaped rather than us. I took some beating and solitary confinement whereas Roy was so well known, I think he could hardly have had a chance to survive.

In the attempt to clear out the jungle [between the evacuation huts of the Bell and Scaff families] we had cut through the trunks of some dozen large trees—though they were laced together by vines high up and thus would not fall. Weeks later a typhoon brought them all down in a heap.

On the morning we were caught, a guerrilla boy with the Bell family had gone out early and spotted the Japanese soldiers coming in the jungle toward our clearing. He rushed back and called to Roy and his family to run. [My wife] Marilee grabbed our baby, Larry, and started to jump out the window. I pulled her back, saying the soldiers were too close. They were shooting at the Bells, who were moving out east and escaped. I was immediately tied up. Later they set our house on fire, released me and had me carry our baby. Marilee walked beside us down the road where we were loaded into a big Japanese truck.

I learned later that Roy had been shot through the leg but had kept running. After the war we learned that all the people who lived in that mountain vicinity had died of malaria.

Sincerely, Alvin

Author note: The Scaff family was shipped to the Santo Tomas Civilian Internment Camp near Manila, where they survived until the war ended.

Notes

Chapter 1. Pearl Harbor Stuns Dumaguete

1. The Japanese executed Major Vesey on July 3, 1942, at a POW camp on Mindanao after four American soldiers escaped. Victor L. Mapes with Scott A. Mills, *The Butchers, the Baker* (Jefferson, N.C.: McFarland, 2000), 155.

2. Ibid., 18.

Chapter 2. Buckling Down to War

1. Later in the war the Japanese captured General Fort on Mindanao and then executed him when he refused to help them obtain the surrender of the fierce Muslim Moros on that island. Victor L. Mapes with Scott A. Mills, *The Butchers, the Baker* (Jefferson, N.C.: McFarland, 2000), 136–144.

Chapter 3. Wives Retreat to Malabo

1. The tower was built by Muslim Moros before the Spanish drove them south to Mindanao, where they are still rebellious.

2. The Japanese eventually sent the students back to Thailand.

3. The abaca plant is similar to the banana tree and is the source of Manila rope.

4. Robert Carson, "Memories of the War," high school report, written in Philippine free territory, December 31, 1942.

5. *Tuba* is a strong, popular alcoholic drink made from coconut blossoms.

6. Ground cassava root was used to make bread.

7. The bolo is a large knife, ten to twenty inches long, that Filipinos use in harvesting sugarcane and cutting brush, and as a weapon against wild pigs, pythons, and carabao that have gone wild and become nasty.

Chapter 4. The Fall of Cebu

1. Ira Wolfert, *American Guerrilla in the Philippines* (New York: Simon & Schuster, 1945).

2. These bees are more ferocious and noisier than U.S. bees.

3. Weiss must have been referring to Lieutenant James H. Cushing, who led a small guerrilla group in that area of Cebu at that time. Cushing and Harry Fenton, a former radio announcer, later promoted themselves to the rank of colonel and controlled a much larger force.

4. Edward W. Weiss, *Under the Rising Sun* (Erie, Pa.: E. W. Weiss, 1995), 58–76.

Chapter 6. Return to Malabo

1. In December 1932 the U.S. Congress had passed an act that called for Philippine independence after a ten-year transitional period. President Herbert Hoover vetoed that bill, but Congress overrode his veto in January 1933. The Philippine Senate rejected the act later that year. Congress then passed a new act in 1934, again calling for Philippine independence after ten years, which President Roosevelt signed. Because of the war, the Philippines had to wait until 1946 for its independence.

Chapter 7. Roy Bell Joins the Resistance

1. Bob Silliman was distantly related to Horace Silliman, the university's founder.

Chapter 10. Forming a Free Government

1. The Southwest Pacific Area (SWPA) was one of two Allied operational theaters in the Pacific region during World War II. Roy and Edna Bell sometimes mistakenly refer to General MacArthur's command as the SWPAC (Southwest Pacific Command) in "Trails to Freedom: World War II Story." In the chapters that follow, quotations from that unpublished manuscript containing this error have not been altered so as to reflect accurately what the Bells and others in the Philippine resistance understood to be true at the time.

Chapter 11. Roy Bell's Journey to Mindanao

1. The general's name actually was Wendell W. Fertig. Roy apparently misspelled and misunderstood or misremembered the full name Fertig gave him at this meeting, though he correctly recorded Fertig's true rank and the fact that he had been in the U.S. Army Reserve.

2. See Victor L. Mapes with Scott A. Mills, *The Butchers, the Baker* (Jefferson, N.C.: McFarland, 2000), for an account of that death march by one of the prisoners.

Chapter 12. Major Villamor Lands on Negros

1. The account in this chapter of Villamor's landing on Negros Island and his conversations with others while on the island prior to meeting Roy Bell are largely drawn from Jesus A. Villamor, as told to Gerald S. Snyder, *They Never Surrendered* (Quezon City, Philippines: Vera-Reyes, 1982).

Chapter 14. Checking on the Cebu Guerrillas

1. Jesus A. Villamor, as told to Gerald S. Snyder, *They Never Surrendered* (Quezon City, Phlippines: Vera-Reyes, 1982).

2. Ibid.

3. The submarine *Tambor*, March 3 on Mindanao; *Gudgeon*, April 30 on Panay; *Thresher*, May 3 on Mindanao and July 9 on Negros; *Trout*, May 26, June 12, and July 9 on Mindanao; *Grayling*, July 30 and August 23; *Bowfin*, September 2 and 30.

Chapter 15. Problems in Negros Oriental

1. Following the Japanese invasion of the Philippines, Manuel Luis Quezon y Molina (1878–1944) was the head of the Philippine government in exile.

2. James F. McKinley with Elizabeth M. McCabe, *Betrayed and Befriended* (Quezon City, Philippines: New Day, 1970).

Chapter 16. Villamor Gathers Island Leaders

1. The account in this chapter of Villamor's meeting with the guerrilla leaders is largely drawn from Jesus A. Villamor, as told to Gerald S. Snyder, *They Never Surrendered* (Quezon City, Philippines: Vera-Reyes, 1982).

Chapter 19. Staying with the Fleischers

1. *Silliman University, 1901–1959.* New York: United Board for Higher Christian Education in Asia, 1965.

Chapter 20. Basay Rendezvous

1. Major Enrique Torres came to Negros with Major Villamor in January 1943. When Villamor returned to the SWPA, Torres stayed with the guerrillas.

2. At the Mitsui labor camp on Tokyo Bay, Japanese guards repeatedly told American POWs that in case of an invasion of Japan, the prisoners would be executed so as to release the guards to fight American forces. Herbert Zincke with Scott A. Mills, *Mitsui Madhouse* (Jefferson, N.C.: McFarland, 2003), 119.

References

Bell, Roy, and Edna Bell. "Trails to Freedom: World War II Story." Unpublished manuscript, Silliman University Library, Dumaguete City, Philippines, 1958.

Carson, Arthur L. "Sa Kabukiran: A Contribution to the War Story of Silliman University." Unpublished manuscript, Silliman University Library, Dumaguete City, Philippines, ca. 1955.

———. *Silliman University, 1901–1959.* New York: United Board for Higher Christian Education in Asia, 1965.

Carson, Robert, "Memories of the War." High school report, written in Philippine free territory, December 31, 1942.

Chapman, James, and Ethel Chapman. *Escape to the Hills.* Lancaster, Pa.: Jacques Cattell, 1947.

Chmielewski, Edward A. "Philippine Adventure." Paper written for English class, Tri-State College, Angola, Ind., 1945.

"A Guerrilla's Wife." *Ladies' Home Journal,* August 1945. (About the execution of the Baptist missionaries on Panay Island.)

Haggerty, Edward. *Guerrilla Padre in Mindanao.* New York: Longmans, Green, 1946.

Jacobs, Abby R. *We Did Not Surrender Manila.* Memorial publication by Robert B. Silliman, Manila, 1986.

Lord, Walter. *Incredible Victory.* New York: Harper & Row, 1967.

Manchester, William. *American Caesar: Douglas MacArthur, 1880–1964.* Boston: Little, Brown, 1978.

Mapes, Victor L., with Scott A. Mills. *The Butchers, the Baker.* Jefferson, N.C.: McFarland, 2000.

McKinley, James F., with Elizabeth M. McCabe. *Betrayed and Befriended.* Quezon City, Philippines: New Day Publishers, 1970.

Murray, Douglas C. "Revision of Recognition Dates, 7th Military District, Commanding Officer, Salvador Abcede." 7 August 1947 Memo, G-3, Philippine-Ryukyus Command, U.S. Army. Washington, D.C.: National Archives.

"Robert B. Kelly, Commander of PT Boat in WWII, Dies." Obituary, *Washington Post,* January 27, 1989.

Silliman, Robert B. *Pocket of Resistance.* Manila: Cesar J. Amigo, 1989.

Villamor, Jesus A., as told to Gerald S. Snyder. *They Never Surrendered.* Quezon City, Philippines: Vera-Reyes, 1982.

Viloria, Ben N. "Roy Bell—Hero of Negros." *Philippines Free Press* (Manila), February 14, 1989.

Weiss, Edward W. *Under the Rising Sun.* Erie, Pa.: E. W. Weiss, 1995.

Willoughby, Charles A. *The Guerrilla Resistance Movement in the Philippines,
    1941–45.* New York: Vantage, 1972.
Winn, Viola S. *The Escape.* Wheaton, Ill.: Tyndale House, 1975.
Wolfert, Ira. *American Guerrilla in the Philippines.* New York: Simon & Schuster,
    1945.
Zincke, Herbert, with Scott A. Mills. *Mitsui Madhouse.* Jefferson, N.C.:
    McFarland, 2003.

Index

A

Abcede, Salvador: in evacuation of American families, 147, 153; Gador and, 68; as head of unified command structure, 115, 125; on Negros' resistance structure, 90–91; Silliman ROTC and, 12, 33

Abellana, Hilario, 110

agricultural produce and production: Bell and, 117, 127; confiscation by Japanese, 116–17; grain supply line, 12–13, 31; guerrillas' seizure of, 120; military reimbursement for, 11; weekly quota for support to resistance, 72, 77

Ainsworth (United States), 163

Aldecoa, Venancio, 77

Almendres, Geraldo, 83

Amblan village, 117–20

Ambrosio (Malabo villager), 35–36

American frontier, *vii–viii*

Amut (guerrilla soldier), 140, 152

Angela (spy), 127

Archer, Leland, 145, 150

Arretas family, 151

Arrieta (plantation owner), 76

Asis, Fernando, 117, 119–20

Aspilla, Julian, 126

Ausejo, Placido, 106, 127, 156; background of, 68–69; on Gador's abuses, 93, 94; on mission to Cebu, 104, 105; on need for civil authority, 75; on need for unified military leadership, 92–93; recruitment as resistance leader, 68, 70–72; on resistance tactics, 69

Ausejo resistance group, 69. *See also* 75th Regiment

automobile fuel production, 81, 127

B

B-17 Flying Fortress, 5

Balolong (Filipino major), 2, 8

Bataan Peninsula, 12, 22, 32

Battle of Midway, 88

Battle of the Solomons, 79

Bavnass (merchant ship), 29

Bell, Donald, 6, 8, 18, 19, 20, 48, 130, 134, 138, 141, 145, 148

Bell, Edna Mae, 25, 35, 37, 38, 53, 137, 140, 142, 144, 152, 160; air raid and, 15–16; concern for student safety, 6, 8, 14–15; on danger to family, 132–33, 134; educational projects of, 77; on evacuation of students, 15; medical clinic created by, 20–21; on need for security watch, 42–45; Norwegians and, 29–30; relocation to Malabo, 16–21; response to Japanese attack, 6; on return to United States, 161–64

Bell, Kenneth, 6, 8, 15, 19, 20, 29, 48, 77, 130, 131, 134, 138, 141, 143, 145

About the Author

SCOTT A. MILLS served in the U.S. Navy as a communications officer during World War II, participating in the invasion of Okinawa and the occupation of Japan. After the war he served with U.S. Army intelligence and later with NASA for twenty years. A resident of Silver Spring, Maryland, he is also the co-author of two books each about an Army Air Corps soldier captured by the Japanese.